Prince
Henry Sinclair

The Arms of the Earl of Orkney. These arms are taken from the *Armorial de Gelre*, 1369–88, an early heraldic work now in the Bibliothèque Royale, Brussels, and are almost certainly those of Henry Sinclair.

Prince
Henry Sinclair

HIS EXPEDITION TO
THE NEW WORLD IN 1398

by Frederick J. Pohl

Clarkson N. Potter, Inc./Publisher   NEW YORK

DISTRIBUTED BY CROWN PUBLISHERS, INC.

Inquiries should be addressed to Clarkson N. Potter, Inc.,
419 Park Avenue South, New York, N.Y. 10016.

Library of Congress Catalog Card Number: 73-79829
ISBN: 505487
Published simultaneously in Canada by
General Publishing Company Limited.

First American Edition published in 1974 by
Clarkson N. Potter, Inc.

Designed by Shari de Miskey

Filmset and printed in Great Britain by
BAS Printers Limited, Wallop, Hampshire, England

Contents

List of Illustrations

Prince
Henry Sinclair

Introduction

THE DETECTIVE SPEAKS

CAN A detective six hundred years after the event reasonably hope to unearth what actually happened in a particular case? Or is a sleuth in history inevitably doomed to failure in attempting to find clues that might enable him to peer with some degree of certainty into a distant past? Time has a dark destroying hand of such efficiency that the chances of being able accurately to reconstruct anything in the fourteenth century would appear hopeless. But he who despairs without trying never feels the thrill that comes to one who ventures against the odds and with patience and good luck succeeds.

These pages record the quest for a fourteenth-century man—to establish, if possible, the facts of his life, to identify the land to which he sailed, and to trace the exploring he did therein; and also to ascertain whether that land to which he and his men sailed was indeed a "New World" and was the land that, a century later, everyone except Columbus began to realize was exactly that.

Strong evidences support belief that there were countless crossings of the Atlantic before Columbus. Most of them have been lost to history because there are no existing records. In all probability there were many crossings made by fishermen, which would seldom, if ever, be recorded. We have only a handful of documented reports that bear upon or hint at such crossings. They point to Irish, Norse, Breton, Basque, and Portuguese fisherfolk. The most persuasive of these are statements by official explorers who have been accredited as first to visit portions of the coast of North America. When Jacques Cartier in 1536 officially "discovered" the islands of St. Pierre and Miquelon south of Newfoundland, he found there "several ships both from France and from Brittany," ships of fishermen. It is obvious from his account that fishermen had named "St. Pierre" years before he sighted that island.[1] So also, Samuel de Champlain, another accredited discoverer and explorer of portions of the North American coastline, and with him Marc Lescarbot, both recorded in 1601, in Tor Bay, Nova Scotia, their meeting with a fishing ship, the captain of which, by name Savalette, from St. Jean de Luz, had crossed from his home port to North America "every year for forty years."[2]

Historians have accepted the honesty and accuracy of Champlain and Lescarbot. Those two men, in turn, did not question the veracity of Captain Savalette. And, if a fishing-ship captain sailed across the Atlantic and back every year for forty years, the father of that captain may have done the same thing before him, and his father before that. Indeed, the historical detective finds a well-authenticated report of fishermen who crossed from north of Scotland, in the Orkney Islands, to North America in the year 1371. The testimonies of Champlain and Lescarbot, of Cartier, and others of the fourteenth century, presented in the following pages, all reinforce this fact. In geometry, three points establish a curve. In history, three similar records establish a pattern. The pattern here is ocean crossing by fishermen previous to crossings by the accepted explorers.[3]

As will be seen in the following pages, expeditions in the Atlantic were described by two members of the Zeno family in Venice in letters written from the Orkney Islands in the years 1390 to 1404. Their letters constitute what is called the Zeno Narrative. Until recently that narrative was under suspicion of being a literary hoax, the boastful story of a Venetian discovery of America in the fourteenth century. However, intensive historical, geological, geographical, and ethnological research has uncovered evidences that establish this narrative as authentic.

The most important part of the Zeno Narrative is the record of a fourteenth-century expedition to North America by a man who was inspired to undertake it by what an Orkney fisherman told him of a land of immense size, with extensive forests, agreeable climate, and waters swarming with fish. That great land was, in the fisherman's words, "a new world."

Such a man, having conducted an expedition to the New World, would have to be considered one of the world's outstanding explorers. Every person in Great Britain may take pride in the fact that a man born in Great Britain crossed the Atlantic to North America and explored extensively, more than ninety years before Columbus. And be it noted that in the telling of this exploration the Zeno Narrative does not make the mistake Columbus made in believing and asserting that what lay on the western side of the Atlantic was the coast of China. And note further that the correct perception that North America was "a new world" was not originally made by the educated fourteenth-century explorer, but by an unpretentious fisherman who had preceded him.

In 1950 when this historical detective published a brief study based upon that narrative,[4] the Arctic explorer Dr. Vilhjalmur Stefansson congratulated him on having taken the spotlight away from the two men of the Venetian family and turned it to where it should be—upon the leader of the transatlantic expedition. This was a proper observation by Stefansson, excepting that the spotlight should also illuminate an un-named Orkney fisherman.

That humble fisherman perceived clearly what Columbus did not. Why don't we know of this fourteenth-century expedition? The explanation may be simply stated: what was given to Columbus, and not to the fisherman or the fourteenth-century explorer, was publicity throughout Europe. With publicity, Columbus opened the Atlantic Ocean to two-way crossing by everyone. Perversity of circumstances denied this to the fourteenth-century explorer. Nevertheless, you will find in this biography of the fourteenth-century explorer an expedition unique among all pre-Columbian transatlantic expeditions in that practically all essential facts in regard to it have been dug out and are known, as definitely as they are in the case of the 1492 voyage of Columbus. We know the purpose of the leader; the number of days and speed of his westbound crossing; the number of days and speed of the returning ships; the year, month, and day of his landing on the coast of North America; the place of his landing identified with certainty; the place of his first meeting with American Indians; the route by which the European visitor explored the country;

the place where he wintered; the place where he built a ship in which he sailed home; the cultural impact he had upon the natives; the permanent memorial he left in the New World; and an actual linguistic link between pre-Columbian Europe and the pre-Columbian New World, in words which the Indians heard from the visitor's lips and preserved in tribal memory. In short, this biography of Prince Henry Sinclair is a new page in history, one of surprising fullness.

Part 1
LORD OF THE ISLES

Chapter One

BOY

IT WAS not easy to pick up the trail of a man who crossed the Atlantic to North America a hundred years before Columbus. Few records survive from the fourteenth century, and only scattered clues to the explorer's activities awaited the historical detective in the man's native Scotland. There were some clues in the Orkney Islands, the Shetland Islands, and Scandinavia; other evidences eventually made possible a geographical tracing of the explorer's footsteps in North America. Occasionally, at places where the man had been, the trail was warm, but more often it was obscured by time's thick veiling and the search at first seemed almost hopeless.

The sleuthing began at the man's birthplace. Eight miles south of the center of Edinburgh is Roslin village. It is one of the most charming places in Midlothian, and draws a constant stream of tourists, most of whom see only the attraction starred in guidebooks—the St. Clair family's burial chapel.[1] That fifteenth-century architectural masterpiece has a unique style of sculptural decoration commemorated in poetry by Sir Walter Scott.[2] Since it is close to a level road where a bus or automobile can deposit tourists at its door, nothing tends to lessen its popularity.

The far side of the chapel, however, which few see from the exterior, is not so accessible, for it stands at the edge of the Esk River Valley, whose steep slopes none but active-limbed youth would venture to descend or climb. Down in the middle of that valley, unseen from the chapel when trees are in leaf, is a much older and more interesting building, which rewards any visitor who takes the time required to reach it. It is the romantically situated Roslin Castle, dating from 1304, the ancestral home of the St. Clair family, and a national monument.

Actually, the visitor to Roslin Castle need not scramble down into the valley, the rim of which is three hundred feet above the river, for slightly to the west of the chapel there is an inclined approach to the castle down a road and along the top of a medieval causeway built out to it. At first sight a beholder would think that the depth of a valley was

Drawn by Frank O. Braynard

Roslin Castle (restored)

an ill-chosen location for a castle. Why was it not on the top of a hill? But before the invention of cannon, the selection of the Roslin Castle site made good sense. Being below the rim of the wooded slopes, it was snug against winter winds. Yet it towered above its near surroundings, and was too far from the valley slopes to be battered by mechanically hurled missiles from those slopes.

Furthermore, the castle was protected on two sides by wide river marshes called the Stanks, which held a foe too far off for effective bowshots. On the southeast the castle rose to a height of eight stories above the river from a rock which itself had a precipitous face. The narrow northeast front was guarded by thick walls, a strong tall beacon tower, and barbican. It was also cleverly shielded by the one-hundred-yard-long embankment or causeway that, in orthodox defensive pattern, led out from the steep side of the valley to in front of the castle, where it made a short right-angled turn close to an arched bridge eighty feet

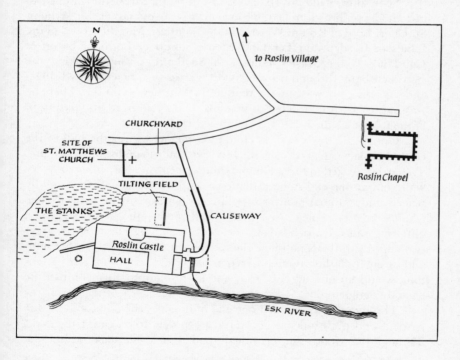

Roslin Castle and Environs

above the bed of the stream below. This bridge gave access to the gateway, which was further protected by drawbridge and portcullis. Only a few enemy attackers could be on the causeway near enough to attack the castle, and, since they carried their shields on their left arms, their unshielded right sides would be exposed to bowshots from the castle.

The name of the castle perfectly describes its position. A "ross" is a promontory or peninsula. A "lynn" is a pool or waterfall. The aptness of the name Roslin (Rosslyn) becomes apparent as one walks over the arched bridge and hears directly beneath it the torrent from the marshes tumbling down over the rocks to rejoin the river below.

Here, in 1345, a boy, the first child of his parents, was born to the lord of the castle. The custom among French-speaking families like his was to give the infant his birth drink, his *boisson natale*, immediately. A few moments after his birth, the hero of our story was no doubt fed a spoonful of toddy, warm, sweet, strong—a taste of his native Scotland.

Soon after, while his sixteen-year-old mother was still confined to bed and as yet not churched, his seventeen-year-old father, Sir William St. Clair, Lord of Roslin, Warden of the Southern Marches, Lord of the Lands of Carden and Pentland Moor, Sheriff of Lothian, Baron of Cousland, Great Master Hunter of Scotland, proudly carried the swaddled baby through the courtyard, across the ancient drawbridge, and over the causeway, up the road to St. Matthew's Church. There he was baptized without delay to save his infant soul from an eternity in limbo in case he died. He was christened Henry.

One of the boy's earliest childhood memories was the hall of the castle, a place of great delight. Its size and splendor thrilled him. Tapestries worked in threads of red, blue, green, and gold hung on every wall, and at one end stood a platform with his father's chair carefully placed under a coat-of-arms of white (argent, or silver) with a black (sable) cross engrailed. Also in the hall, above the fireplace, was a glittering object suspended on the wall, a shining claymore, a great two-edged sword. Its polished blade reflected the dance of the firelight, and surely his father, upon observing that it had caught his son's attention, would lift him up close to it and let his chubby fingers touch the gleaming golden hilt.

Through the windows at one end of the hall, the boy could see the garden, and the branches of a dark green yew tree against the sky.* Through the windows at one side of the hall he could look out into the

---

* The yew tree, seven hundred years old, is a mighty giant, whose branches were used to make bows for archers.

courtyard. But he no doubt remembered most vividly the thrilling view from out the windows on the other side where one could see the awesome drop down to the river in the bottom of the ravine.

When he was old enough to be clad in a long gown of green motley or homespun, with a red biggin to cap his yellow curls, and a brown leather belt to bear a gilded wooden dagger, his father told him how his great-great-grandfather had won the Battle of Roslin Moor, one of the first victories of the Scots against the English. And he told how the boy's great-grandfather had also used the great claymore at Bannockburn, a famous battle of nearly forty years gone by, when hundreds of English nobles had been captured and held for ransom, and miles of loaded wagons had fallen into the hands of King Robert the Bruce. The invaders had lost thirty thousand men; the Scots only four thousand. No doubt the boy made up his mind that when he grew up he too would fight with valor against the English and all other natural enemies.[3]

Unfortunately for Scotland the northern counties of England were least populated, and Scottish raids could not penetrate far enough south to destroy the centers of real strength in England. On the other hand, the southern lowlands, which were exposed to swift English raids, were the most populous and progressive sections of Scotland. Scottish forays had only a retaliatory and nuisance value.

Another story his father would have told him was that Henry's great-grandfather Sir Henry was among the signers of a letter to Pope John XXII on April 4, 1320, asserting the independence of Scotland. Signing it was an act of courage, for the letter was addressed to a pope who had excommunicated all adherents of King Robert the Bruce. In view of the previously enforced submission of the Scottish nobles to King Edward I of England, any man's signing of such a letter was, from the English point of view, an act of high treason, as it denounced the "burning, slaughter, robbery and barbarities" committed in Scotland by King Edward I. It contained these ringing words: "We will never submit ourselves to the dominion of the English; for it is not glory, it is not riches, neither is it honour, but it is liberty alone that we fight for and contend for, which no honest man will lose but with his life."

Both in historical setting and spirit, this document was comparable to, indeed a direct forerunner of, the American Declaration of Independence.

Life in a fourteenth-century castle was not luxurious, but there were two very special features at Roslin. One was a large structure that covered a square hole in the floor. Dishes of hot food were placed on a tray in the kitchen and brought up to the hall by a pulley rope. Henry heard it said that this lift for hoisting food three floors from kitchen to hall was the first such device in all the world, and had been created by the ingenuity of one of his forefathers. The other was a small wooden tube that went down somewhere. When the chief server spoke into it, another man's voice promptly answered from below, according to Henry's mother, from deep down in the cellar.

The time came when the boy went exploring into the dark sub-basement through a door under the yew tree, leading down a flight of steps carved out of the living rock upon which the castle stood. He found himself at the beginning of a fearsome corridor about one hundred feet long, one wall of which, like the floor, was solid rock. In that wall were recesses for crusie lamps. The other wall was built of great stones with doorways into rooms or cells. Each of these cells was lighted by a narrow slit from out of doors. One cell was provided with running water from a spring that gushed out of the solid foundation rock which formed one wall of the corridor. It flowed in a groove across the corridor and into and across the cell floor to a drain in the outside wall. By this clever use of what nature supplied, anyone in the cell or the corridor could scoop up spring water whenever he was thirsty.

Further along near the end of the corridor in the pantry next to the kitchen was the bottom of the food lift, a square opening in the ceiling out of which hung two strands of rope, one of them tied to the handles of a broad hoisting tray. There also was the bottom end of the small wooden speaking tube, about the height of a man's head.

A heavy door closed off the end of the corridor. When this door was open, a gust of warm air brushed one's face, and one smelled a delicious whiffle of roasting. The great kitchen was a vaulted room with a huge fireplace ten feet wide and seven feet high in the center. In it the boy often saw a spitted ox suspended, or a fat buck his father had shot with a well-aimed arrow. A scullion with a long ladle stood by to baste the roasting flesh. The boy watched the runoff of juices and fat in the channel cut in the stone at the bottom of the fireplace. The channel was divided into a narrow deep groove for gravy, and a broad shallow groove for grease, to be used to make tallow candles.

A cook with a potstick stirred broth in a cauldron. On a dressing board in the middle of the kitchen, another scullion minced meat with a cleaver. Along the walls in racks were iron pots and pans. There were rows of knives and fleshhooks, a gridiron and a scummer. On the boards were posnets and pots, platters and saucers and spoons, a basket of eggs and a pepper-quern and a heap of plucked fowl. Next to the kitchen was a bakehouse, with an oven eight feet in diameter and five feet high, for bread and pastry.

Henry became familiar with every nook in the cellar. He knew the vault where wines were stored, and the room with a shelf in the stone wall for monks' books. Later came the day when his father, after he had sent everyone else out of the cellar, showed him the secret entrance to the passage that went down and under the river and came out in a cave in the glen.

Many a time in the hall after supper, a jongleur with fiddle or lute sang of border battles or the valorous deeds of heroic knights. The tale that Henry loved best was one he heard more than once from his father's lips. The boy appreciated it all the more after he was breached, and began to ride agallop and go hunting with his father on the hills where it all happened.

It was the story of how King Robert the Bruce had many times pursued the chase upon Pentland Hills, and had often started a "white faunch deer" which to his extreme annoyance had always outrun his hounds. Having been so frequently disappointed, the king asked the nobles with him on the King's Hill whether any had hounds fleeter than the royal hounds. No courtier ventured to affirm that he had swifter hounds than the king's, but young Sir William St. Clair of Roslin, who had two very fleet red fallow hounds, cast aside all caution and boasted: "I'll bet my life on't, my two favorite hounds, Help and Hold, will kill the deer before she can cross the March Burn!"

King Robert instantly took up the challenge of this unwary brag, and bet the entire Forest of Pentland Moor against the life of Sir William —a royal wager indeed!

As the old tale had it: All the hounds were tied up, except a few ratches or slow hounds, to put up the deer; while Sir William, posting himself in the best situation for slipping the dogs, prayed devoutly to Christ, to the Blessed Virgin, and to St. Katherine, who was the saint who had worked a miracle at a brook.

The deer was shortly after roused, and came off the black hills, and while Sir William said: "Help! Hold! begin ye may, or Roslin loses his head this day!" the hounds were slipped, Sir William following on a gallant steed to cheer his dogs. The hind, however, reached the middle of the brook; upon which the hunter threw himself from his horse in despair, and lay flat on his face. At this critical moment, Hold stopped the deer in the brook, and

Help coming up, turned her back, and killed her on Sir William's side.[4]

The king descended from the hill, embraced Sir William, and bestowed on him the Lands of Kirkton, Logan-House, Earncraig, and Pentland Moor in free forestrie.

The winning of the great bet not only added much land to the Barony of Roslin but it gave the St. Clair family all hunting and fowling rights thereto.

With a boy's curiosity, Henry may have wanted to ask his father whether, if the hounds had failed, King Robert would have cut off the head of his friend Sir William. But he no doubt knew the answer when his father told the aftermath of the story, how in gratitude to St. Katherine

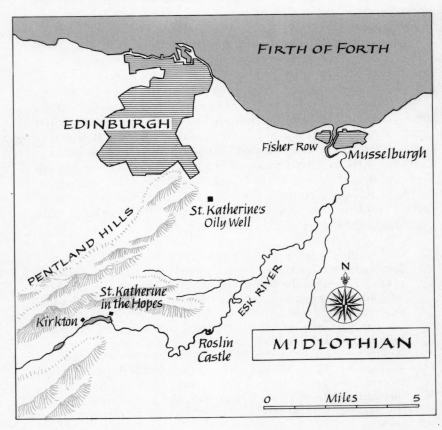

for her miraculous intercession at the brook by which his life was saved and he came home the new owner of lands larger than his wildest imagination could ever dream of possessing, Sir William built the Church of St. Katherine in the Hopes,[5] on the spot where he made his last despairing devotion to her before the deer was killed.

Chapter Two

MAN

A BOY who craved adventure and the thrill of peril would not long stay cooped up in Roslin Castle. It was a safe hold and Henry was proud to know that it would someday be his. He also knew that ambition would require his often traveling away from it.

His playmates were his cousins, some sons and daughters of vassals, the wards of his father, and his sister Margaret, until her marriage. His parents kept a cleric for the saying of prayers for all the family, and for teaching the children Latin.[1] The young people also spoke French, and read the French romances and poetry. The boys were trained in all manner of physical skills, and management of arms, of bow and spear and sword, horsemanship, sport, and outdoor life. The girls were trained to govern the household, to brew medicinal potions and perform surgical operations on the wounded, and to nurse the sick. Both boys and girls could ride, leap, and swim. In addition to this practical knowledge these young people of the fourteenth century were taught music with singing and dancing. Above all, they were taught table manners and social behavior in hall and bower. They were instructed in how to behave at tournaments, with the proper etiquette, so that they could hold their own with all comers, native or foreign, either in valor among the lists or in good taste among the spectators.

Henry learned correct bodily posture, to hold his head erect, to look fearlessly, to keep hands and feet at rest. In short, he learned to bear himself with dignity as future Lord of Roslin.

Before meals, after he had washed his hands and cleaned his fingernails, he was not permitted to rush rudely into the hall, but had to enter at easy pace and stand attentive until his father, the Lord of Roslin, had said grace and was seated. Then, as he himself sat to the board and began to eat, he was required to give thought to poor men. As the good manners book said:

> *For the full stomach ever faileth*
> *To understand what the hungry aileth.*

He must not eat greedily or cram his mouth as churls do, but must chew small morsels. He must keep his knife sharp and carve his meat decorously. He had to learn to handle the new instrument called a fork. He must tell no foul or dishonest tale at table, nor be scornful. He must keep his cheer, "humble, blithe and merry, never chiding as if ready for a fight."

He must not break bread, but cut it with his knife. He must eat pottage with his spoon quietly, and not leave the spoon in the dish. He must not bring his meat into touch with the salt in the saltcellar, but must properly lay salt on his trencher.

When the meal was ended he must clean his knife, and remain seated until the servers had brought basin and water for him to wash his hands. Then he would rise, go to his lord's table and stand there until the ending grace be said. He was told that if he observed all these good manners, folk would say of him after he bowed himself out: "A gentleman was here today."

His training was to fit him to become the head of a family with repute, a family that well deserved to be called, centuries later, by Sir Walter Scott, "the lordly line of high St. Clair."[2]

Henry learned from his father how the St. Clairs began. Since we know the facts, perhaps as accurately as Sir William did, we can imagine the conversation:

"In Normandy there was a hermit named Clare. He was martyred and later was made a saint. The place where he had lived became a shrine, by which the region thereabouts took its name. Our family dwelt nearby, and so we called ourselves 'of St. Clare', now 'St. Clair.' We were among the first families to assume a surname. We had more French blood than most Norman families."

"How came we to Roslin?"

"By strong arms. Nine St. Clairs fought in the Battle of Hastings, in the charge that won the day for the Conqueror of England. Five of them were first cousins of the Conqueror, one of whom, our ancestor, came to Scotland."[3]

"Why did he so?"

"Through no love for his cousin. He took refuge here with King Malcolm."

"What was his name?"

"Sir William."

"What was Sir William like?"

"He was a handsome man. They called him 'the seemly.' At Queen Margaret's Court he became the first high steward."

"I thought the high steward was the ancestor of the Stewart family."

"The Stewart family came from another and later steward."[4]

There were gay times in the castle at Christmas and Twelfth Night feasts. On the first of May everyone rode out after supper to the hills to see the bonfires lighted, and to watch the cattle being driven between two of the fires to immune them against murrain.

A jollier time than any, the gayest of all was a tournament. The jousting field was immediately north of the castle wall, down below the causeway. In keeping with custom a tourney would have been held on the afternoon of the wedding of Henry's young sister.

First came the grand procession: the musicians marching with bagpipes and bugles and kettledrums. Then came the squires in the colors of their masters' liveries, each holding aloft his master's pennon; then the ladies gowned in a rainbow of colors with sweeping trains; and then the knights in jousting armor carrying gilded basinets with waving plumes. They were followed by armorers who bore files and hammers and chisels ready to open dented basinets or bashed-in collar pieces and visors. Last of all came Sir Thomas Stewart, Earl of Angus, escorting his girl bride, Margaret of St. Clair, seven years of age, with her hand clinging to the arm on which he wore the embroidered sleeve of his lady love, his mistress, who resided in a castle near Dundee. Thus Sir Thomas brought before the company Henry's sister, now his countess, who was to be, in spite of her tender years, the honored Queen of the Tourney.

A great blare of trumpets sounded when little Margaret took seat. Another came as she signaled the heralds to announce the names of the contestants. Then, two opposing knights mounted their steeds and took their places at the ends of the tourney field on opposite sides of the long fence. They lowered their visors and set their lances. At the final trumpet signal, they heeled with their rowels, spurring their horses, and manfully came to the clash, doing each other whatever damage they could. Many gallant blows were struck. After several knights had been unhorsed, refreshments were served. Then more knights were unhorsed, and any who lay unconscious were carried into the castle to be bled.

Pipers played that evening all through supper. After the supper the boards were cleared and removed, and flambeaux lighted the hall. In addition to the bagpipers and drummers were men with fiddles and harps, viols and rebecs, flutes and oboes, and at least one with a great trumpet. To distinguish them from the Roslin serving men, dressed in red scarlet gowns and black coats, the musicians would wear tunics and caps of other colors.

The knights strutted about in tight hose and in tunics with rising collars and bulging sleeves. The noble ladies wore low-necked tunics with straight long sleeves, and dresses of all colors, red and blue and green and purple, furbelowed with gold or silver buttons and bright ribands and bows. The noblemen and ladies alike had their hair banded with gold or silver circlets.

Before the dancing commenced, young and old engaged in a jolly game of forfeits, with laughter and chattering. Then, with hilarious shouts, the children and some of the grown-ups played Hot Cockles. In this game, one person was blindfolded and knelt with his hands behind him, and the others one at a time struck his hands, and if they could, knocked him over backward by the weight of a blow, and he must guess who.

The dancing began, with music sweet and lusty. The air throbbed with the beat of drums and the shrill of clarions, and there were heavy stompings and loud merriment. The flashing torches flickered as the whirling figures passed, and the tapestries swayed when brushed by a dancer's shoulder.

Late at night pasties of small birds were served, and there were steaming liquors to drink toasts to the earl's marriage and to the fertility of Margaret, when she was old enough to bear.

Henry's ancestors were strong supporters of the kings of Scotland.[5]

His grandfather, Sir William, born about 1310, was famous in the circumstances of his death. With his brother John and with Sir James Douglas, he vowed to fulfill the wish of the dying King Robert the Bruce to have his heart buried in Jerusalem. The three young warriors, bearing the embalmed heart of Bruce in a silver casket, started for the Holy Land. When their ship put into a Spanish port, they learned that King Alfonso was at war against the Saracens in Spain. The three Scotsmen chivalrously volunteered their assistance. In the Battle of Theba on the plains of Andalusia on August 25, 1330, the St. Clair brothers went in too far. Sir James, for the moment in no personal danger, observed that the brothers were "sorely beset," and dashed in to their rescue, but all three were slain. Thus Henry's grandfather perished too soon to inherit the Barony of Roslin, but he left "an infant son"—William, our hero's father —heir to the barony.

If Henry had in his turn become merely another Lord of Roslin, his name today would be significant only to the extent that he played a part in border warfare. The desire, the determination, and the opportunity necessary to conduct an expedition across the Atlantic to explore and take possession of new lands, shows a man who was something more than Lord of Roslin; a man acquainted with ships, in possession of ships, accustomed to sea voyaging, and able to command the services and loyalties of ship captains and their crews.

Roslin was only seven miles from the sea. It was but a short ride to the mouth of the Esk River where Henry smelled the salt air and saw the wide water. He saw fishing ships at their wharves, and some in midstream at anchor. On one side of the river was the town of Musselburgh, where the delectable molluscs that gave it its name were always in good supply. On the other side was Fisherrow where the salmon and herring fishermen lived. As a boy Henry had ample opportunity to observe the activities of the waterfront. He watched sailors haul up a ship, caulk her seams with flax wicking soaked in resin, and coat her hull with black pitch to keep sea worms from boring holes. He saw sailors at work in the rigging, and fishermen mending their nets. It was exhilarating to watch a ship when its captain gave command to raise the sails. The crew sprang to their task and sang lustily to the rhythms of their toil as the lifted sails filled and the ship moved bravely out of the harbor. It was a life very different from that at Roslin, and Henry began to look to a wider horizon than he could see from the castle tower. His interest in ships was to become a lifelong passion that would shape his career and prepare him for crossing the Atlantic Ocean.

His interest in the sea grew from something within himself. But the position that was to give him the power to follow this interest and use his knowledge of the sea came to him through his mother, Isabella. She was the daughter of Malise Sparre, Earl of Orkney, who had died before Henry was born. She had in her veins the blood of a king of Scotland, Malcolm II, and of two kings of Norway, Magnus I (died 1047), and Magnus V (died 1280). When she was fifteen, her father, on his death-bed in Inverness, had called in her uncle, the Earl of Ross, and had entrusted to him the arrangement of her marriage. On May 28, 1344, the dying earl had affixed his seal to a document that declared her, his daughter Isabella, heir to the Earldom of Orkney, failing male heirs of himself and her mother Marjory. This document was of much conse-quence; for it gave Henry claim to many islands, and if this claim were allowed by the king of Norway, Henry would of necessity have much to do with ships.

The St. Clairs, who had known better days, suffered much through the unhappy border conflicts with England that repeatedly brought havoc to Scotland. Pressured by the English, who advanced their claims under the terms of Edward de Baliol's preposterous grant to England of all Scotland south of the Firth of Forth, our Henry's great-grandfather, Sir Henry, on October 13, 1335, forfeited one-third of his Barony of Roslin, and died the following January. On September 10, 1336, his widow Alice was forced to forfeit her dowry. It was not until Henry's time that the family recovered from these reverses.

Everyone suffered from the plague, or Black Death as it was called; it destroyed more than half the population of England, and at least a third of the population of Scotland in the years 1348–1350. Though the Black Plague generally struck men of the meaner sort in much greater proportion than the affluent who could afford more sanitary habits, everyone was panicked. The St. Clairs at Roslin made daily intercession at their St. Matthew's Church, and prayers there were reassuring. But their greatest source of confidence was intercession at St. Katherine's Holy Well.[6]

The "Balm Well" of the St. Clair family's saint was four miles north of Roslin. It was held to be an inexhaustible fountain of healing, con-stantly renewed by St. Katherine; for there was in it a black oil believed to be "a precious oyle . . . from her bones."[7] The oil sprang up so abundantly that no matter how much of the "viscous fatty balsam" was cupped up out of the well, always the same amount remained.[8] This was clearly a supernatural sign of the spiritual working of the saint. No one thought of the possibility of a natural cause.[9] Men said the oil had singular virtue against all manner of canker and scabs and dolors of the skin, and was a cure for asthma, paralysis, dislocations, inflammations, blows, burns, contusions, and sprains. Since the black oil was remedy for so many ills, it must surely save from the Black Death all those who venerated St. Katherine, and especially those who made proper offerings to her at her "Oily Well."

In still another invasion of England, King David II of Scotland had been captured, and Scotland was compelled to pay a huge ransom of one hundred thousand marks, an almost impossible sum since the ravages of the plague had left Scotland with a population of only about two hundred thousand. Every nobleman felt the pinch; for he had to assume a share of the burden, and squeeze the money out of his lands as best he could. The first yearly instalment of the ransom was due on June 25, 1358.

Seven weeks before that date, on the sixth of May, Henry's father procured a safe conduct to go into England on his way abroad to Prussia to fight in foreign wars. His hiring out of himself and his vassals to fight was apparently the only way he could raise his share of the ransom payment. He was accompanied by Sir William Keith, Marshal of Scotland, and by Sir Alexander Lindsay, Sir Robert Clifford, and Sir Alexander Montgomery, each with sixty horsemen and a strong body of footmen. They went to join a great crusading expedition which the Teutonic Knights were preparing to launch against infidels; for East Prussia was a frontier of Christendom. The plague had taken a heavy toll throughout the continent, and wars in the German lands had killed many knights. Hard pressed by the Lithuanians, the Teutons centering at Marienburg called for aid, offering the incentive of free booty, and the appeal of pleasing God by performing the righteous deed of killing those who denied the Faith of the Cross.

Warfare was one of Great Britain's principal exports. If when passing through London on his way to Prussia, Sir William St. Clair was seen by the poet who was beginning to write the *Canterbury Tales*, he might have been a living model for Chaucer's description of the knight who "loved chivalry" and was a leader in the war "in Pruce."

When Sir William rode away from Roslin, Henry was thirteen years of age. When "shortly thereafter" unhappy tidings were brought back to the castle that Sir William had died, the grief and shock fell hardest upon the boy who was suddenly called upon to face a man's responsibilities.

GENEALOGY OF HENRY SINCLAIR

Sir William St. Clare, Baron of Roslin,
won Battle of Roslin Moor in 1303.

Sir Henry St. Clair, at Bannockburn, 1314;
signed letter to Pope declaring Scotland
independent, 1320.

Sir William St. Clair, won Pentland Hills
on a bet with King Robert the Bruce. Died in
a battle in Spain, Aug. 25, 1330.

Sir William St. Clair = Isabel, daughter
of Malise, Earl of
Strathearn, Caithness,
and Orkney.

PRINCE HENRY SINCLAIR = Janet Halyburton
(1345–1400),
1st Sinclair Earl
of Orkney

| William | Elizabeth
= Sir John
Drummond
of Stobbhall | Mary
= Sir
Thomas
Somerville
of Carnwath | Jean
= Sir John
Forester of
Corstorphine |

John
= da. of Waldemar
King of Denmark

Sir Henry,
2nd Earl,   =   Egidia, granddaughter
Admiral   of King Robert II.
of Scotland,
died 1420.

Sir William, 3rd Earl, builder of
Roslin Chapel, died 1446.

Sir William, 4th Earl, resigned
his right to the earldom in 1470,
after Orkney came under Scottish
rule in 1468–1469.

B

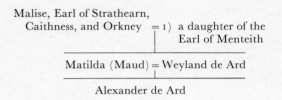

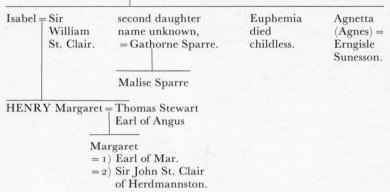

Marjory, second wife of Earl Malise, was sister to Euphemia, who married Robert Stewart, who became King Robert I of Scotland. Prince Henry was grandnephew to that king, and was cousin once removed to King Robert II.

Henry's young shoulders were forced to carry a weight that many a man would have failed to sustain. Becoming Lord of Roslin when the St. Clair family fortunes seemed to be at their lowest in centuries, Henry needed every advice that his uncle Thomas and his mother and the retainers could give. He had been counseled to heed correction and advice from inferiors who knew better than he in their several fields. Of course he would not welcome advice from equals outside the family, for he had to maintain the family standing before such equals; but advice from an underling was part of what each vassal within the limits of his knowledge owed him.

Most help had to come from his own mind and heart. In learning this, he thought of his father's saying: "To hold reins over men, the rider must bridle himself." Henry had to hold himself to a sharper discipline than he demanded of his retainers and vassals. He had stood at attention in the hall in his father's presence. Now, when he stepped upon the dais to occupy the lord's seat, he gave careful concern to his own proper behavior, so that every man was constrained to show him respect.

He was just old enough to know how to reach for inner strength. His sense of need must have often taken him to St. Katherine's Well. When he looked upon the "black oil swimming," he always somehow had the encouraging belief that it was a sign of personal good fortune. It would not be surprising years later, on the other side of the ocean, when his men reported that they had found a brook flowing with black balsam, that he would feel it to be a special revelation of St. Katherine's benevolence toward himself. He would be likely to interpret it as her particular invitation and proof of her guidance, and he would be irresistibly drawn to see with his own eyes the black oily brook.

Chapter Three

CHECKMATE

HENRY SINCLAIR, to use the better-known form of the surname (a name for which there have been ninety-seven different spellings) was compelled by the death of his father to begin his education in practical affairs. He was legal heir to the earldom of Orkney, but his claim was under cloud, since his grandmother Marjory had been the second wife of Earl Malise and his mother had been the second daughter of her father. A rival claimant was the son of Matilda (Maud), the eldest daughter of Malise by his first wife.[1] There was also a third daughter whose son, Malise Sparre, became a factor in the competition for the earldom. Since Malise had left no male heir, the question was whether his grant of heirship to the Orkney earldom to his second daughter would stand against the claim made by the heirs of the eldest daughter. The earl had died about the time Henry was born, and his earldom, which included both the Orkney and Shetland islands, had reverted to the crown of Norway at that time.

Orkney was the only earldom in the Norwegian kingdom. In Norway the "jarl" was all but equal with the king. It had been established by royal decree that the Norwegian earl took precedence over everyone except princes of the royal family. The Earl of Orkney ranked higher in Norway than any Scots earl in Scotland or English earl in England.

When Henry was only a boy, an enterprising Swedish nobleman, Erngisle Sunesson, married Agnetta (Agnes), a daughter of Earl Malise. By proclaiming that she was the rightful heir, and using not a little political chicanery, he procured nominal possession of Orkney. He had himself installed as governor of Orkney, at first without the coveted title of earl, but he took up residence in the Orkneys, and soon got the title from the king of Norway. Possession being nine-tenths of the law, it looked as though Erngisle had permanently captured the prize. The ambitious hopes of the Sinclair family seemed to be foiled.

Erngisle, however, was overreaching. He made the mistake of becoming involved with a Swedish party that sought to depose King Magnus II of Sweden. King Magnus, as regent of Norway, sequestrated all of Erngisle's Norwegian estates and declared his title of earl forfeited in 1357. When this happened, Henry Sinclair, twelve years old now, again became an active claimant. His family, realizing what a difficult game he must play, began to move the pieces on the political chessboard in his name. It was his cousin Alexander de Ard, son of Matilda, eldest daughter of Earl Malise who attempted to checkmate him.

The right of an eldest child today would be paramount. In the fourteenth century, the idea of primogeniture was not yet universally recognized. Earl Malise had specifically willed the inheritance of the Orkney earldom to Henry's mother and her heirs. However, the struggle for the earldom between Alexander de Ard and Henry Sinclair continued in dispute through twenty-two years.

On November 25, 1357, a manifesto was issued to the people of Orkney by Duncan Anderson, as bailiff, in support of Alexander de Ard, warning all taxpayers that he had under his guardianship the true and legitimate heir of Earl Malise. He told the people not to let revenues be taken out of the islands, or they would have to recompense the proper heir.

This was the state of affairs at the time of the death of Henry's father.

The game now to be played out between the two cousins involved the claims of seniority against those of a bequeathed heirship. If Henry was to win, it must be by superior qualities of character and ability, which he must make evident to Norway's king. Through education, training, and experience, he must try to better his cousin. It would be fatal to his cause, even if it were not repugnant to him, to use the ugly method other Scots nobles had employed to advance their ambitions. Robert the Bruce, to make sure of the throne, had stabbed his rival, John Comyn, the Balliol heir, in a church. William Douglas, whose family motto was *Never at the Rear*, had cleared the path to becoming 1st Earl of Douglas by murdering his godfather and kinsman, the Knight of Liddesdale, in Ettrick Forest. Liddesdale, called "the Flower of Chivalry," had previously starved to death Sir Andrew Moray. The future 3rd Earl of Douglas, Sir Archibald the Grim, wielded a two-handed sword seventy-four inches in length, which no other man could lift and swing, and with this instrument of personal force carved his career. In 1360, Henry's brother-in-law, Sir Thomas Stewart, whose family motto was the vindictive *No One May Touch Me With Impunity*, was suspected of having instigated the murder of Catherine Mortimer, the king's favorite, and for this was imprisoned in Dunbarton Castle until he died.

In contrast to the Douglas and Stewart mottoes, the Sinclair family motto, *Commit Thy Work to God*, had a religious emphasis that implied a Sinclair would keep in mind that his activities were in the sight of God and that he ought to do work acceptable to God.

For Henry to attempt to destroy his cousin Alexander would be to admit that he himself had an inferior right to the earldom. The king of Norway could bestow the earldom on whomsoever he chose. Henry's game must be to win that choice by deserving it.

To that end he learned all he could about the Orkney Islands. He studied their history, and the politics of the Scandinavian kingdoms, and prepared himself in the necessary languages. He awaited his chance to go to Scandinavia, which came in 1362 when he was eighteen.

Haakon VI had been king of Norway, and now had also become king of Sweden. The Princess Margareta, daughter of King Waldemar of Denmark, was to be married to King Haakon in 1362, and Henry took ship to Copenhagen to attend the wedding. This marriage would bring together all the royalty and nobles of Scandinavia, and it behooved Henry to make the best impression he could, and lay the foundation for political preferment. He went as ambassador from Scotland. It was foreseen that Margareta, the future "Semiramis of the North," might someday become ruler of the three kingdoms, and unite for the first time the thrones of Denmark, Norway, and Sweden. At the time of her marriage she was ten years of age.

Henry's relatives and representatives busied themselves in Copenhagen on his behalf, and laid his claim before the assembled monarchs. We are told that his ancestors got from those princes a confirmation of the lands of Orkney. This was recognition of the Sinclair claim to ownership of lands which Earl Malise had personally owned and had the right to bequeath; but Earl Malise could not bequeath the title of Earl, since that was something which only the king of Norway could bestow. Though confirmation was a step forward it fell far short of what the family hoped for, since it did not secure the earldom. It meant only that the king of Norway would let the Sinclair family show what they could do with the Orkney Islands, the administration of which presented many thorny problems. The first concrete result of the Sinclair family's diplomacy was the installation of Henry's uncle Thomas as "Bailivus," or agent for the Norwegian king in Orkney.

Three years later, Henry received the honor of knighthood, at the customary age of twenty-one.

The Sinclair family administrator of Orkney, in his efforts to win the earldom for Sir Henry, actually proved harmful to his cause for he began by placing relatives and friends in positions of power in the islands. What King Haakon feared most was that the Orkneys, so far from his shores and so close to the coast of Scotland, might fall under Scottish influence and be lost to Norway, in spite of their predominantly Norse population, just as the Hebrides had been lost one hundred years before. Although it was geographically inevitable that there be some influx of Scotsmen into the Orkney Islands, Norway now sought to put a stop to it altogether. The king of Norway requested the king of Scotland to prevent attempts to settle the succession to the earldom by force and intrigue, and acceding to this request, King David of Scotland forbade his subjects to pass into Orkney on any errand other than lawful commerce.

The situation in the Orkneys was more than a struggle between the Norse and the Scots; it was complicated by the interfering hand of a churchman, William, Bishop of Orkney and Shetland. This cleric had appropriated land rents due to the king of Norway, and had quarreled "in various matters" with representatives of the king. Seeing in what direction the wind was blowing, Bishop William tried to make it appear that he was not opposed to the king of Norway but was opposed to Scotsmen. He endeavored to identify his interests with those of the native

Orkney and Shetland landowners, who were Norsemen. Under pressure, Bishop William came to an agreement on May 25, 1369 in Kirkinvaghe (Kirkwall) with the king's governor, Haakon Jonsson, by which both promised to return the persons they had seized from among each other's partisans. The bishop would return the king's butter, in which form the land rents had been in part paid, and 112 "true golden coins" of Norway and "21 nobles," gold coins of Scotland. The bishop and the governor agreed to make atonement for any injury either might do to the other in the future, "unless they both prefer to settle it between them." Their supporters were to be safe from each other, except as they might proceed by lawsuits. The bishop and the leading landowners were to be foremost in all councils, and the bishop promised to "have good native men of Orkney and Shetland in his service" thereafter. One of the witnesses to this agreement was "John Sincler."[2] In spite of this agreement, the bishop continued his villainous activities.

Some credit for having had a share in settling the quarrel evidently belonged to Henry, but in any case, immediately afterward he sent ambassadors to King Haakon requesting that the administration of the earldom be confirmed to him personally. The next year the king granted the confirmation to him, but still did not give him the title of earl.

During these years, 1362 to 1370, Henry was acquiring political experience at meetings of the Scottish Parliament at Scone and elsewhere, but he had much more to learn, for he had not yet come to grips with the complexities of the actual situation in Orkney. He let the king's governor, Haakon Jonsson, serve as his prefect, and left Orkney affairs largely in his hands. This proved to be a mistake; for his cousin Alexander was actively intriguing against him and brewing trouble.

Henry meanwhile was kept very busy in Scotland. When King David died, Robert Stewart, who had been chosen to be his successor, established the Stewart dynasty. The new queen, Euphemia Ross, was Henry's great-aunt. Henry went to court to do homage, and to carry out his hereditary duties as guardian of the throne. He might have supposed that his relationship to the queen would further his claims to the earldom, but actually it militated against him. The king of Norway began to question whether it would be wise to let anyone become permanent master of the Orkneys who was so closely related to the throne of Scotland as Henry was.

According to Father Hay, "a marriage was concluded" in Copenhagen between Henry and Florentia, a princess of Denmark, daughter of King Magnus, and a sister to King Haakon. Jacob Van Bassan, who has a reputation for genealogical inaccuracy (having been called "a pure fabulist") doubts this marriage. Following Van Bassan, Douglas's *Peerage of Scotland* says: "The fable of his having married Florentia is exploded." Father Hay, however, was in a position to know the facts.

It is probable that there was such a marriage. Henry's family would have sought such a marriage, and it would not have been seeking too high. The marriage was possible within surviving records of the royal genealogies, but "daughter" of King Magnus may have meant grand-daughter or great-granddaughter.[3] Magnus Ericsson, King of Sweden 1350–1359, had a daughter who died young, and King Waldemar and Helwig, daughter of King Magnus, had two daughters who died young. Those who were married in infancy or childhood were not bedded until puberty.

Considering the ages at which Henry's forebears had married, he would have been quite the exception if he had not married at about the time he first went to Copenhagen. In his family on the male side, beginning with his great-grandfather, there were four generations in seventy-nine years. On the female side, from his great-grandmother, through his grandfather, mother, sister, and niece, there were five generations in eighty years, an average of less than fifteen years each. Henry's sister Margaret bore her first child at the age of thirteen. This was not unusual, though it is the earliest maternity of record in the Sinclair family, in which the earliest paternity of record was that of a boy of fifteen.

In our hero's day there were many compulsions to early parent-hood: the need of assuring heirs before the male got killed in battle; the desire for children through whose early marriage a family's ambitions could be more rapidly advanced; and the uninhibited notion that puberty gave sanction to an immediately active sex life. The decimation of many of the population by the Black Death was still a further incentive, and, after all, life expectancy in the fourteenth century was only thirty years.

If Henry married a Danish princess, she would have had to be one who died in infancy. All we are told is that she was one "by whom he had no issue." It has also been said that he made a second marriage with "Elizabeth, co-heiress of Strathearn."[4] If this marriage, of which there is no record, occurred, he had no heir by it. In any case, the time came when he made arrangements for a marriage of which we do have a record.

As Lord of Roslin, Henry had very probably been compelled by his family to marry the Danish princess for political reasons. His family would have given no consideration to any personal inclination he might have had. If he did marry the Danish princess, she died before she was old enough to be bedded with him. Since marriage into royalty had not brought him the earldom, there seemed to be no point in seeking another such marriage, especially since he was now closely related to royalty, being grandnephew to the new king of Scotland. While any match he made would have to be one of which the king as well as the Sinclair family would approve, Henry was determined to marry a girl of his own choosing. She must not be an infant, but one ready for child-bearing. In the midst of his journeys hither and yon, he had eyed many beautiful damsels. Now he was in love with the fairest of them all.

Her name was Janet. She was the daughter of Sir Thomas Haly-burton, lord of Dirleton Castle, twenty miles from Roslin. He asked her father for her hand and received the parental consent. Since the match was thus settled, Henry, wishing to meet the girl and to declare his love, must have felt irked that his fervor must yet be curbed by the conventions insisted upon by gentlewomen. But a nobleman's direct wooing must conform to custom. It was a custom to which we are given a clue by a poem, the *Roman de la Rose*. The *Roman* enjoyed such popularity in the fourteenth century that two hundred manuscript copies of it have survived. It set the pattern for courtly love upon which all ladies of rank and breeding were resolute.

Henry was probably familiar with the *Roman* from his boyhood, but probably scorned it as being of interest only to girls. Being a man, he did not realize that what it expressed was women's protest against male conceit, male notions of superiority, and male possessiveness. Nevertheless he must abide by its code.

In accordance with the *Roman*, his meeting with Janet had to be in a garden. Fortunately, Dirleton Castle had a most beautiful garden. Henry, we may believe, stepped forth on the greensward blithely, aware, however, that he must not declare his love at this first meeting alone with Janet, but must let converse carry to better acquaintance. The girl, of course, did not at once come into the flowered walk, but kept him wait-ing. He may have marveled that she did, if he did not know the *Roman* well enough. The delay gave him time to look about him. He must have felt as others did that Dirleton Castle in its garden setting was a place of singular charm, and he would have agreed enthusiastically with the nobleman who esteemed it "the pleasantest dwelling in Scotland."[5]

But he had eyes for naught else than the girl he had come to get when he turned and saw her near him; for of all creatures that ever lived she seemed to him the most breathtakingly lovely. In accordance with custom, she at first appeared not to have seen him, no more than if he were a gardener, but when she reached up and broke off a rose from its stem and laid the blossom in a wicker basket at her feet, Henry with courtly form bowed and spoke her name, and she blushed to match the rose.

If in an ecstasy of adoration he yielded to the temptation to brush aside etiquette, and immediately avow that he was quite enraptured by her blue eyes, her golden hair, her gay lips and her sweet smile, she answered him with banter, saying that if she had such beauty, it should have made him tongueless. If he took oath that she was the most beautiful girl in Scotland, she challenged him to be honest, since he had seen the damsels at court. Over his protest, she would have reminded him that the king's daughter, Giles, was universally deemed the most beautiful Scotswoman. In any case, Janet as woman wooed, would have brought him back to decorum and the proper and prescribed ritual.

Dirleton Castle Ruins

As Henry and Janet strolled together through the garden, he found words to praise her flowers. When she took seat on a bench at the end of the garden, it was permissible for him to sit beside her.

She gave ready ear when he told her news of the court and spoke of his ambition and hopes in regard to the Earldom of Orkney. In the midst of his telling, she sought to school him according to the *Roman*. Suddenly she said she missed her purse and must have left it in her flower basket. Eager to serve her, his passion making him her willing slave, he did not think to call a lackey, but ran back to the spot where they had met and like an underling fetched her basket to her.

He told her many things about his family that day. When the afternoon shadows lengthened, he, ever more distractedly impassioned, came away from his own talk warmly aglow like the western sun. Her father's guest for the night, he deliciously anticipated talking with her again on the morrow, and shaped the words by which he would then declare his love.

On the second day, when the romantic ritual permitted him to tell her that he had her father's consent and that he wished to marry her, she asked him why. This he took as an opportunity to say he had chosen to marry her for the best of reasons—because he loved her. In a torrent of words he told her he had been smitten by the god of love beyond all curing save through her acquiescence. If he had supposed this would conclude his courting, he was mistaken; for a wise woman before she said yes enjoyed a power she feared she would never afterwards have. It was her instinct to make the most of it while she could, and so she quoted from the *Roman*, posing the question:

> *Think you a man gains woman's love*
> *Who sets himself as lord above*
> *Her will and ways?*

Being a man, he probably failed to understand her; for it was a point of view very difficult for any male to comprehend. Since it made him feel that he had failed to convince her that he did love her, he redoubled the ardor of his wooing, with extravagant avowals. She then disconcerted him. Without committing herself, she told him that his saying this day that he loved her was no more than he had told her yestreen. When he denied that he had been rude enough the day before to tell her that he loved her, she said he had told her it with certainty. When in astonishment he defied her to show how he had declared his love the first day, she said it was by his running like a lackey to fetch her basket. If he had not been in love, he would have walked. And to make sure that he, a man, would not miss her meaning, she wagered that his father, from the time Henry was of age to observe, had not run or even so much as walked, or bestirred himself at all to fetch something for his wife, if a lackey were within call.

She asked him whether he thought dreams foretell the future. When he replied that he did, for it was a common belief that dreams had a controlling influence over human lives, she told him she had dreamed of a husband who would love her beyond the nuptial love. Then he implored her to believe that he wanted nothing so much as to fulfill her dream. He said it, and swore to it, and at the moment believed it.

It was the most a woman could get. And so, having planted in one man this idea which noblewomen hoped would grow in all men until someday it might flower into a garden of paradise, Janet told Henry that there was another question he must ask her, before she could give answer to his suit. By indirection, she led him into asking her the question that was a woman's privilege to hear if she had managed the conversation with sufficient skill. She reduced him to asking her if she loved him. When he asked that, it did not take her long to say she did.

Henry Sinclair and Janet Halyburton were joyously wed.

Shortly after his marriage, Sir Henry's attention was occupied by a personal problem concerning his niece Margaret Stewart, his sister's eldest child. His niece had married the Earl of Mar, but had been left a widow and childless at the age of fifteen. After her father, the Earl of Angus, died, young Margaret became a ward of Sir William, first Earl of Douglas, who was married to her father's sister. She lived in the earl's castle. Lord Douglas should have been seeking to arrange another marriage for his ward, for she was an earl's daughter with two titles, Countess of Angus and Countess of Mar, and thus eminently eligible. She was also extremely beautiful. But that was precisely why Lord Douglas, a strong and lusty man, was dilatory, if not deliberately stalling. Folk said he was so enamored of the beauty of his wife's niece that he was unwilling to part with her. He was constantly with her and was obviously becoming so infatuated with her that it was likely that he would make forcible advances. Her mother was deeply disturbed about the situation and consulted with Sir Henry. Aroused by what his apprehensive sister told him, Sir Henry in turn discussed the matter with his aunt the queen, but the queen felt she could not interfere; for the Earl of Douglas' son James was married to her own daughter Isabel. However, much as

Henry would have liked to remove his niece Margaret from proximity to her dangerous guardian, he did not wish to quarrel with William, Earl of Douglas.

Henry gave his approval to the remarriage of his widowed sister, aged thirty-one, to Sir John St. Clair, of another branch of the family (see Note 2, Chapter 3). Lord Douglas, perhaps to win favor with his wife's niece, gave the dowry for her mother's marriage, in the form of a charter of the lands of Herdmannston (Hermiston) and of Carfrae, to his "beloved cousin John of St. Clair." This marriage was welcomed by Douglas and was precisely what he wanted, for it removed young Margaret's mother from the Douglas castle so that she could no longer keep a watchful eye on her daughter.

When the young countess was twenty years of age, she ceased to resist her guardian, and gave herself to him. The fruit of their union was a son, George, and later a daughter, both born out of wedlock; for the wife of the Earl of Douglas lived, and indeed, lived to survive him.

Henry's disapproval of the illicit connection was ridiculed by Margaret's ardent lover. What really angered Henry was Earl William's calling him "Henry the Holy."

Shortly thereafter, Janet bore Henry a son and heir who was named after him. She also bore him two other sons and three daughters. Then, on June 30, 1375, King Haakon removed Henry's administrators and appointed Sir Alexander de Ard governor of Orkney and commissioner for the king.

This was a blow and a bitter humiliation to Henry. It forced him to ask himself wherein he had failed. Probably, under the circumstances, it was inevitable.

There was a ray of hope, however. King Haakon had set a time limit, a period of one year, as the term for which Henry's cousin was commissioned. Evidently the king was not convinced that Alexander de Ard should be given permanent control of Orkney. Henry cheered himself with the thought. Meanwhile, family agents in the Orkneys would make as much trouble for Alexander as Alexander's agents had been making for him. And, above all, now that the struggle between himself and his cousin had come to this pass, he would see to it that there was firmly planted in King Haakon's mind the idea that Henry Sinclair's claim to the earldom was to be preferred to Alexander's.

A year later Henry had reason to feel that both steps had been effective. King Haakon sent a notice to the people of Orkney that Alexander de Ard was to come to the king's presence "to give evidence of what right and reason he asserted he has the lordship of the earldom, and to prove to us and our council how the contest between the bishop of Orkney and him is turning out." We do not know how Alexander responded to this command, but we do know he lost his case. The removal of Sir Alexander de Ard from the governorship of Orkney strengthened the argument of those lawmen who supported Henry's claim that inheritance should be on the basis of bequeathed heirship. King Haakon had given each of the rivals an opportunity to show what he could do with administrative authority, and Alexander had revealed inadequacy.

It may be that King Haakon had no other choice; on the other hand, Sir Henry's abilities and character may have been what ultimately convinced King Haakon that he was the man to be entrusted with the great task. Henry would at last checkmate his cousin.

Chapter Four

EARL

HENRY SINCLAIR'S rise to what was practically the status of royalty is a most romantic story.

Ever since the death of his grandfather, Earl Malise, there had been no settled government in the Orkney and Shetland islands. Without an effective ruler, the islands had fallen into lawlessness. The royal commissioners, the Orkney bishop, the local officials, and the fishermen were continually at odds.

It was a period of confusion throughout Europe. The Papal Schism began in 1378, to the shame of all Christendom. For seventy-three years the papacy had been "captive" at Avignon in southern France, under the control of French kings. At the death of the Avignon Pope Gregory V, in 1378, the College of Cardinals in Rome elected Pope Urban VI, but then declared his election null and instead elected Clement VII, who fled to Avignon thus taking the papacy once again from Rome. The great question for all Christians was which pope should they accept.

By the time King Haakon of Norway had made up his mind which pope he preferred, he had also decided which of the rivals to the Orkney earldom had abilities commensurate with the responsibilities. A strong man was needed to take the reins in the islands, one whose training was outstanding and whose character would command respect. But it must also be a man of whose loyalty he could be sure.

Froissart, chronicler and poet of the time, characterized the perfect knight: "gay, loyal, gallant, prudent, secret, generous, bold, determined, enterprising." Gay meant vivacious, brisk, lively, spirited, vivid, responding and rebounding quickly. Secret meant capable of retaining confidences. Most knights were more than sufficiently bold and enterprising, but few exemplified the kind of chivalry that was above prowess in the field, and consisted of self-restraint and consideration for others. The virtue found most rarely in a knight was gentleness—"high erected thoughts seated in a heart of courtesy."

Sir Henry Sinclair did not fall far short of Froissart's "perfect knight." He certainly possessed the qualities of judgment and leadership requisite for the work he would be called upon to do. He was thirty-three when he learned that he was to be invested with the title of earl. Maturity had brought him a new attitude, a readiness to separate himself for long periods from the comforts of his barony and the amenities of a nobleman's life in Scotland. He was prepared to deny himself many pleasures. Hardest for him to forego would be the woodland delights of stag and boar hunting while he was in the treeless islands of his earldom. There was hunting there on the open moor, but that was never so exciting as hunting in the glades of forested hills. He was nevertheless ready to devote himself to his duties as earl, though he knew it would mean long separations from his friends. With his beloved Janet he was willing to live anywhere.

His task would be to rescue the Orkney islanders from a reign of violence and corruption and to extend the king's authority over all. In the just settlement of land disputes, he would have to adjust himself to island laws and customs. As Earl of Orkney he must be faithful to the king of Norway, while as Baron of Roslin he must at the same time remain loyal to the king of Scotland. He would have to be a master of the art of human relations. In him the Norwegian Crown secured a vassal who took a serious view of his obligations.

The terms under which the Orkney earldom would be bestowed on him were carefully prepared by lawmen. He himself procured, if not the wholehearted support, at least the active cooperation of his disappointed cousin Alexander. With prudent sagacity, and perhaps persuaded by a gift or promises, Alexander agreed to serve as an agent for Henry.

The Deed of Investiture of Sir Henry Sinclair as Earl of Orkney is interesting in all its details. Its full text is given as a note,[1] but for the reader's convenience, here is a brief summary of its terms:

1.   If requested, Earl Henry pledged to serve the king of Norway with one hundred armed men.

2.   He would defend the islands with all available force.

3.   He would help the king of Norway in war.

4.   He would not build castles in the islands without the king's consent.

5.   He would cherish the rights of all persons in the islands.

6.   He would not sell or give as pledge any of the islands.

7.   He would hospitably receive the king or his followers on visits to the islands.

8.   He would not initiate any war that might damage the islands.

9.   He would answer in person for any injury done to anyone in the islands.

10.   When summoned he would come to counsel the king in person.

11.   He would not break the king's peace.

12.   He would make no league with or establish friendship with the Orcadian bishop.

13.   His heir would not inherit the earldom except as the king of Norway were to grant title.

14.   His payment for the title of earl was to be one thousand gold pieces.

15.   His cousin Malise Sparre would disavow any claim to the earldom.

16.   His cousin Alexander de Ard would also.

There follow pledges of hostages and agreement to procure the promises of Scots nobles to recognize Sir Henry as earl of Orkney, and an added term,

17.   Earl Henry would not take lands or rights belonging to the king.

Finally, the penalty for breach of any of the terms would be loss of the earldom.

The installation of Sir Henry Sinclair as Earl of Orkney is chiefly of importance to us because it gave Henry the opportunity to acquire the knowledge and power that enabled him to become in his day a discoverer of North America. But his installation is of great importance to historians because it is unique among medieval documents of infefture. Historians had assumed that the terms of a feudal grant were dictated by the overlord and accepted in toto by the vassal. But Henry's installation bears the touch of lawmen from his native Scotland as well as those from Norway. It clearly shows that there must have been a negotiation between the Norse and the Scots on the terms of the deed back and forth across the North Sea.

The installation took place on August 2, 1379. One of its terms is the following:

> Further, we promise in good faith that we shall be bound to pay to our abovesaid lord the king, or to his official at Tunisberg, on the next festival of St. Martin the bishop and confessor, a thousand golden pieces, which are called nobles, of English money[2] in which we acknowledge us to be bound to him by just payment.

This one thousand nobles was the price Henry paid for his feudal investiture. But on the same day, by a document quite separate from his installation, he was bonded to make another payment at another place. This requirement was patently for another purpose.

> Let it be clear to all by these presents that we, HENRY SINCLAIR, Earl of Orkney, are bound and firmly held to Haquin Johnson [Royal Bailie for the king of Norway] to pay 200 nobles of good gold to him or his sure attorney, who must hold in their hands the present letters, with the letters of receipts by Haquin. The sum of the said gold must be paid at Kirkwall within Orkney in equal portions of 100 nobles at Pentecost next and St. Martinmas thereafter. If it happen that we fail in payment of the 200 nobles as is promised to be done, we bind our heirs and executors to completely pay the sum of gold faithfully to Haquin or his deputy, as is preferred, without any trick or fraud. In testimony of the matter, our seal is appended to the presents. Written at Marstrand, 2nd August, 1379.[3]

Because this bond was deemed of major importance, it was examined by the chapter of the canonical church of Bergen and the chapter of the canonical church of the Twelve Apostles of the same royal city.

"Let all know whose interest it is, that we have examined the letters of a noble and illustrious lord, Henry Sinclair, Earl of Orkney, and they are not damaged nor cancelled nor vitiated in any part, and are confirmed by his certain attached seal. We have carefully read them, their tenor following word for word. . . . [The above bond is here entered.] In Testimony of this matter the seals of our chapter were appended to the present document. Written within the eighth of the Nativity of the Virgin, that is, September 9, 1380, at the canonical church of Bergen."[4]

What was the purpose of this carefully examined bond? Why must the two hundred nobles be paid in two portions at two separate dates at Kirkwall within Orkney? Could it be for any other reason than that King Haakon was determined that the man he had chosen for earl should not shirk the onerous problems in the islands, should not be merely a figurehead, a title holder, but an actual ruler who must take permanent possession of the main Orkney island, the one called Pomona? Earl Henry was bound to deliver the money in Kirkwall, the principal town in Pomona, in 1380, half of it seven weeks after Easter and the other half on November 11.

Both king and earl clearly saw what the duties of the earl would be. The Orkneys, to say nothing for the moment of the Shetlands, had for decades been riven by disputes over land ownership and boundaries. The bishop's tax gatherers were still in open conflict with the king's, and often triumphant over them. The bishop was prepared to use force against any attempt by the earl to advance the king's cause. The church situation was complicated by the Papal Schism. The Orkneys were often being raided by "wild Scots" (Highlanders). The water passages around and between the islands swarmed with smugglers and pirates. Most of the Orkneymen were defiant of the king's law. Earl Henry would have to build up an effective military force to restore the islands to obedience and order. Including the Shetlands, there were one hundred and seventy islands in the earldom, fifty-three of them inhabited. To meet the responsibilities of Earl of Orkney would be no easy task.

As Earl of Orkney, Henry's power in the islands was near to that of a king. However, so as not to arouse jealousies and antagonism in his native land, he tactfully and wisely accepted equality there with other earls. He could not neglect his Scottish baronies, and so in Scotland he called himself merely "Comes," the Latin for the title of earl held among Scots nobles.

In his seagirt kingdom, Henry was "more honoured than any of his ancestors, for he had power to cause stamp coins within his dominions,[5] to make laws, to remitt crimes,—he had his sword of honour carried before him wheresoever he went:—he bore a crowne on his head when he constituted laws, and, in a word, was subject to none, save only he held the lands of the king of Denmark, Sweden and Norway, and entred with them, to whom also it did belong to crowne any of those three kings, so that in all those parts he was esteemed a second person next to the king."[6]

Close links to royalty came with the marriages he arranged for his three eldest children: His son and heir, Henry, married Giles (Egida) Douglas, granddaughter of King Robert II. Earl Henry's second son, John, married Ingeborg, a daughter of Waldemar, King of Denmark.[7] His eldest daughter, Elizabeth, married Sir John Drummond of Stobhall (of Cargill in Perthshire), the brother of Annabella, queen of King Robert III.

With these royal alliances, Earl Henry strengthened his position as the head of what was to all intents and purposes a buffer state. In Orkney he was an independent ruler, a prince, practically a sovereign. He was limited only by his commitments to the king of Norway.

He had to sail stormy seas of statecraft, with strong political currents that might at any moment run him on the rocks. However, he seems to have steered his course without shipwreck, firm ruler over himself. He must have often whispered to himself the words of his patron St. Katherine, who in the midst of controversy had quoted the ancient wise man: "If thou be ruled by the body, thou shalt be a slave, but if by the spirit, a king."

Henry had reason to feel exultant when as titled earl he entered among his wide-flung islands. The many bays, sounds, and firths broadened the distances so that his sea dominion was one hundred and seventy miles in length from the southern tip of the Orkneys to the northern tip of the Shetlands, and about thirty-five miles in width, extending over an area of six thousand square miles. He was thrilled with the spaciousness as he sailed to Orkney, flanked on its western side with elevations almost as high as those of the Pentland Hills. He saw lordly vistas of wild seaboard, of towering cliffs and spume-girt headlands. It was the realm of sea-kings, tameless spirits of the past:

> *Land of the whirlpool-torrent foam,*
> > *Where oceans meet in maddening shock;*
> *The beetling cliff—the shelving holm—*
> > *The dark insidious rock.*[8]

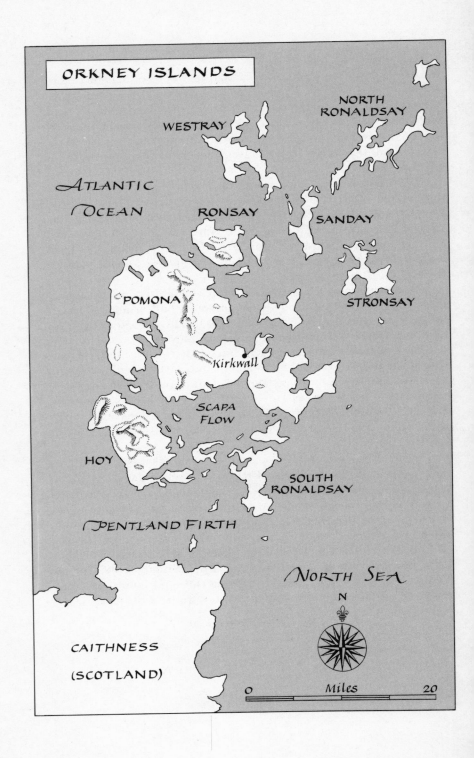

Waves clawed at the reefs, while gulls and kittiwakes wheeled and screamed. Back of the cliffs black ravens soared over green moors that reached into blue-gray mists. Birds called petrels, black and white like his Roslin coat-of-arms, dived for fish in broken water. Any Orkneyman would have told Earl Henry they were harbingers of storm.

To the eye of a Scotsman from thickly wooded Midlothian, the bare windswept Orkneys were shelterless and forbidding. But their grim strangeness yielded upon acquaintance as one experienced their moods in changing lights and shadows. When the sun in a fitful break between showers brightened the meadows and touched the reefs with gold, they wore a mantle of beauty.

Though almost treeless, the land was rich, excellent for grazing cattle and sheep. Upon its moors roamed deer and rabbits. A huntsman's hawks could there bring down wild geese, wild duck, plover, curlew, and teal. Otters were plentiful along the streams, and seals along the shores. The Orkney seas swarmed with lobsters and crabs, with ling, haddock, keeling, skates, flukes, whiting, turbot, and sole. Though the islands of the whole earldom comprised only 926 square miles of land, their fisheries were of major importance to Europe and brought in great wealth.

Henry had come to stay, except as his duties required his presence in Scotland or Scandinavia. He would have to do battle with entrenched violators of the king's law, illegal tax collectors, pirates and smugglers to make the islands really his. In granting him the title of earl, all that King Haakon had been able to give him was the right to win the islands, by whatever armed might he could command. He had been invested merely with an opportunity.

To procure the obedience of the islanders, Henry must prove himself their effective overlord. He would have to quell dissensions, put a stop to violence, and maintain justice. He would have to fight through many a precarious passage to restore respect for the king's law and to establish his own tenure.

When Malise Sparre, son of the third daughter of Earl Malise, and Alexander de Ard, listening to the public reading of Henry's Investiture in Marstrand, first learned that they were to be held in Scandinavia as hostages for the fulfillment of Henry's promises, they doubtless scowled. It was all they could do at the moment. They had been neatly trapped. Their retention in Scandinavia had been a masterly move, as much to King Haakon's liking as to Henry's; for it kept those two troublemakers temporarily out of the way, giving their cousin a cleared field, at least briefly, in which to secure his earldom. Even if it embittered them, though Henry felt it should not since some of his real friends were also hostages for the faithful performance of his obligations, it did not make them more his ill-wishers than they already were.

Now Henry could concentrate on the thorny problem of making himself master of all the islands.

Chapter Five

CASTLE

HENRY'S FIRST and foremost requirement as a base from which to enforce the king's law in Orkney was a strong castle. Like all his peers, he thought in terms of a castle, for he was accustomed to power stemming from a stronghold, with footmen and cavalry. He had many reasons for building a castle in Kirkwall. He wanted a safe home for Janet and the children. They could not be expected to live, as some Orkneymen did, in a windowless two-room house under the same roof with pigs. He demanded comfort in Kirkwall comparable to what his family had in Roslin. Furthermore, a castle was a prerequisite to extending adequate hospitality to important visitors. Above all, he needed a castle to establish in men's minds the reality of his position as lord of the isles: It would be a symbol of his authority. It must be a fort in which to house retainers and hold soldiers in constant readiness to serve the king, and it must be an armory for weapons and a center where loyal men could assemble in an emergency. Its location must be near the shore in order to give safe cover to the landing of ships.

The second provision of Henry's investiture pledged him in these words:

> If any wish to attack or hostily to invade, in manner whatsoever, the lands and islands of the Orkneys, or the land of Zetland [Shetland], then we promise and oblige us to defend the lands named, with men in good condition whom we may be able to collect for this solely, from the lands and islands themselves, yes, with all the force of relatives, friends, and servants.

Any lawman, Norwegian as well as Scottish, could have argued the incompatibility of this with any withholding by the Norwegian king of consent to build a castle in Kirkwall. It would be patently impossible for the earl to gather a force of islanders to defend the islands effectively without a fortified stronghold as a base.

Before his installation, Henry or his lawmen had surely stated the need for a stronghold in Kirkwall from which to initiate operations against the law-breaking bishop of Orkney, who had brazenly assumed the license and dignity of a petty sovereign. The bishop resided in a fortified palace with turret rooms, standing inside a massive wall that enclosed a square wherein he had many armed retainers. There was no question of the necessity of giving the earl permission to build a castle at Kirkwall, and there is no implication that there was any argument by the Norwegian Crown that a castle in Kirkwall would be superfluous. What points directly to the contrary is the implication, in the twelfth term of the Deed of Investiture, that Earl Henry was not to make any league with or establish friendship with the antagonistic bishop. There is every reason to believe that the king of Norway conceded the necessity of Earl Henry's building a castle if he were to become the effective ruler that the king desired him to be. But if the earl did succeed in taking physical possession of the Orkneys, with a castle there, he would become a very powerful person, strong enough to break away from his overlord. This was King Haakon's anxiety. This is why the king insisted upon the fourth provision, fifth paragraph in Henry's Investiture:

> We promise in good faith that we must not build or construct castles or any fortifications within the lands and islands beforesaid, unless we have obtained the favour, good-pleasure, and consent of our same lord the king.

The question obviously was not whether the earl should have a castle, but what he must do to win the king's consent to its building. Did

Earl Henry violate this agreement?[1] Or, as the language of the pledge distinctly says he must do, did he obtain the "consent" of the king of Norway?

King Haakon was understandably worried over Norway's possible loss of the Orkney earldom. Perhaps King Robert of Scotland, wishing to eliminate smuggling and pirating activities so close to Scotland's northern shores, had dropped a hint or threat that the Scottish Crown might be impelled to seize the Orkneys and restore law and order in the islands if King Haakon did not soon appoint an earl. In appointing as earl a man who was not by birth one of his own subjects, but a man born in Scotland, King Haakon's fear was that under pressure from Scotland the earldom of Orkney might be seized by Scotland.

Henry Sinclair, after he had become Earl of Orkney, had to set this fear at rest. He did so by obtaining two commitments in Scotland one month after his investiture. The first was a contract entered into by King Robert of Scotland making formal resignation of any right in the Orkney earldom, and recognizing King Haakon's action in giving the earldom "to our beloved relative, Henry, Earl of Orkney" (*"dilecto consanguineo suo Henrico Orcadie"*).[2]

The other commitment was made by Earl Henry, a pledge to which he procured a host of witnesses. It is important enough to quote in full:

> To all sons of holy Church to whose notice the present letter shall come: Henry de St. Clair Earl of Orkney and Lord of Roslin in Scotland sends greeting in the Saviour of all men. I inform all of you by this present letter with all fidelity I do promise to the most excellent prince and my lord, the Lord Haakon, King of Norway and Sweden, the illustrious, that I shall in no way alienate or pledge or deliver as security the lands or islands of the country of Orkney away from my lord the aforesaid king, his heirs and successors, or surrender them without the consent of my lord the above-mentioned king, his heirs or his successors.
>
> And that I shall faithfully observe all the promises given above, the venerable fathers in Christ and lords, Lords William and Walter, Bishops of St. Andrews and Glasgow; William and George, Earls of Douglas and March; William Ramsay, Walter Halyburton, George Abernethy, Patrick Hepburn, John Edmundstone, Alexander Halyburton, John Turribus and Robert Dalzell, barons and knights, also have promised.
>
> In testimony of all which things our seal is appended, and we have procured to be appended to the present the seals of the said bishops, counts [earls], barons, and knights.

Given at St. Andrews on the first day of the month of September, in the year of grace one thousand and three hundred and seventy-nine.[3]

The leading Scots nobles were thus not only witnesses to the fact that Earl Henry was a vassal to the king of Norway and bound by feudal law to the preservation of the earldom of Orkney to the Norwegian Crown, but they added their promises to his that it would be so preserved. They made their promises by all that men held most sacred: their religion, their knightly pride in their own word of honor, and their relation to each other within the feudal code which together they upheld.

King Haakon could not have asked for any stronger assurances. There is no reason to doubt that Earl Henry did by these two commitments win "the favour, good-pleasure, and consent" of the king of Norway to the building of a castle in Kirkwall. There is no record of any greedy opportunism in Earl Henry, or any willingness to snatch at an illegitimate goal by gross deception.

We are not making an unwarranted pleading of the case. Several writers who have not read the terms of Henry's Investiture carefully, have charged Earl Henry Sinclair with treachery and deceit because he built a castle in Kirkwall. It is in defense of his character that we cite the facts.

It is unimaginative to suppose that Henry Sinclair, within his first twelve months as earl, would have deliberately incurred the penalty for violation stated in the last paragraph of his Investiture, and would have put in jeopardy his title and the rights of his heirs to inherit the earldom. Hugh Marwick, in *Orkney* (1951), obviously not having reflected upon the implication of the language of the fourth provision of Henry's Deed of Investiture, says: "It may have been partly in consequence of Highland raids that Earl Henry, in direct contravention of his charter from the king of Norway, erected a formidable castle in Kirkwall, but it is equally probable that he had in view a fortress in Orkney from which he might be able to defy his Norwegian liege-lord if occasion should arise."[4] This imputation of base motives to Henry Sinclair was a careless repetition of a similar charge made by Fred W. Lucas in 1898. There is no indication that Earl Henry ever entertained any such motive. There is every evidence to the contrary. He never showed any spirit of disloyalty to Norway. If he had not begun his castle in Kirkwall in 1380, King Olaf, who came to the Norwegian throne the next year, would undoubtedly have requested him to build one as soon as he could, because kings in all countries were frightened by the terrifying reports of the Wat Tyler revolt, the revolutionary uprising of the common people of England in 1381.

Kirkwall means "Church Bay." The Orkney Cathedral of St. Magnus sat near the shore of the harbor, which was formed by a long spit, originally a shoal. This shoal had been built up to a mole that extended nearly across the harbor, leaving a narrow entrance. Today, that entrance is closed and the old harbor is a lake.

The bishop's palace was about two hundred feet to the south of the cathedral. Henry's castle was about one hundred yards to the north of the cathedral, on a slight elevation at the shore and extending out into the bay. It was actually a reconstruction of an old stronghold of the Norse earls, as it was on the same site. Its foundations below water and up to the level of the highest tides were necessarily of dry masonry, since salt water would attack mortar, at least such mortar as the fourteenth century knew how to make. It was certainly inferior to that of the ancient Romans who had the secret of a mortar or cement resistant to salt water. Henry's castle had an arched water entrance for loading and unloading ships, and the cellar was partly used as a warehouse. Since it was at the site of a viking fortress, it was where ships could be drawn ashore, and in the opinion of Mr. Evan MacGillivray, county librarian of Orkney, it was where ships could be inverted above a hollow out of which stones had been dug.

Rising above the waterline to a height of sixty to ninety feet, Henry's castle was built of ashlar. The stones, which had something of the striated appearance of masonry, were probably not laid in courses as in later dressed ashlar work, and this may have been the secret of the great strength of the walls. There were rounded turrets later used for gun emplacements. The walls were of such vast thickness that they had barrack rooms within them.[5]

The stoutness of its walls was such that two centuries later, a man who laid siege to it with cannon said: "I protest to God the house has never been biggit without the consent of the devil, for it is one of the strongest holds in Britain—without fellow."[6]

A well that was lined with dressed freestones supplied the castle with water. This well still exists, though covered over. The water in it is clear, not like the present Kirkwall reservoir water, which is discolored by contact with peat-bog earth. This clarity of the well water indicates that close to the castle were broad sands.[7]

Above the gate of the castle was the Sinclair Orkney coat-of-arms, cut in a block of red stone.[8]

The castle was surrounded on three sides by the water of the bay. On the land side there was a moatlike channel, over which was a drawbridge. The castle was a fortress perfectly protected from foraying horsemen.

Henry built adequately for his purposes. Since his Investiture in its twelfth provision required that he oppose the Orcadian bishop, "be for help to him [the king] against that bishop," and since that enemy bishop had a palace that accommodated a large garrison within its

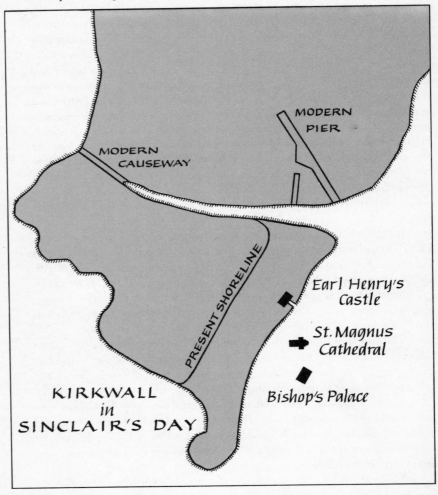

walls, a military force that the bishop used to accomplish unjust seizures of lands and rents, it was necessary that Henry have a residence stronger than the bishop's. Orkneymen approved when they realized the purposes of the castle and Earl Henry's intentions. Henry's castle did not separate him from the people of Orkney but brought him closer to them.

The building of his castle was preliminary to his squaring of accounts with the vexatious prelate. The antagonism between the king of Norway and the bishop of Orkney had several aspects. One of them was nationalistic. The king of Scotland had complained of the way Scotsmen were being mistreated in the Orkneys, and also that enemies of Scotland were being harbored there. Scotsmen were becoming numerous and some of them influential in the islands. Norway's complaint was that the Scots, whom the islanders called outlanders, "utlenske menn," were being favored by Bishop William of Orkney, who was himself Scottish. In the agreement between the king of Norway and the bishop in 1369, the bishop had promised thereafter to favor native Orkneymen.

Now the conflict between king and bishop broke out afresh, intensified by the national rivalries involved in the Papal Schism. France, Scotland, Spain, and the Kingdom of Naples recognized Pope Clement VII at Avignon, while England, Portugal, Norway, and other northern countries recognized Pope Urban VI at Rome. The Church in Orkney and the bishop stood with Scotland and the Avignon pope. Earl Henry represented Norway in politics and therefore supported Urban and fought for the land rights of the king of Norway against the Kirkwall bishop.

But the complaint that the secular nobles throughout Europe had against ecclesiastics was not based solely on national rivalries or the Papal Schism. It was a struggle for land control. For centuries, in every country, many pious souls had been bequeathing to the church estates that previously had been yielding taxes to monarchs. As church lands, their rents were collected by the church, which never died and never bequeathed anything. Fourteenth-century bishops were often wealthier than kings. King Haakon's father, King Magnus, had been in such financial straits that at one time he could not provide the royal family with enough to eat.

The landowning situation throughout Europe was in crisis. The corruption of the clergy was accurately described some years later by the author of *Il Principe*, who blasted exploitation of the people by churchmen.[9]

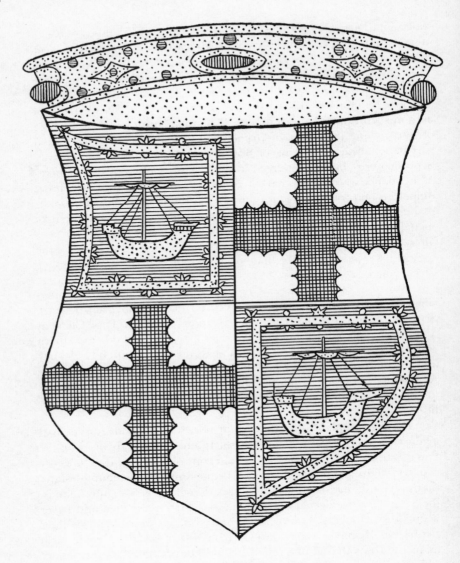

Sinclair Coat-of-Arms

An early Sinclair coat-of-arms, from Orkney. The colors on the arms
are indicated thus: red (*gules*) by vertical lines; blue (*azure*) by
horizontal lines, yellow or gold (*or*) by dots; black (*sable*) by cross-hatching.

The higher clergy had become unpopular. They were too rich, to put it mildly. They had come into possession of many baronies and attached them to bishoprics. They were in politics, held state offices, and were neglecting their religious duties. Their church activities had degenerated into simony, a traffic in the sale of church appointments. They treated repentance as a means of filling church coffers. They sold pardons for varying sums always nicely adjusted to a man's wealth, so that every Christian could afford to sin, and be properly milked for it. All in all, they were hated by the nobles, and feared by laymen.

In England, a theological professor at the University of Oxford was preaching what most men were thinking. John Wycliffe was advocating the return of church endowments to impoverished laymen. Many nobles who had records showing rights of inheritance from those who had made bequests to the church would recover property if church holdings were confiscated. William Langland wrote in *Piers Plowman*: "Take their lands, ye lords!"[10]

It was a period when barons were closer to the people than bishops. Barons were at first delighted to see the people attempting to take power from the bishops, but of course no sane man could sympathize with a French Jacquerie or a bloody uprising like that of the year 1381 in England. That had started in fishing villages in Essex and Kent—a fact to give caution to the overlord of the Orkney and Shetland fishermen. Fishermen, often smugglers on the side, were of all common folk the most successful in resisting serfdom. The blood of the English fishermen was up, and they roused the country. The peasants, resentful of oppressive taxes, would not pay the new poll tax, and they chased away the king's commissioners. It was called the "hurling time."

Wat, the tiler of Dartford in Kent, killed with a blow of his hammer a tax collector who insulted his daughter and by this act became the leader of a rising which culminated in an invasion of London by one hundred thousand men of Kent armed with pitchforks and clubs, rusty axes and crossbows. The king, the nobles, and the Archbishop of Canterbury took refuge in the Tower of London, while the mob killed tax collectors, burned John of Gaunt's palace, roared their indignation, but righteously refrained from looting.

When the fifteen-year-old King Richard II went out to the men of Kent and talked with them, they asked for freedom and an end of serfdom; he made unlimited promises, which they accepted joyfully.

They did not think of themselves as opposed to the king. The man they hated was the head prelate of Kent, the Archbishop of Canterbury,

C

who had enriched himself at their expense, and whom they took out of
the Tower and beheaded.

The next day, when the mayor of London stabbed Wat Tyler, the
men of Kent were angry enough to aim their crossbows at the king, but
the boy king spurred his horse forward, and by his manly courage and
royal prestige won them by promises and persuaded them to go home.
Having gained time to collect his forces, King Richard then led an army
of forty thousand into Kent and Essex, where he captured, then tortured
and hung thousands of the country folk. But the lesson of the rising was
not lost, and the English nobles began to take the complaints of common
folk more seriously.

It has been said that the exploiting class in England in 1381 could
not credit a rising without precedent. But there had been precedents
elsewhere—the Jacquerie in France, and the rising in Florence—of
which the English were becoming aware. It is therefore more accurate
to say that the ruling class was just beginning to learn. Modern society,
of course, has been strengthened by experience with revolutions, which
have taught policy makers why violent upsets occur and how they could
be avoided.

Henry, in opposing the Orcadian bishop, was expressing what all
Orkneymen felt against that prelate. He was dealing with forces that
were to go further than he intended.

Bishop William had often shifted positions. He had been against the
king's agents, then temporarily with the king's agents, and then again
against the agents. He had been for Scotsmen against native islanders,
and (by the written agreement he had been forced to make in 1369) for
native islanders against Scotsmen. He had in turn opposed Erngisle
Sunesson, the Sinclair family, Alexander de Ard, and now Earl Henry.

The bishop was consistent in only one thing, his thirst for riches. He
was not for the Church, not for properly constituted secular authority,
not for the people, but for himself, for the filling of his own purse. Aside
from his control over the church lands, he possessed wide bishopric lands,
acquired in part through declaring marriages within the fourth degree
of cousinship as incest and by appropriating the property of those thus
pronounced guilty. He and his predecessors through a long course of
years had also appropriated lands from the king, and had taken over
much of the "auld earldom" lands that rightfully belonged to Henry.
He had even alienated church lands—that is, had sold church lands for
his own private profit.

The building of Henry's Kirkwall Castle gave renewed hope for justice to Orkneymen who had been dispossessed. Their hatred of the bishop was intense. Henry did not plant the hatred, but every legal move he made to curb the bishop and to recover stolen lands brought nearer a day of reckoning that neither the bishop nor Earl Henry foresaw. It was in 1382, just a year after Wat Tyler's rebels had executed the Archbishop of Canterbury, that opposition to the bishop of the Orkney Islands broke out into violence. "Then was heard the mournful tidings that Bishop William was slain in the Orkneys."[11] All that the sparse record tells is that he was "killed or burnt by his flock."

His flock was Norse. The lesson was not lost on the church in Orkney. Terrified by what had happened to the bishop, and realizing how strongly the sympathies of the people of Orkney and Shetland were with Norway in its choosing to support the Roman pope, the Chapter of the Cathedral of St. Magnus in Kirkwall quickly broke away from the Scottish Church and its support of the Avignon pope, and they asked Pope Urban in Rome to nominate John, the parish priest of Fetlar, to be their new bishop. The chapter had another practical reason for doing what they did, for peasants in Shetland were bequeathing lands to the monastery at Bergen, instead of to the Orkney Church.

However, a relative of Henry's, Robert Sinclair, dean of Moray, was appointed bishop of Orkney by Pope Clement in Avignon in 1383. At the same time, another Scotsman, William de Lancea, was appointed by Avignon to the archdeaconate of Shetland. Although both Avignon appointees were merely titular and never got possession, there were two bishops of Orkney for a long time. During this disputed succession, Earl Henry, using Kirkwall Castle as a power base, recovered some of the filched earldom lands and restored to the king's holding lands rightfully belonging to the Norwegian Crown.

The major portion of his duties, however, could not be performed merely by aid of a castle. To extend the king's law throughout the many islands and to protect the fishermen in all the waterways and to put down piracy, Earl Henry needed also an effective fleet.

Chapter Six

FLEET

THE RESTORATION of lands in the Orkney Islands to their rightful owners required much scouting of the moors to locate the markers of ancient boundaries. Earl Henry found more peat bogs than plowed meadows. The heath, however, was natural shelter for the nesting moorfowl that scattered before his horse's hoofs. The desolate wastes seemed unrelieved except where rivulets in small ravines were "fringed with dwarf bushes of birch, hazel, and wild currant, some of them so tall as to be denominated trees, in that bleak, bare country."[1] The winds blew hard, seldom letting Henry and his men forget how near they were to the sea, even where they were out of sight of it.

The Orkneys were exposed to sudden storms from the ocean. Once Henry was caught in the blast of a dreaded wester, he learned the wisdom of seeking shelter in the nearest crofter's house, though it be but a lowly homestead in unenclosed fields, with one small kale-yard fenced about to keep animals from rooting. The humble dwelling had thick stone and sod walls and a thatched roof lashed down with binders weighted with boulders, amid which black oats sprouted green above the rooftree. Built into one end of it was a cow barn into which Henry's men led their horses.

A latchstring of tanned hide dangled from the house door, and when Earl Henry stepped inside to warmth and a welcome, the honored host swiftly made a seat for him before the peat hearth. The children, excited and wide-eyed at seeing the lord of the island in their home, perched on the low partition that walled geese and pigs from the kitchen. The smiling goodwife reached for a crock from the shelf and offered rye cakes, then bustled about to stir up a savory pottage or a slot of fish roe beaten to cream.[2] On the other side of the fireplace the household spinster wound flax and made her spinning wheel periodically whir:

> Till—lill—ēē—arum
> Tēēdon ooden, Tēēdon ooden,
> Till—lill—ēē arum, Tēēn ōōden ah,
> A tow and a tēēdon, A tow and a tēēdon
> A tow and a tēēdon, Tēēn ōōden ah.[3]

The wind howled in the chimney, but the room was weathertight and snug. Henry learned many a word of Norse speech while sitting out a storm, especially terms of the sea. He learned to call a strong wind a *gro*, and a dangerous squall a *flan*, and a swift narrow shore current a *roost*.

From hearing them often repeated, he knew almost by heart the tales of audacity and daring crossings of the seas in the songs of the former earls of Orkney. He knew it would be with men like his host, born and bred to the sea, that he would sail from island to island to establish the king's law. He did not yet know that with such men as crews on his ships he would someday cross the wide ocean.

Amid talk of winds from *gussel* to *gro*, he might hear the housewife repeatedly inquire of her man whether the tide had begun to flow. If at first the husband said no, the wife did nothing, but when at a later asking the man said yes, the woman started churning, for it was believed that with a rising tide the butter would come more quickly and plenteously.

All Orkney folk insisted that they had met dwarfs on the moors. They claimed to have seen *Drows*, the Little People, who did not always remain concealed or slink away under the sorrel, but sometimes, amid sedges, bogbean, or wild mustard, openly faced human beings and cursed them with angry mutterings.

Whenever Henry asked his hosts if they had also seen strange things on the sea, they said in God's truth they had. They told of seals changed into mermaids, and mermaids to seals; of sea serpents longer than ships; of islands that floated; of a whirl-stream that could suck a ship under. Henry, listening, now and then almost forgot where he was, in wonder at the tellings.

He observed that Orkneymen treated their wives with respect, almost as their equals. Man and wife consulted together on everything that was to be done. He recalled what he had heard of hot countries like those south of Rome and in the land of the Turks. There the weather was so warm that the room in the house used for cooking was too hot for a man's comfort, and therefore the husband chose to sit down in a cooler part of the house, thus seldom seeing his wife at her domestic tasks. In cold and windy Orkney, when a man who had been out in a boat or on the moors came home, he wished to sit where it was warmest —before the hearth where his wife was bustling about. And so in northern lands where men and women spent evenings and winter days together, there was more understanding between the sexes.

Sometimes there was too much understanding, Henry thought, among young people of opposite sex in Orkney. During St. Olla's Fair at Kirkwall, an unmarried youth and a maiden could associate in complete intimacy and even live together on an experimental basis. It was the custom. Folk called them "brother and sister," and no one minded, but if the girl was got with child, they married.

There was no tendency toward dwindling population in the islands. Henry estimated that more than twenty-five thousand people lived in Orkney, and he was told there were as many in Shetland.

All the islands did a thriving trade, selling fish, pork, sheep, and hides to the Hanseatic merchants and to Scotland. They imported timber, pitch, wax, salt, pewter wares, and raw flax. Of all vegetable products, flax had the most varied uses. Out of it were made clothing, sails, fishing and hunting nets, sewing thread, ropes, bowstrings, measuring lines, bed sheets, sacks, bags, and purses. Because of their prosperity the islanders could more readily pay the king's taxes.

He approached the humble crofters of Orkney with geniality. He was a good-humored man and he had a generous nature that endeared him to the islanders, but he also commanded their deep respect and strict obedience, because when the occasion called for it, he acted with firmness and dispatch. Closely as he came to know the people of Orkney, he maintained the dignity of his position. He had no uncertainty as to the proper functioning of a lord. Without a lord, common men would not stand uninjured, nor would churls abstain from slaying one another. He had heard it said that the devil, who is subtle and full of artifice, labors day and night to cause bloodshed wherever he finds peace and quiet.

If the power and might of rightful lords were withholden, then was malice free, and goodness and innocence never secure. There was present instance in Flanders, where the simple men of Ghent, having driven their lord the earl out of his country, were endeavoring to be themselves masters everywhere, and were destroying gentleness. Henry had no doubt that if burghers or villeins or fishermen got the upper hand, all noblesse would perish.

He knew that a lord, by rightful law, hears and determines causes, pleas, and strifes, and ordains that every man have his own. He draws his sword against malice, and puts forth his shield to defend innocents against evildoers, robbers, and reivers.

A rightful lord uses his power not after his own will, but to halt war, battle, and fighting, and brings to accord them that be in strife. He is a name of peace and surety. Convinced of this, and the justice of the king's cause, Earl Henry was confident that any man who might dare assail his lordship or break his peace, should be made to feel the full severity of the law.

Henry was a man of remarkable personal force. He was the right man for the work to which he had been assigned. Under his rule, the islands began to enjoy the most successful and prosperous period in their history. Instead of squeezing and impoverishing the islanders, he was receptive to their customs, and he helped solve their problems.

Earl Henry's greatest problems stemmed from the differences in land tenure. Some of the earl's estates paid no tax to the king, while other earldom lands near the harbor paid a tax called the *scatt*. Except for the estates of the king, the bishop, and the Church, most Orkney holdings were in no way feudal but were in independent ownership. This was under a Norse system called *Odal*.

Odal land was the property of a family. All the children inherited equal shares. If one heir sold his share outside the family, the rest of the family had prior rights of redeeming the land at a fair price set by a proper judge. In Norway this rule tended to keep a farm in the possession of the same family for a thousand years or more. It worked well where a farm in a fjord was isolated and limited in size by impassable cliffs at both ends, a farm large enough for only one successful unit. In the Orkney and Shetland Islands, however, Odal lands got subdivided under the law of equal sharing by the heirs, until each share was too small to support a family. Yet this had been tolerated because so many men made their living not on the land but at sea by fishing. And so, individual Odal holdings became smaller, until no one was rich enough to buy back all his family's former property. This was what had already happened, and in Henry's time many an Odaler who fell to poverty was forced to sell his small holding. Shrewd Scotsmen began to buy up lands in scattered parcels, and in this way themselves became Odalers. Earl Henry was part of the inevitable Scotification of the islands.

The people of the Orkneys needed more fertile land. In times gone by, when Scandinavia had become overcrowded, men of the *viks* (fjords) had sailed out of their home waters and had attacked and slain the inhabitants of coastal areas in other lands, in Russia, France, England, and the Mediterranean. Then they had taken the lands of the slain and had settled on them. Those much-feared vik-men had settled also in Iceland and Shetland and Orkney and the Hebrides and Ireland, and to the north and west in the far-off country called Greenland. But now all the islands everywhere, large and small, were filled.

Henry heard blood-stirring tales of the viking adventurers. Though these tales aroused no wish that time could go backward, he did wish there were still new lands free for the taking.

With his castle as a base, Henry gained physical control over the main island of the Orkneys, but he could not extend his power over the many lesser islands except with a fleet. He had, therefore, begun to lengthen his arm and multiply his presence with ships, which he started building as soon as he finished his castle in Kirkwall.

His shipbuilding was slowed by the absence of timber in the islands, and he had not been able to obtain the needed timber in Norway. Except in the northern part of that country, where pine was used, it had been the accepted practice to use oak for the larger members of a ship's hull: the keel, prow stem, stern post, ribs, and outside planks, or strakes. More easily replaceable parts such as thwarts and the mast might be of pine or other wood. Primitive methods of procuring the desired pieces of oak were extremely wasteful, however, and had consumed oak trees faster than new ones could be grown in Norwegian forests. A tall straight oak would make one keel. Another oak, the trunk of which had grown with the proper curvature, was needed for a prow stem. The same was required for a stern post, and still another curved oak trunk for the ribs.

The only known method of getting out the timber was to split an oak log down the middle by ax strokes; for the water-powered saw had not yet been invented. Each half of the log was trimmed by ax and adze into a plank of the proper thinness. Thus most of the wood of a tree was chopped away in small pieces to leave only two planks. These planks, in the early viking ships, were about three-fourths of an inch thick.[4] The vikings and those who followed in their tradition built flexible ships, the most graceful ever constructed. For all the oak trees required to build them, they were much lighter in weight than any other ships of like dimensions in all the world's history. They were clinker-built, with thin overlapping planks in a technique called lapstreak.

By the fourteenth century the fine lines of viking ships were being lost to shipbuilding. Clinker-building was displaced by carvel-building, with planks laid edge to edge. Ships had a higher freeboard and deeper draft, with bluffer, less-pointed hulls. They were more tublike. Warships had thicker planking, and high wooden towers or castles fore and aft. Being decked, ships were more than twice as heavy per length as ships of the viking type, and their construction required twice as much timber, which simply did not exist in Norway near to water.

Henry had to look to Scotland and his barony there for wood. Pentland Forest, in Henry's Scottish barony, had much good oak and pine. And so Earl Henry developed a battle fleet of thirteen vessels: two undecked ships rowed with oars, one long decked battle ship, and ten decked barks.[5]

Proud of his war vessels, it is likely that Henry adopted a new heraldic coat-of-arms, which retained the Roslin Sinclair family's engrailed cross and included a galley. Later he or his son and heir adopted a quartered coat of arms, which kept the engrailed cross in the second and third quarters, and had in the first and fourth quarters *azure*, an armed Orkney galley *or*, within a double tressure counter-flowered *or*. The galleys spoke of his sea power, and the double tressure border indicated affinity to royalty.

Because it had been necessary for him to supervise the building of his fleet, Henry was alert to the latest development in naval warfare, the use of cannon on ships. Fire artillery, like the "crakys of war" used by King Edward III, had at first been employed only in sieges. Then, at the Battle of Crécy in 1346, bombards—small cannon propelling stones or other missiles—had been used for the first time in field warfare. It began to appear that foot soldiers with field artillery would be more than

Probable forms of 14th century ships

a match for heavily armored knights. And so it was with the parallel innovation of using cannon in naval battles. The effectiveness of cannon on ships was strikingly illustrated while Henry was completing his castle in Kirkwall. Before the end of 1381, he heard of a great naval victory of the Venetians by which armed galleys had saved their city. Because it was to have an intimate connection with his own fortunes, the story of that victory is no digression.

The city of Chioggia, at the mouth of the southern waterway leading to the open sea from the lagoon in which Venice lay, had been seized by the Genoese. The Genoese had fifty galleys, carrying mortars (bombards), with which they blockaded Venice. The Venetians made futile attempts to break through. Most of their heavily armed galleys were somewhere in the far eastern Mediterranean under Captain Carlo Zeno. Urgent messages were sent to him but there was no reply. Food supplies ran low and the people of Venice faced starvation. The Doge and the Council were in despair. They announced that the city would have to surrender by New Year's Day, 1381, unless the eastern fleet had by then arrived.

It happened by chance on that very day, the first of the year, that Carlo Zeno arrived with fifteen galleys loaded with provisions. He also brought "potent succor" to Venice in fire power. With his galleys armed with cannon, he attacked the Genoese at Chioggia and laid siege to them. When their mercenaries panicked, Carlo enlisted the mercenaries on the Venetian side, and eventually forced the entire Genoese fleet to surrender. Genoa never recovered from the blow.

The victorious hero of the War of Chioggia was rewarded by the grateful citizens of Venice. They made him an admiral, "Capitano Generale d'Armata," and affectionately called him "Carlo the Lion," because the balconies on the facade of his palace and the top of its court-yard stairs were adorned with sculptured lions. He was given permission to erect two pyramids on the roof, symbols granted only to military generals and admirals. Carlo's fame spread throughout Europe.

And so, admiring the hero from a long distance, Earl Henry sought to learn how to install on his warships such cannon as Carlo the Lion had contrived. From ancient times in warfare men had used various devices to throw firebrands into an enemy's fortress. The projectiles were fire, or some form of fire-producing material. Then in the mid-fourteenth century men began to use the explosive force of gunpowder. They required a stronger tube. At first cannon had been made in the way a cooper made a barrel. Some cannon had actually been made of wooden staves bound tightly with leather. This kind of cannon was mentioned by Petrarch, who died in 1379. Since wood and leather could not resist a large explosion of gunpowder, men began to use other materials for cannon barrels. They made cannon with staves or bars of metal around the bore in concentric layers welded together with iron rings or hoops shrunk on over them. The "barrel" was open at both ends. It was loaded at the breach, and that end was stopped with plugs of wood and metal, or with one large piece of iron shaped to cork in snugly. Of course, such cannon, called bombards, blew their breach stoppers about as often as they projected missiles toward an enemy.

The idea of projecting fire persisted in the heating of stone missiles until they were red hot before they were put into the cannon barrel, and then there was the problem of keeping the gunpowder in the barrel from choosing its own time to explode prematurely.

Then men got the idea of using hard missiles of stone or lead and eventually iron to batter down walls. These would be as effective cold as hot. But the word "fire" persisted. Men "fired" cold missiles. They ran into difficulty, however. The particular problem with cannon on a ship was recoil. The recoil would toss the cannon back across the deck and it would smash things, doing more certain damage to its own ship than to the enemy. To avoid this, the cannon on a ship's deck would have to be firmly fixed; but if they were so fixed, the only way one could aim them at a target would be to maneuver the ship, and that was impracticable. Also cannon could not be mounted on a forecastle; for if they were they would have to be fired when the ship was bearing down directly on the target, and in such case, after the firing, the ship could not be brought about fast enough to avoid collision with the target. Besides, in a light wind, the recoil of cannon on the forecastle might cause the ship to luff, and thus throw it out of control at a critical moment in a battle. What Henry wanted was cannon that could be swung around on a ship's deck and aimed, and would not easily burst. It appeared that cannon must be mounted amidships, but the seemingly insoluble problem was how to mount them so that their firing and recoil would not be destructive to the ship and crew, and would not interfere with steering the ship.

Chapter Seven

POLITICS

HENRY'S ACTIVITIES were not confined to his earldom. In June 1384 he was at Roslin.[1] In the same year, Sir William, first earl of Douglas, died, leaving his wife and lawful heir, and also leaving his lady love, Henry's niece Margaret, with her two children. Under the circumstances, Henry as Margaret's uncle was the one who had to give her advice and protection.

The next year King Richard II invaded Scotland with a large army. Henry spent anxious weeks in the defense of his baronies, and supported the strategy of retreat by which the English raiders, unable to bring the Scots to decisive battle, were constantly harassed until they were forced to withdraw. The Scots in turn ravaged Cumberland and Westmorland and laid siege to Carlisle. This warfare kept Henry away from the Orkney Islands for many months.

The death of King Olaf left three thrones vacant. As Earl of Orkney, Henry was an elector for the three kingdoms of Norway, Sweden, and

Denmark, and his presence was now required in Scandinavia. He sailed, probably in November 1387; for he was in Scandinavia at the beginning of February 1388, and it is unlikely that he would have crossed the North Sea after winter had set in.

King Olaf's mother, Margaret, the princess whose wedding Henry had attended in Copenhagen, became the sovereign of the three Scandinavian countries. At a council meeting on February 2, 1388, she was elected for life as queen of Norway and Sweden, and as rightful heir and regent of Denmark. She was thirty-five years of age, very beautiful, and a woman of immense influence. Her political shrewdness was revealed by her quick recognition that the action of Earl Henry and the other electors was in part a personal compliment. She knew that Scandinavians preferred a king to a queen. She was flexible-minded enough to see that her power would not be diminished and might be all the more secure if she found a young boy who could be made king of her three countries, during whose minority she would be actual ruler.

She therefore adopted the five-year-old Eric of Pomerania, her grandnephew, and two weeks after her own election, the council at her request recognized Eric as rightful heir to the three crowns.

In the council's diploma proclaiming Eric as heir to the throne of Norway, the order of signatories is Vinold, the Archbishop of Drontheim; Henry Sinclair, the Earl of the Orkneys; James, the Bishop of Bergen; Augustine, the Bishop of Oslo; Olaf, the Bishop of Stavanger; and many others.

Henry's duties required his being frequently in each of the three geographical areas: Scotland, Scandinavia, and the Orkney earldom. This necessity was complicated by the distances involved and the uncertainties of travel.

We do not know whether he remained in Scandinavia between the time of Eric's election in February 1388 and Eric's becoming king of Norway in September 1389, or whether he went home and returned again that second year. There is no evidence of his having been in the Scots raid that invaded England and fought the Battle of Otterburn (Chevy Chase) on August 14, 1388. His sons were as yet too young for battle, and if Henry had been at Otterburn he almost certainly would have been mentioned. In any case, he was at Helsingborg in Sweden on July 9, 1389 when Eric was acclaimed king.

Also in 1389, Scotland and France made peace with their mutual enemy England. This peace removed the international tensions that had kept Henry from accomplishing all that the king of Norway desired.

The passing of long periods of time—especially five to six hundred years—makes many a biographical search futile. Records are lost and important incidents are forgotten. Yet a biographer always hopes to find factual evidence that will replace supposition with certainty. Evidence of that fortunate kind suddenly appeared in a document that had seemed to deserve a place only in a textual note.

On July 9, 1389, at Helsingborg in Sweden, Earl Henry was required to bind himself to Haakon Jonsson, royal bailiff of Norway:

> Let it be known by these presents that we, Henry Sinclair, Earl of Orkney and Baron of Roslin, with our heirs, are held and bound to a man of the nobility, Haquin the son of John, or his successors, in £140 sterling of Scottish gold, to be paid to him or his heirs or sure deputies at the Church of St. Magnus the Martyr in Tingwall in Shetland, at terms of the year, without fraud or trick; that is at the first term, being St. Lawrence's Day, 1390, £40, at the second term same day of 1391, £40, at the third term the same day of 1392, £40, and at the fourth term the same day, £20, all at the same place. If we or our heirs fail to pay Haquin Johnson or his successors, they may seize all our rents for their loss and the delay, with escheats from the islands of Sanday and Ronaldsay in Orkney, not lessening in any way the said sum of £140, and they will enjoy the rents and escheats till fully paid. Our seal is appended at Helsingborg Palace.[2]

The significance of this document was that the king of Norway must have deemed Earl Henry's power sufficient to attempt to extend the king's law to the Shetlands. That is why he was bound to make the four annual payments "all at the same place," a place that was inland, in the very middle of the main island of the Shetlands. If he failed to take possession of the main Shetland island and hold it throughout the named years and thus was unable to make the four payments at Tingwall, the penalty was to be loss of revenue from two sizable islands, Sanday and Ronaldsay, which were in the Orkney group. Here is evidence that by 1389 Earl Henry Sinclair had become effective ruler over the two northernmost Orkney islands, and presumably, therefore, over the entire Orkney group. The bond did not name islands in the Shetlands whose rents would be withheld as penalty, for the obvious reason that Earl Henry did not yet have possession of any of the Shetlands.

After conferring the earldom on Henry in 1379, Norway, lacking sufficient naval power, had waited ten years while Henry established his firm authority in the Orkneys and had built a fleet, preparatory to making himself master also of the Shetlands, in the king's name. Thus far Earl Henry had been trying at long distance in every way he could to make his influence felt in the Shetlands, but nothing short of his physical possession of those unruly islands could command proper respect for the king's law.[3] When by 1389 Earl Henry had built up a force of soldiers and ships to transport them, so that it seemed probable that he could make himself master of the Shetland Islands, the Norwegian Court demanded that he should no longer postpone their conquest, and should obligate himself to achieve the task the very next summer. His being bonded to do it was a reminder to all men of his right to do it. The criterion of his success would be whether the king's fiscal agent would be able to go about the king's business openly in the Shetland main island, and without local interference receive Henry's four yearly payments there.

This was the same sort of mandate as had been in the bond Henry was compelled to sign on the day of his installation. We have already seen how that old bond, in specifying that he was to make payments of gold on two separate dates "at Kirkwall within Orkney," had required him by those dates to be in physical possession of the Orkney main island. The new bond required him to gain physical possession of the Shetland main island in 1390, and to hold that possession for four years, time enough for him to establish his suzerainty permanently.

Part 2

THE MAKING
OF AN EXPLORER

Chapter Eight

THE RESCUED
CAPTAIN

EARL HENRY Sinclair had reason to feel apprehensive about the outcome of his attempt to invade the Shetland main island. The opposition there might well defeat him. Though he had confidence in the justice of his undertaking, and trusted that God would be with him, he knew he faced overwhelming odds. Even before he came to land he might have to fight a naval battle with the fishermen of Shetland. And to fight through on land, he might not have soldiers enough, for the Shetland main island had a population of about twenty thousand and might resist him with as many as two thousand fighting men. There is no way to estimate the number of armed men he could transport. It was certainly several hundred. If he pressed into service all available ships and Orkney fishermen's boats, he may have had more than five hundred soldiers.

There was no possibility of surprise. What he intended to do had been obvious for months. Some Orkney fishermen had surely slipped word to Shetland fishermen as to what was coming. Would Orkneymen put their hearts into fighting to subdue their cousins in Shetland? He felt reasonably sure they would, but he no doubt would take a stout core of Scotsmen with him also.

He had gathered all the forces he could. There was disquiet in him nevertheless, because he had been unable to install in his fleet improvements that existed in a more advanced part of the world, like triumphant Venice. If he had been able to obtain information as to how to construct superior cannon and how to mount them, he would control the northern seas. As it was, he might well be defeated. With thoughts such as these he finished his preparations for the attack on Shetland.

At the appointed time he departed with his fleet from Kirkwall, and steered northward toward Shetland. It was in the first half of the sailing season of 1390, probably in late May or early June. It could scarcely have been earlier, for he had undoubtedly been at Scone in the spring of that year to render homage to King Robert III, who had become king of Scotland on the nineteenth of April. Henry had to begin his naval operations as early as possible, since the whole military undertaking, to be successful, would have to be concluded before St. Lawrence's Day, which was the tenth of August.

He had given himself enough extra time to make a landing on Fer Island lying slightly more than halfway between the Orkneys and Shetland. Since it was an island that was included in Dunrossness Parish of the main island and thus belonged to Shetland, it was strategically his first point of attack. Landing on it and taking possession would give his sailors and soldiers practice and confidence for the hard struggle ahead. And so Earl Henry went to that small island in 1390 with his whole fleet of war vessels and with many more soldiers than the total number of that island's inhabitants.

Departing from that island afterwards would depend on the winds. Winds were often contrary, and he might be detained there for several days. His ships sailed only with the wind; even if they could head a point into the wind, they would lose as much from sideway drift. So he had to allow for possible delay after completing his easy and quick work of bringing the king's law to that midway island.

There on that remote island came a moment that was to have great consequence.

On his trail centuries later, I was on the main island of Shetland. As I was about to leave, I went down to the tiny wharf at Lerwick, to the ship that was to take me as a passenger to Aberdeen, and was thrilled to see on her prow the name of the man whose career I was reconstructing—*St. Clair*.

The purser and the captain had no knowledge as to why their ship had been so christened. They thought it was because so many persons in the islands bore the family name St. Clair, or Sinclair. The captain, however, was so interested in hearing the story of the one particular member of that family who had originally established it as the most distinguished name in the Orkneys and Shetlands that he invited me to visit with him on the bridge.

The *St. Clair* was plowing ahead through rain and thick mist. The North Sea has busy ship lanes and many trawlers everywhere, and even with the foghorn blowing, it seemed perilous that the captain dare go full speed ahead when there was so little visibility. His confidence was not based on foolhardiness, however, but on the radioscope. That instrument indicated all clear ahead. It also showed some object off to starboard. The captain knew what that object was, and its distance—fourteen miles. It was a piece of land which, he said, was called Fer Island, the island Henry had taken over en route to the Shetlands.

This island has always been feared by mariners as one of the most dangerous spots in all the waters of the world. Officially belonging to the Shetlands, it has a rocky coast that is completely exposed either to the full fury of the Atlantic, or to the almost equally violent North Sea. It is three and a half miles long and half a mile wide. Along its perimeter there are only three possible landing places, two on its east coast, and one at its south end. Reefs and shoals are offshore, and it is in the midst of tempestuous tidal currents. Its original name, of which Fer Island is a modification, meant "Isle of Sheep." A more apt name would be Isle of Shipwrecks, for it has been the scene of many sea tragedies. It was the grave of the flagship of the Duke of Medina Sidonia of the Spanish Armada. A navigator of a sailing boat that raced from Newport, Rhode Island, to Marstrand, Sweden, told me that he considered the greatest hazard of the voyage was getting safely past Fer Island.

On Fer Island in the year 1390 there occurred by chance a dramatic meeting of two notable men from very different parts of Europe. The presence of these particular men at the same time on such a small and remote island was most extraordinary.

One of them was Earl Henry, who was now also called Prince Henry out of respect for his political power and alliances and relations with royalty and his stature as a practically independent ruler.[1] He was in the process of taking possession of the island in the name of the king of Norway. While he was negotiating with some of the inhabitants, he was surprised to see them suddenly snatch up their weapons and all start running in one direction.

The natives, as you may have guessed, were running because a shipwreck was imminent. "Among the Shetlanders formerly, a stranded vessel was considered quite as lawful a capture as a stranded whale."[2] Dwellers along a Shetland seacoast, eager to enrich themselves from a wrecked vessel, would customarily slay its crew in order to possess its cargo.

Nobody had very far to run. There was no particular coincidence in the fact that Prince Henry and his men were close to the shore where the ship struck the rocks.

It was a terrifying sight. Under the dark lowering sky, amid the thunder of breakers, a large decked vessel had been driven fast upon a reef. Its two masts had snapped at the moment of impact. In the bows the crew were clinging desperately to the rails and fallen rigging. With

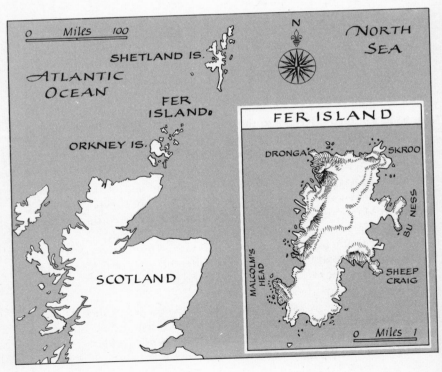

each wave, a foam-white wall of seething water raced over the deck from stern to prow and threatened to wash them off into the sea.

Strong swimmers unencumbered with weapons might have made it from ship to shore. None of the crew risked it, however, for good reason. A menacing crowd of men and women gathered along the water's edge, brandishing spears and fish knives, and shouting in gleeful anticipation of slaughtering the sailors and gaining possession of the wreck. The ferocious islanders were more cruel than the sea.

Prince Henry led his followers into instant action. He dispersed the loot-hungry natives, driving them off so they could do nothing but stand on the hilltops as frustrated and cursing spectators. He then sent swimmers out to the ship, who gestured to the men on board to throw them a line, by which the crew were all brought safely to shore.

The men Prince Henry saved were shorter than Orkneymen. Most of them had darker hair and were more swarthy than the fair-complexioned islanders. Their ship looked like those that sailed from the Mediterranean. He guessed they might be Gascons, or perhaps natives of Marseilles, and so he spoke to them in French. They did not understand him.

Not knowing how else he might question their captain, Prince Henry used the language educated men of all countries understood. He asked in Latin: "Whence come you?"

In the same tongue, their captain, a gray-haired man, responded: "We are from Italy."

And when Henry asked him, "From what city?" he was astonished to hear the captain say: "We are from Venice."

From Venice, of all seaports in the world! It seemed too good to be true! Prince Henry counted it the best of good fortune to be able to converse with a ship captain who had come directly from the city that was reputed to be the fountainhead of knowledge and skill in naval matters. But how had the captain and his men happened to sail from far-off Venice into these northern parts, these island passages north of Scotland? For what purpose had they come? And what purpose of his own, Henry thought to himself, could their presence be made to serve?

He courteously asked the Venetian captain his name.

"Nicolò," was the answer, "Nicolò Zeno."

Tremendously moved at hearing the name Zeno, Henry introduced himself.

From a letter which Nicolò Zeno wrote home to Venice, we can reconstruct the conversation that was held between the two leaders.

Prince Henry asked hopefully: "Captain Nicolò, are you by any chance cousin to that great man of your city, your master of the galleys, and savior of your city, that famous hero, Carlo Zeno, called the Lion?"[3]

Captain Nicolò's worn features must have broadened into a vivacious smile as he replied: "Carlo the Lion is my brother."

Henry was overjoyed. He could barely contain himself; for the seemingly impossible had happened. The captain he had saved from the sea was actually a brother of the naval hero of the War of Chioggia! As such he would know all the secrets! He would know how the best kind of ship's cannon were to be made. He would know how they should be mounted. The meeting with Captain Nicolò was most timely. Captain Nicolò had a well-trained crew, and he and his men would be of invaluable assistance.

Himself an elector of the kings of Scandinavia, Henry soon found out that Captain Nicolò had been an elector of the Doge, and one of the twelve "Orators" sent by the Venetian Senate with five galleys to Marseilles to transport the pope and his court to Rome. He had been the captain of a galley in the war against the Genoese. The return on his loans to his native city for the War of Chioggia and some war profiteering had made him one of the richest men in Venice. He had been Venetian ambassador to Ferrara in 1382, and was the first of three city magistrates ("Sindaci") elected in 1388 to take possession from the Lord of Padova of the city and territory of Treviso.

Why had a man of such wide experience come into Orkney waters? Henry asked him whether he had come as merchant.

"No, my lord," Nicolò answered.

"Why then have you come?"

"To see the world."

"On a pilgrimage?"

"No indeed, but to get acquainted with the different customs and languages of mankind."

"What gave you that desire?"

"Citizens of Venice, among them Ser Marco Polo, have told of wonderful sights in their travels. My blood was stirred."

"Why came you to these parts?"

"I came where the winds carried me. I sailed from Venice and through the Mediterranean westward, and passed the Strait of Gibraltar. For several days on the ocean all went well. I steered a northward course, intending to visit England and Flanders. But when I came into waters between those countries, we were hit by a frightful storm. I was for days so tossed about with the sea and the wind that I did not know where I was. At last when I saw land across the bows, I could not bear up against the violence of the tempest, and was cast on this island."

Perceiving that Messire Nicolò was a man of judgment, with great experience in naval and military matters, Henry took him into his service.

"I would like to have you go on board my fleet with all your men," said Henry. Then he charged the fleet captain: "Give Captain Nicolò Zeno all respect. In all things take advantage of his advice and experience."

Henry's confidence was not misplaced. Captain Nicolò knew how to navigate with use of the compass. He knew every trick of sailing. He knew also of a recent invention of drawn wire that mariners could use to replace ropes in the shrouds and as stays.

Captain Nicolò showed the Orkneymen how to construct the newest and best types of cannon to be fired from on board ship.

Captain Nicolò eventually showed Earl Henry how to cast the latest type of cannon, which had a closed breach and a small touchhole for setting off the charge, and were to be loaded through the muzzle. He showed how the recoil of a ship's cannon could be resisted. He knew how to do this by having two iron pivots or trunnions attached to and under the barrel. Before these trunnions were firmly lashed to ringbolts in the deck, they furnished a means of swiveling or turning and aiming the cannon, so that the pointing of the cannon at the enemy did not have to be accomplished by maneuvering the ship. No one knew how to eliminate the practical problem of compensating for the roll of the ship in aiming a cannon, except by practiced skill in timing the firing.

In one of his letters home to Venice, Nicolò Zeno said that at the time of the shipwreck his rescuer was on "the island of Frislanda." He gave the name as that of a single island. In spite of this, there has been speculation that Frislanda was the Faeroe Islands, two hundred and fifty miles north of Kirkwall. This assertion has been repeated in histories and encyclopedias. Among the natives of the Faeroe Islands, however, there is no record and no tradition of their ever having been under Earl Henry Sinclair's control.

The Frislanda of which Nicolò Zeno spoke was a single island. By introducing a single "e," Frislanda becomes Fer Islanda. In line with all the known facts, it was unquestionably Fer Island. There can be no doubt as to Earl Henry's whereabouts at the most fateful moment of his career.

With Captain Nicolò's men in his fleet, and perhaps with cannon saved from the wreck of Nicolò's ship, Henry sailed from Fer Island toward the main island of Shetland. With Captain Nicolò Zeno at his side Earl Henry had the help of a "keen Italian intellect, the source of so many novelties."[4]

Chapter Nine

THE WINNING OF SHETLAND

NICOLO WROTE home that from Frislanda to the main island of Shetland their course was "to the westwards."[1] By advice of the Orkneymen, the fleet avoided, as all mariners sought to do, the dangerous current around Sumburgh Head, the southern tip of the main island. They steered well westward of it and then north into a bay. With little opposition Prince Henry landed on the western side of the main island and gained possession of a place that Nicolò called "Ledovo." In Shetland, a "voe" is a bay. Ledovo was the name of a bay, or a place in a bay, but there seems to be no possibility of identifying it now.[2]

While Earl Henry and his soldiers marched overland, the fleet was active and captured what Nicolò called "Ilofe" and other small islands in a bay he called "Sudero." They captured some small barks laden with salt fish, in a harbor he called "Sanestol." This name suggests Sandesting, the country west of Scalloway on the Shetland main island, or possibly Sandness farther west.

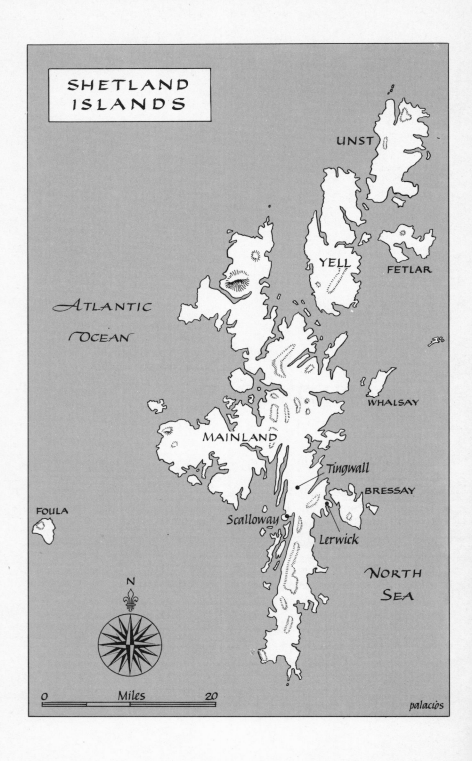

SHETLAND
ISLANDS

UNST

YELL

FETLAR

ATLANTIC
OCEAN

WHALSAY

MAINLAND

Tingwall

BRESSAY

Scalloway

Lerwick

FOULA

NORTH
SEA

N

0   Miles   20

palacios

Earl Henry meanwhile had fought his way overland to Sanestol. There the fleet rejoined him and landed supplies for his soldiers. He had conquered with ease all the country through which he came, because he had not yet encountered the forces of the main island that had assembled to resist him.

The fleet remained at Sanestol only a little while. Then again the land forces and the fleet separated. The fleet went farther westward, to the other cape of the bay. Then turning back, the fleet brought certain other islands and lands into Earl Henry's possession.

The waters through which they sailed were full of shoals and rocks. All the Orkneymen afterwards declared that the fleet would have been lost with all hands if the Venetian mariners had not been their pilots. Orkney fishermen knew their own local waters, but in the general navigation of ships were less experienced than the Venetians who, according to Nicolò, "had been, one might say, born, trained up, and grown old in the art of navigation."

The captain of the fleet, by Nicolò's advice, decided to go ashore at a place, the name of which Nicolò caught as "Boudendon." He wanted to find out what success Prince Henry had had in his fighting on land. There to everyone's great satisfaction they heard that the earl had fought a decisive battle and put to flight the combined forces of the whole island. In consequence of this victory, ambassadors were being sent from all parts of the main island to yield the country up into his hands, and the people in every town and village had taken down their ensigns.

The natives of Shetland main island, called Mainlend everywhere, capitulated to the earl's legal authority. Most of them were glad to submit to him, the king's representative, since his coming promised order and justice.

The fleet awaited him. On his arrival, there were demonstrations of joy over the victories by land and sea, and the Venetians were given utmost praise. Earl Henry was a great lover of valiant men, and he was pleased to hear reports regarding Captain Nicolò's nautical skill. He sent for Captain Nicolò, complimenting him for his zeal and ability, by which two things he acknowledged himself to have received a very great and inestimable benefit, that is, "the preservation of his fleet and the winning of so many places without any trouble to himself."

Then Henry, in his capacity as prince, conferred on Nicolò the honor of knighthood. He rewarded Sir Nicolò's men with very handsome presents.

After that, Henry and the fleet went triumphantly toward the chief town[3] of the main island, a town on the southeast side of it, lying inside a bay. This was where many ships were loaded with salted fish to supply Flanders, Brittany, England, Scotland, Norway, and Denmark, a trade that brought the island great wealth. This chief Shetland port was at the site of the later-founded city of Lerwick. For centuries the port had been the principal center for herring, ling, cusk (torsk), and cod. Its hardy fishermen were accustomed to sailing great distances in the North Atlantic. On one occasion, more than two thousand fishing vessels were there at one time, from Holland and other countries. The fishing season began near the end of June and lasted until the end of December.

The laws and system of landholdings in Shetland were the same as those in Orkney, but many of the legends and customs were different. Shetlanders were predominately Norse, with some Picts and Gaels, but almost no Scotsmen as yet to boil the brew.

Named for the Celts who were there when the Norsemen first came, the islands were called "Hjaltar," equivalent to "Celtae" or "Galatae." "Hjaltland" was the Norse form of the name Shetland. The Norse language has persisted among some of the people, for the present writer has met persons there who can understand and speak nothing else.

The Shetlands have more severe winters than the Orkneys, but summers with less fog and more days of sunshine. They are more barren than the Orkneys and are swept by more violent winds. Like the Orkneys they are an ancient land, with house ruins from the Stone Age and Bronze Age, and with Pictish forts. There are numerous standing stones that, folk say, will cure insane, bewitched, and deformed persons who visit them at the right moment. Unfortunately, no one knows just when that moment is.

In Henry's day the people had practically no money to use for exchange. They paid the king's taxes in butter, fish oil, and homespun woolen cloth called *wadmal*.

Some of the men who fought against Henry's invasion did so merely for love of battle. There was a lingering viking tradition that accounted it a great virtue to die fighting one's enemies. A "straw-death," on a bed of sickness, was ignominious. Death on a battlefield or on a ship ensured a hero's entrance into Paradise. In viking times, a dying leader had himself placed on a galley into which his followers flung flaming brands, and then his floating funeral pyre was launched, so that he would go to the halls of Valhalla in a fire-boat burial, while his friends sang a war song on the shore.

Henry made the fishing port of Shetland one of his chief naval bases.

His strategic problem was to have a striking force where needed and when needed. With one hundred and seventy scattered islands, there were many points vulnerable to attack from the sea. An extended signal system was necessary, so he decided to make Fer Island an important station. In clear weather a smoke signal on Sumburgh Head at the southern tip of Shetland could be seen by observers on Fer Island and from there relayed to watchers on Ronaldsay (Ronald's Island) in the Orkneys. Thus the fleet, wherever it was, could be swiftly apprised of a piratical attack on either island group.

He now had done what he had come to do: He had won the place and the time; he had brought the Shetland islanders back to their allegiance. The Norwegian king's fiscal agent could now land on the main island without hindrance. The roads were safe and both the king's agent and his own agent could travel unmolested to their appointed meeting at the Church of St. Magnus at Tingwall. Henry made his first payment there according to the absolute terms of his bond, on the tenth of August; it was visible proof that the main island was restored to the king's authority.

It is possible that he finished his work in Shetland much earlier in the summer, and left his agent to make the payment; for he would have wanted to be present at Scone at the coronation of King Robert III on the fifteenth of August.

Sir Nicolò, whom Henry had made captain (admiral) of his navy, remained in Shetland. Henry went back to Kirkwall, and doubtless to Scotland.

Sir Nicolò wrote home from Shetland to Antonio, a younger member of his family in Venice. His letter was probably carried across to the continent by one of the foreign fishing boats, and the rest of the way on a Venetian trading ship. More than one hundred and fifty years later this letter, torn and with ink faded, was not all clearly decipherable. The names of the places and persons were unfamiliar to a descendant of his who attempted to read it. Here is what the sixteenth-century relative thought Sir Nicolò had written of Earl Henry: "He is a great lord, and possesses certain islands called Porlanda, lying not far from Frislanda to the south, being the richest and most populous of all these parts."

What was "Porlanda"? The best guesses would seem to be "Pomona" or "Pentland."

Sir Nicolò's penmanship, the damaged condition of the letter, and a naive deciphering of it caused several misreadings. Sir Nicolò named the prince ("*Principe*") in his letters, but in Venice more than one hundred and fifty years later the name was misread. For four hundred years thereafter historians were greatly confused by what appeared in type when a copy of this letter was sent to the printer by Nicolò's sixteenth-century descendant and namesake in 1558: "His name is Zichmni, and besides the said small islands, he has lordship over the land of the Duchy of Sorano, situated on the side of them towards Scotland (*posta della banda verso Scotia*)."

The misreading of "Sorano" for "Roslin" was not too surprising.

But who was "Zichmni"? This name in what is called the Zeno Narrative became one of the most troublesome misspellings in literary history. No one had ever heard of a "Prince Zichmni" on the islands north of Scotland, or anywhere else on earth. For more than two centuries there was no explanation. Then in 1786 the historian Johann Reinhold Forster came to the conclusion that "Zichmni" was a muddled misspelling of "Sinclair." This identification was found to fit the facts so well that it was accepted by the translator of the Zeno Narrative, Richard Henry Major, in 1873, by most nineteenth-century historians, by the *Dictionary of National Biography*, and by the leading encyclopedias. In 1898 this identification was challenged by a skeptic, Fred W. Lucas, who advanced elaborate but baseless arguments against it.[4]

The key to the solution of the Zichmni puzzle is the fact that Sir Nicolò would not have called a prince by his family name. It would not have been in keeping with fourteenth-century practice to write "Prince Sinclair." Sir Nicolò would have called the prince either by his first name, "Principe Enrico," or by the name of the earldom over which he ruled, "Principe d'Orkney."

Now we shall see how the spelling Zichmni happened:

In medieval Italian letter forms given by Capelli,[5]

"d'O" would most likely be written as

In the Marciana catalog in Venice, capital Z of "Zeno" is written thus:

"d'o" and "Z" in Italian Script

The major portion of the second form is identical with the first form, so that the "d'O" could easily be misread as capital "Z".

Since in Italian an initial Z calls for a vowel to follow it, the second letter in "Orkney," the "r" would be read as the vowel which most closely resembles "r" in script—"i".

In "Orkney" and in its variant spellings, "Orknay" and "Orkeney," there are two letters which do not occur in Italian. Substitutions for those two letters would necessarily have been made, either by Sir Nicolò or by his sixteenth-century descendant in Venice.

One letter in "Orkney" that never occurs in Italian is "k". What takes the place of k in Italian is "ch."

Nor does the letter "y" occur in Italian. What takes the place of y in Italian is "i."

All that remains to be said is that the up and down strokes in hand-written "ne" or "na" or "ene" could easily be mistaken for the strokes in "mn."

| Thus we have the name— | d'O | r | k | ene | y |
| read by an Italian as— | Z | i | ch | mn | i |

There is a certain inevitability to this equating.[6]

Sir Nicolò in his letter home requested Messire Antonio Zeno to find some vessel to bring out to him. As Antonio later wrote: "Antonio, having as great a desire as Sir Nicolò to see the world, and visit various countries, and thereby make himself a great name, bought a ship, and directing his course that way, after a long voyage in which he encountered many dangers, at length joined Sir Nicolò in safety. Sir Nicolò received him with great gladness, not only as his brother in blood, but also in courage."

We shall later see how the "brother" relationship falls under question.

Now that Earl Henry was in actual possession of the Shetlands as well as the Orkneys, he eliminated all possible rival claims. At Kirkwall the next spring, on April 23, 1391, he issued a charter to his half brother: "To all who shall see or hear these presents, Henry Sinclair, Earl of Orkney and Lord of Roslin, safety in the Lord! I concede to my brother, David Sinclair, for life, because of his claim through our mother Isabella Sparra in Orkney and Shetland, all the lands of Newburgh and Auchdale in Aberdeenshire, to return to me if his heirs fail."[7] With this land grant, Henry eliminated the potential claim his half brother might have to the Orkney earldom.

Three months later in the Shetlands Earl Henry was faced with a problem that could not be so peacefully settled. It came up at the legislative and judicial assembly at Tingwall. The annual assembly, called the Lawthing (or Lawting), met there on an island in a small lake. Access to the island was by a stone causeway one hundred and forty feet long. The Lawthing Holm, or island, was not fortified, since it was a place to which all men could come to procure justice. Odalers were obliged to convene at the Tingstead when called by the chief magistrate. They came, of course, on horseback. Their horses were grassed in the neighborhood, on two adjacent farms of Grista and Astar, whose proprietors were given seats in the assembly to repay them for the grass the horses ate.

A lawthing was, as well, a meeting of all currents of thought, and "to some extent took the place of literature, for it promoted the arts of narration and minstrelsy. There were songs and games and dances."[8] Far more serious business of a lawthing was to consider questions of public discipline, to hear complaints and petitions, and to witness pledges. A lawthing was comprised of locally selected representatives whose decisions were legal and binding. It was a democratic institution, of Norse origin, which initiated its own procedures, and at which the king or earl or his representative presided, but did not dictate.

At the Lawthing at Tingwall in 1391, the case of Malise Sparre was brought to judgment. Malise had waived all rights in favor of Henry at Henry's installation. Although Malise had signed an agreement with his cousin, he evidently had not given up the lands he had seized in defiance of the king's ruling. John and Sigurd Hafthorsson were the lawful heirs, and put their claim before the lawthing. Malise displayed a recalcitrant attitude, which was equivalent to a threat of open war or rebellion.

Malise was summoned to appear before the lawthing. It is not known whether he came there with his armed followers, or whether Henry brought him there as a prisoner, but his armed followers gathered there to help him escape the law. Perhaps he thought he could win the assembly to his point of view. Evidently he failed and just before judgment was passed against him, he or his men forcibly resisted it. It may have been then that Henry took him prisoner.

One writer says: "It seems the Earl was about to hold a court to settle the legal rights of the parties concerned. A conflict taking place, the dispute was terminated by the strong hand."[9]

Armed resistance to the lawthing was comparable to what would now be called an attempt to overthrow the government by force. It was treason. Justice in such cases was swift and stern. There was a fight and some of Malise Sparre's men fled toward the port of Scalloway. All we know is what a laconic record tells us:

"Malise Sparre, with seven others, was slain in Hjaltland by the Earl of Orkney. He had previously been taken prisoner by him. From that conflict there escaped a man servant, who, with six men, got safely away to Norway in a sixareen."[10]

Tradition does not hint at any tyranny in the slaying. From the point of view of the lawthing of Shetland, and from the earl's point of view and the king's, it was a legal execution.

One writer says: "The standing stone of gray granite close to the road between the Loch of Tingwall and the Loch of Asta was probably erected to mark the spot where Malise Sparre was slain."[11] This standing stone of the Bronze Age, mistakenly ascribed to a fourteenth-century origin, makes a popular appeal to tourists.

The reports of Henry's swift victory in one short summer in Shetland, and the efficiency of his fleet, made a great impression in Norway. Earl Henry, aided by his Italian advisers, had acquired a tremendous reputation as a master of naval construction and strategy.

He did not engage in naval adventures in 1392. In that year on the tenth of March a safe conduct was granted by King Richard II to "*Henry Seintcler, Comes Orchadie, et Dominus de Roslyne*" to come into England with twenty-four persons in his retinue. This safe conduct was valid until Michaelmas, the twenty-ninth of September. It specified that no one who was a fugitive from English laws should be of the company.

Why did Henry go into England this year? To perform some secret diplomatic mission for the king of Scotland? To procure ship-rigging material recommended by Sir Nicolò and Antonio Zeno? To make a Canterbury pilgrimage while the *Canterbury Tales* were being written? Or was it merely to travel for pleasure because he could now take a vacation from his many duties and labors, having consolidated his island possessions?

The facts point to another explanation. Norway had completely lost sea power. In 1392 Queen Margaret was reduced to leasing from England, since she had no means to buy, three war vessels to replace the national fleet that had been a long time ruined. Who better could be sent into England to choose good ships than Earl Henry, loyal to the Norwegian Crown, and possessing the latest knowledge as to ships and naval guns? It seems probable that he went into England bearing a commission from Queen Margaret, to use his best judgment in her service. Very likely he took with him Sir Nicolò Zeno, or one or two of the other Italian mariners as advisers. That was probably why the English, not knowing who these Italians might be, added to his safe conduct the specification regarding fugitives from English laws.

In 1393, Henry's fleet "with much warlike preparation went out to attack" another land, presumably the Faeroe Islands. The record is confused. What Sir Nicolò wrote is that after the fleet had begun to attack the other land or islands, they broke off the attack when they heard "that the king of Norway was coming against them with a great fleet." A storm then drove Henry's ships upon some shoals, and many of them were wrecked. Sir Nicolò wrote that report had it that the "great fleet" from Norway was "utterly wrecked and lost" in the same storm.

There is no record in Norwegian history of this fleet action or disaster, and there certainly would be if it had occurred. Sir Nicolò was relating a rumor of something else. The "great fleet" may have been a Faeroe Island fishing fleet returning home, but it was probably something more dangerous.

King Olaf of Norway had lacked power to hold the Faeroe Islands, and in 1386 they had become the property of Denmark. Henry, in 1393, may have been attempting to restore them to Norway. Norway had no "great fleet." To the contrary, Norway was too weak to defend her own coasts against pirates. Stockholm was held by Germans whose large forces were being supplied by privateers called the Victual Brothers. These Victualleurs of Stockholm had begun to procure by piracy the supplies they sold at high prices in the Swedish city. They harassed the shores of all Scandinavia. In 1393 these Baltic pirates extended their operations to the coast of Norway and seized and sacked the important town of Bergen. Their depredations were so wide-flung that Norwegians for three years abandoned the fisheries on their own coasts. Knut Gjerst in *History of the Norwegian People* says: "The Victual Brothers gravely endangered all commerce, not only in the Baltic, but also in the North Sea."

What Earl Henry heard and Sir Nicolò recorded was undoubtedly a warning from someone who had fled before the pirates, that the pirates were coming out from the coast of Norway to attack the earldom of Orkney.

The pirate attack on the Orkneys did not materialize. As soon as Henry had repaired his ships, he sailed with the intention of landing in "Islanda" (Iceland), "which together with the rest was subject to the king of Norway." This was undoubtedly at the request of Queen Margaret, who had become unpopular in Iceland, where there was widespread disapproval of Eric, her adopted child king. In 1392 she had attempted to levy a new tax in Iceland, but the "best men" there had refused it. Having no power to enforce the demands of the Norwegian Crown, she would naturally have asked Earl Henry with his fleet to do what she could not do. It appears that he attempted to carry out her orders. When he found Iceland "well-fortified and defended" and perceived that it would be too much for his reduced fleet to conquer, "he was fain to give up that enterprise." As an alternative employment, he used his fleet to take possession of the lesser islands of the Shetlands. What Sir Nicolò wrote about the fleet maneuverings is confusing but will provide entertainment to those who love puzzles.[12]

Immediately thereafter, Sir Nicolò remained to finish the "fort in Bres" for Earl Henry. Bres was Bressay, the island lying to the east of the Shetland main island and, with it, forming Bressay Sound. "In Bres" meant within the shelter of Bressay, that is, in Bressay Sound where the fishing ships anchored. The site of Henry's fort was in all probability where a later fort was built in the seventeenth century, at the water's edge in Lerwick.[13]

Chapter Ten

VOYAGES
TO GREENLAND

ORKNEY HAD been divided by the Papal Schism, but not so Shetland. Shetlanders unitedly clung with Norway to the Roman pope. After Earl Henry had become the actual leader of both groups of islands, he deemed it politic to accede to the insistent religious preferences of the Shetlanders. With Henry favoring the move, the Orkney bishopric in 1392 gave submission to the archbishopric of Nidaros (Trondheim) in Norway and to the pope in Rome.

Bishop Henry of Orkney had made enemies in his diocese, and Earl Henry, who desired to have him removed, may have been instrumental in getting the Roman pope to take action. In the *Orkney and Shetland Records* we are told what happened. In 1394, the year in which Pope Clement VII in Avignon died of apoplexy in anger at the proposal that he and the Roman pope both abdicate, Pope Boniface IX in Rome ordered the exchange of the bishops of Orkney and of Greenland. Bishop Henry of Orkney was to go to Greenland, and Bishop John of Greenland was to come to Orkney.

The population of Greenland was not large and the Norwegian hold on Greenland was loosening and soon to break.[1] Norway had endeavored to send one trading ship annually to Greenland, but was not always physically able to do it. Merchants of Lynn in England, and the Hanseatic merchants carried on much more trade with Greenland than did Bergen.

Henry had attended the Scottish Parliament which met at Perth in March 1392 and in October 1393. He attended parliament twice in 1394, in March at Scone and in August in Edinburgh. It thus seems likely that having in 1393 fulfilled his bond to the Norwegian king and made the fourth and final payment at the Church of St. Magnus at Tingwall in Shetland, he did not in 1394 go in person to the Shetlands. He had left Admiral Nicolò in charge there.

Sir Nicolò and Antonio Zeno had remained over the winter at the fort in Bressay Sound. Messire Antonio wrote to Carlo in Venice about Sir Nicolò that "being left behind in Bres, he resolved (*si dilibero*) the next season [1394] to make an excursion with the view of discovering land."[2] Accordingly, he fitted out three small barks in the month of July, and sailing towards the north arrived in Engroneland [Greenland]."

Sir Nicolò's daring was in his blood, for Venetians of the name Zeno were said to have come from a noble Roman family, and in all probability also had some Norse ancestry. Pietro, the father of Sir Nicolò, was called "Dracone," because he carried a dragon on his shield. This family insignia, which suggests Norse origin, was no doubt used by Sir Nicolò to adorn the prows of his three barks.

The papal order to interchange the bishops of Orkney and Greenland had nothing to do with Sir Nicolò's voyage. Bishop Henry did not leave Orkney for Greenland until 1395, and it was not until the following sailing season that Bishop John of Greenland reached Orkney. The transfer of bishops was probably accomplished by one of Earl Henry's ships directly from Kirkwall. The dates emphasize the delays and hazards of sea voyaging to and from Greenland in those days, though it is possible that one of the bishops may have wintered in Iceland en route.

The Greenland diocese with its cathedral at Gardar was on the west coast of Greenland. Sir Nicolò, however, went far up the east coast of Greenland, north of Iceland. It seems unlikely that he could have visited the Norse Settlement on the west coast without having made mention of it. While it is possible that he did mention it and that the record was lost, it is just as reasonable to assume that he did not visit the west coast.

Antonio reported afterwards: "In Greenland, Messire Nicolò found

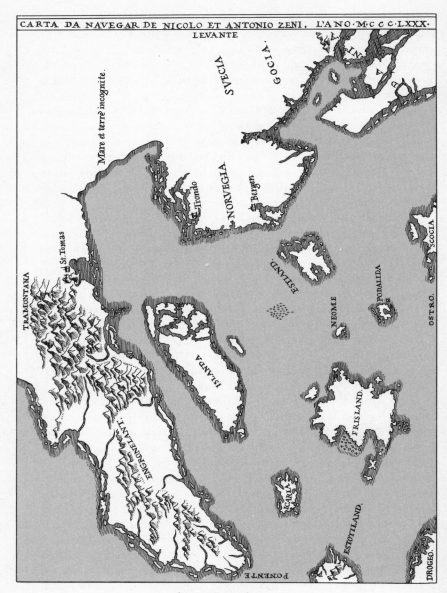

Zeno Sea Chart

with omission of latitude and longitude lines

a monastery of the Order of Friars Preachers,[3] and a church dedicated to St. Thomas, hard by a hill which vomited fire like Vesuvius and Etna. There is a spring of hot water there." The Zeno Sea Chart shows where the Monastery of St. Thomas was, and the volcano.[4]

The nineteenth-century scholar Dr. Luka Jelic tells us that in 1329 collectors sent out by Pope John XXII reported that there were two ecclesiastical centers in "Grotlandia" (Greenland), one called Gardensi (Gardar) and the other Pharensi (the name suggesting the glow of the volcano like a lighthouse or Pharos).

When Sir Nicolò returned from the east coast of Greenland, he told Antonio what he had seen there. Messire Antonio wrote it down for Earl Henry and also sent it in a letter to Carlo Zeno in Venice. The essence of Sir Nicolò's report is that he had found the church and monastery of the Black Friars heated by piped-in hot water from the spring. He gives a very accurate description of Eskimo kayaks. Though the report has no direct bearing on the story of Earl Henry, the full details are in themselves historically interesting.[5]

Several archaeologists in the twentieth century, among them Alwin Pedersen, Helge Larsen, and Lauge Koch, established the existence of formerly active volcanoes and hot springs between 72° and 75° north latitude on the east coast of Greenland. Dr. William Herbert Hobbs, a geologist of the University of Michigan, identified the region in which Sir Nicolò Zeno found the monastery as Gael Hamke Bay at about 74° north latitude. With reference to what Sir Nicolò described—the populous settlement of Eskimos, the monastery of friars, the volcano, the hot springs, and the summer shipping—Dr. Hobbs said: "Evidence for all these has been found there."[6]

Some years after Sir Nicolò's visit to Greenland, Antonio Zeno drew a sea chart that included a well-drawn map of Greenland showing the coasts on both sides. Sir Nicolò has been credited by some enthusiasts with the geographical exploration that supplied the information that went into this mapping of both coasts of Greenland. Messire Antonio, however, made no such claim for Sir Nicolò. He specifically said that the exploration of "the coasts of both sides of Greenland" had been made by the prince. It is quite certain that the exploration was not done by the Prince of Orkney in person. It is to be assumed, therefore, that Messire Antonio acquired the conception of the coasts of Greenland from a map furnished him by Earl Henry. The mapping may have been copied from a map brought to Orkney by Bishop John, who had been in Greenland since 1382. This copy may have come through Earl Henry's hands to

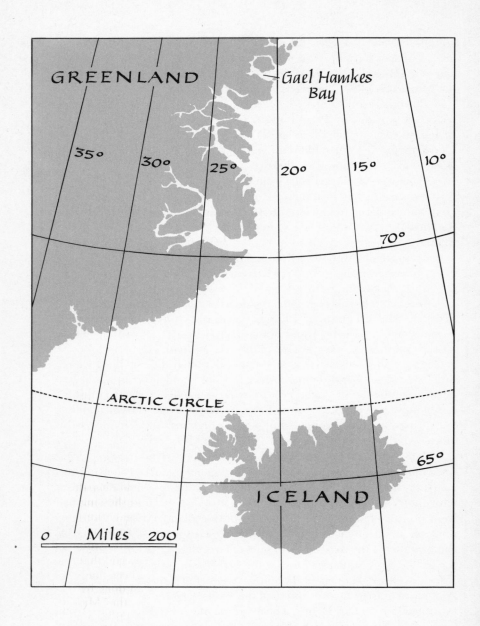

GREENLAND

Gael Hawkes
Bay

35°   30°   25°   20°   15°   10°

70°

ARCTIC CIRCLE

65°

ICELAND

0   Miles 200

East Coast of Greenland visited by Sir Nicolò

Antonio's. It is possible that some of the exploration of the coasts of Greenland was carried out by an expedition commissioned by Earl Henry, perhaps by the ship or ships that transferred the bishops.[7] But the bishops of Greenland of course had a fairly accurate map of that country in the fourteenth century. The Zeno Map was not the first to show the fairly accurate contour of both sides of Greenland. Indeed, the drawing of the Zeno Map appears to have been greatly influenced by or copied from other maps.[8]

At the end of his letter to Carlo, in which he gave Sir Nicolò's description of the Monastery of St. Thomas in Greenland (St. Tomas on the map), Messire Antonio added the unhappy news: "At length Messire Nicolò, not being accustomed to such severe cold, fell ill, and a little while after returned to Frislanda, where he died."

At the time of his death in 1395, Sir Nicolò was about sixty years of age. Antonio, who had married in 1384,[9] was in all probability at least twenty years younger. Sir Nicolò and Antonio had been together in the islands for four years. Antonio remained there for ten years more.

In a study of the official references to the Zeno family in Venice, Andrea da Mosto says the fourteenth-century Nicolò and Carlo Zeno were brothers, but that there is no surviving record of their having a brother Antonio. Sir Nicolò did, however, have a son Antonio.[10]

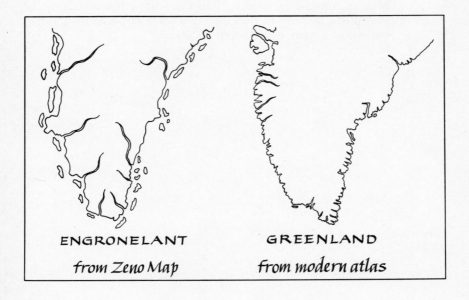

ENGRONELANT   GREENLAND

from Zeno Map   from modern atlas

Antonio's descendant in the sixteenth century may have mistakenly assumed that Antonio was Sir Nicolò's younger brother. It would be the kind of mistake frequently made in genealogy, a field in which it is extraordinarily easy to fall into such an error. In the absence of complete records, Antonio as the son of Sir Nicolò fits far better than if they were brothers, certainly in view of the presumed disparity in their ages. It seems safe to accept Antonio as a son who joined his father and later succeeded him as admiral of the prince's fleet, and wrote letters to his uncle Carlo.

According to his subsequent letters home, "Messire Antonio succeeded Messire Nicolò in his wealth and honors." Earl Henry made him captain (admiral) of his navy, but there is no record of his having knighted him. During the last ten years he remained in the islands, Messire Antonio immensely enjoyed the one summer when he participated in the great adventure of crossing the Atlantic, but aside from that, he complained constantly. The editor of his letters expressed it thus:

> Although he strove hard in various ways, and begged and prayed most earnestly, he could never obtain permission to return to his own country. For the Prince Zichmni, being a man of great enterprise and daring, had determined to make himself master of the sea. Accordingly, he proposed to avail himself of the services of Messire Antonio by sending him out with a few vessels to the westwards, because in that direction some of his fishermen had discovered very rich and populous islands.

Chapter Eleven

FISHERMAN'S TALE

FISHERMEN HAVE a reputation for tall tales. Everyone knows they are prone to exaggerate the size of a catch. But how about a fisherman who sails away toward the west and is not heard from for a quarter of a century, is presumed dead, and to everyone's surprise returns home? Must his description of the lands where he lived all these years be discounted as imaginary and boastful? What motive would he have for lying?

It seems safe to assume that before the invention of printing in the fifteenth-century, fishermen throughout the centuries had discovered many lands, knowledge of which was common gossip along the waterfront but which never came to the attention of university professors. Sailors often saw islands and coasts of which scholarly geographers and cartographers long after remained in ignorance.

Henry Sinclair was not a university scholar tucked away in a medieval campus. Perhaps more than any other ruler in his day, he spent much time on ships in daily contact with sailors and fishermen. He was close enough to his islanders to give credence to the story one of them brought back from the western side of the Atlantic. The fisherman would not lie to his prince. Of that, Henry could feel certain. The man's story could be, maybe would be, checked and verified. The man must have told the literal truth in his account of the new lands he had seen across the ocean. Henry gave good heed to the fisherman's tale.

The discovery the fisherman had made, Messire Antonio, in a letter to Messire Carlo, relates in detail in the following manner:

> Six and twenty years ago four fishing boats put out to sea, and encountering a heavy storm, were driven over the sea in utter helplessness for many days; when at length, the tempest abating, they discovered an island called Estotiland, lying to the westwards more than 1,000 miles from Frislanda.
>
> One of the boats was wrecked, and six men that were in it were taken by the inhabitants, and were brought into a fair and populous city [town], where the king of the place sent for many interpreters,[1] but there were none could be found who understood the language of the fishermen, except one that spoke Latin, and who had also been cast by chance upon the same island. On behalf of the king he asked them who they were and where they came from; and when he reported their answer, the king desired that they should remain in the country. Accordingly, as they could do no otherwise, they obeyed his commandments, and remained five years on the island, and learned the language. One of them in particular visited various parts of the island, and reports that it is a very rich country, abounding in all good things. It is a little smaller than Iceland.

Newfoundland is very close to the size of Iceland, but slightly larger. Iceland has an area of 39,688 square miles, and Newfoundland, 42,734 square miles.

> It is more fertile; in the middle of it is a very high mountain, in which rise four rivers which water the whole country.

The Annieopsquotch Mountains, over 2,000 feet high, are in the interior of Newfoundland, and would have seemed high indeed to an Orkney fisherman. The highest mountain in the island is 2,673 feet, about six miles inland from the Gulf of St. Lawrence. Compare the contour of Estotiland, allowing for its clockwise shift on the Zeno Map, with the contour of the eastern side of Newfoundland. The points of close similarity are too numerous to be mere coincidences.

> The inhabitants are very intelligent people, and possess all the arts like ourselves; and it is believed that in time past they have had intercourse with our people, for he said he saw Latin books in the king's [tribal chief's] library, which they at the present time do not understand.[2] They have their own language and letters. They have all kinds of metals, but especially they abound with gold.[3] Their foreign commerce is with Greenland, from which they come (*di dove traggono*) with furs, brimstone, and pitch.[4]
>
> He says that towards the south there is a great and populous country, very rich in gold. They sow corn and make a drink (*bevanda*) of a kind that northern people take as we do wine. They have woods of immense extent. They make their buildings with walls, and there are many towns and villages. They make small boats and sail them, but they have not the loadstone, nor do they know the North by the compass.
>
> For this reason these fishermen were held in great estimation, insomuch that the king sent them with twelve boats to the southwards to a country which they call Drogio, but in their voyage they had such contrary weather that they were in fear for their lives. Although they escaped the one cruel death, they fell into another

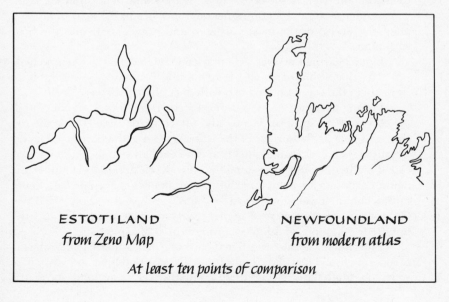

ESTOTILAND
from Zeno Map

NEWFOUNDLAND
from modern atlas

At least ten points of comparison

of the cruelist; for they were taken into the country and the greater number of them were eaten by the savages, who are cannibals and consider human flesh very savoury meat.

The fisherman who lived to tell the tale had the horror of seeing most of his companions killed by ritualistic slaughter, and their flesh roasted and eaten by their captors, who believed they would thus acquire the heroism and strength of the mysterious white strangers. The fisherman no doubt expected the same fate.

But there had been something in his boat when he was captured that excited the curiosity of the savages. The men of the tribe drew it out of the boat and stretched it on the ground, a device of knotted ropes nearly two hundred feet long. The Indian chiefs cautiously felt it with their fingers and took counsel together as to what it might be. Was it dangerous? Was it evil magic? Was it a weaving by which a white god wrought a spell that brought pestilence? It was not a war weapon. Did the white men hold prisoners tangled up in it until they were ready to eat them? None of the sachems could conceive its purpose.

Their curiosity was so great that they had the fisherman brought to them. Instead of binding him to a tree to serve as a target for arrows, they pointed to the crosswork of ropes and with gestures and lifting of eyebrows indicated that they wanted him to show them how it was to be used. He pointed into the boat and drew the shape of a fish in the sand. They understood, and let him stow the ropework in the boat in his own manner; several of the most daring young braves went into the boat with him.

Upon hearing the story, Antonio Zeno related what had happened:

"As that fisherman and his remaining companions were able to show them the way of taking fish with nets, their lives were saved."

Fishing with nets was a well-developed art in Orkney and Shetland. A net was about sixty yards long and fifteen yards wide. While the top edge was held at the surface of the water by floats, the bottom edge was weighted with heavy stone sinkers at each end, and smaller stone sinkers called bighters, at intervals along the edge. Each stone was held in a fine mesh. Part of such a net is on exhibition in the Ethnographical Museum in Stockholm. Twenty nets made a "fleet" and each vessel carried two fleets of nets. The nets were set at night and hauled at sunrise. Frequently, hundreds of pounds of fish were brought in at a single haul.

The Indians of the eastern seaboard of North America knew the art of spearing fish. They also caught fish with hook and line, and with stake weirs on tidal flats. Using these comparatively slow and inefficient methods, an Indian might fish all day and catch barely enough to feed his family. The Indians who had captured the Orkney fisherman had never seen anything so marvelous as these long nets that quickly drew into his boat great numbers of fish, food enough for several days for a whole tribe. They set great value on the life of a man who was such a prolific provider.

The Zeno Narrative tells us:

As this man's fame spread through the surrounding tribes, there was a neighboring chief very anxious to have him with him, and to see how he practiced his wonderful art of catching fish. With this object in view, he made war on the other chief, with whom the fisherman then was, and being more powerful and a better warrior, he at length overcame him, and so the fisherman was sent over to him with the rest of the company. During the thirteen years he dwelt in those parts, he says he was thus sent to more than twenty-five chiefs, and became acquainted with almost all those parts.

He says it is a very great country, and like a new world (*grandissimo e quasi un nuovo mondo*).

The people [along the coast of Florida?] are very rude and un-cultivated, for they all go naked, and suffer cruelly from the cold, nor have they the sense to clothe themselves with the skins of animals that they take in hunting. They have no kind of metal. They live by hunting, and carry lances of wood, sharpened at the point. They have bows, the strings of which are made of beasts' skins. They are very fierce, have daily fights, eat one another's flesh. The farther you go southwest, however, the more refinement you meet with, because the climate is more temperate, and accordingly there they have cities and temples dedicated to their idols, in which they sacrifice men and afterwards eat them. In those parts [Mexico or Yucatán?] they have some knowledge and use of gold and silver.

Now this fisherman, after having dwelt so many years in these parts, made up his mind, if possible to return home, but his companions despairing of ever seeing home again, gave him God's speed, and remained themselves where they were. Accordingly, he bade them farewell, and made escape through the woods in the direction of Drogio, where [in the woods] he was welcomed and very kindly received by the chief of the place, who knew him and was a great enemy of the neighboring chieftain; and so passing from one chief to another, being the same with whom he had been before, after a long time and with much toil he at length reached Drogio, where he spent three years. Here by good luck he heard from the natives that some boats had arrived off the coast, and full of hope of being able to carry out his intention, he went down to the seaside, and to his great delight found they were from Estotiland. He forthwith requested that they would take him with them, which they did very willingly, and as he knew the language of the country, which none of them could speak, they employed him as their interpreter.

He afterwards traded in their country to such good purpose that he became very rich, and fitting out a vessel of his own, returned to Frislanda, and gave an account of that most wealthy country to this nobleman. The sailors, from having had much experience in strange novelties, gave full credence to his statements.

The psychology of the sailors was well expressed. The habit of truthtelling was strong among the islanders. Men who had honestly reported on things they had seen, but had been doubted by landlubbers, had learned that what appears fantastic to stay-at-homes might be literal truth.

As for our believing the fisherman's story, it has received some corroboration from archaeology.[5] Also, the entire biography of Henry Sinclair in its internal credibility is further corroboration.

The fisherman of Frislanda who had traveled extensively along the coast of land on the western side of the Atlantic, and had succeeded in returning home, had indeed "during the thirteen years he had dwelt in those parts" seen enough to justify the descriptive statement that he made in the presence of Earl Henry: "It is a great country, and, as it were, a new world." This was the earliest use of the term "new world" as applied to any part of the Western Hemisphere. As we shall see, it was thus first applied to the continent of North America.

Part 3
WORTHY OF IMMORTAL MEMORY

Chapter Twelve

"NEW WORLD"

MESSIRE ANTONIO wrote that the prince proposed to send him out to the westward across the ocean to the lands that the fisherman had seen. The discovery of those lands was the fisherman's; the conception of the transoceanic expedition was Earl Henry's.

We can fairly read Henry's mind. The fisherman had mentioned "woods of immense extent" where the natives "live by hunting," and he had described it as "a very great country" and "fertile," and one that comprised "a new world." With such spaciousness there was room for newcomers, a great territory that would solve the land problem of Orkneymen and Shetlanders. It was almost fifty years since the Black Plague. The population of the Orkneys and Shetlands was again close to the limit of the food supply in the island areas. The fisherman's report of such large new lands was very welcome. It was worth investigating. And so Earl Henry planned to send "a few small vessels." But as he reflected on the matter he began to see other possibilities. A new land with extensive woods would supply ample material for shipbuilding. With untapped timber resources near where ships could be launched, he could add to his fleet, enhance his power, and literally become "master of the sea."

In his several trips into Scandinavia he had no doubt encountered vague rumors that the Norse Colony on the western side of the coast of Greenland had long ago procured timber from a land that the Norse called "Forestland" (*Markland*), which lay somewhere to the southwest of Greenland.[1] But the tale told by the fisherman of great new lands on the western side of the Atlantic came as a fresh discovery—one brought directly to himself—and it presented an opportunity commensurate with his wildest dreams. And so, as Antonio later wrote:

"This nobleman is therefore resolved to send forth with a fleet towards those parts, and there are so many who desire to join in the expedition on account of the novelty and strangeness of the things, that I think we shall be very strongly appointed without any public expense at all."

The business grew until it promised to be of such major importance that the prince of Orkney decided to lead the expedition himself. As Antonio put it: "I set sail with a considerable number of vessels and men, but had not the chief command, as I had expected to have, for Zichmni went in his own person."

Henry felt free to put the width of the ocean between himself and his earldom for a whole year because he was in undisputed possession of all the islands, and there was at the moment nothing on the political horizon to threaten the peace. He knew well the hardships and dangers of an ocean expedition. His decision not to sit at home in comfort is a measure of the man. To him the amenities of his position as earl were incidental: He was no idler, no lover of luxury, but a born adventurer. Prince Henry's decision was more than a debonair gesture. With the opportunity of crossing the Atlantic, the soul of an explorer was awakened in him.

His ships had sailed great distances in the open ocean. His mariners and Antonio knew various ways of ascertaining latitude. That does not mean that they counted latitude by number of degrees, though they may have done so. They could tell approximately how far north or south they were, within a distance of what we call one or two degrees, by the shadow of the gunwale on a thwart, when the sun was shining at midday and the ship not too violently rolling. With the astrolabe they could measure, within a degree or two, the altitude of the sun. Their most accurate instrument for determining latitude at sea was the sun-shadow board. This was a wooden disk marked with several concentric circles. A wooden pin through its center could be set at varying heights to function in accordance with tables of the sun's declinations at different times of the sailing season. This contrivance was floated in a basin held in the hands of one of the crew, who would keep the basin as level as he could, to compensate for the rolling and pitching of the ship. Observations at the midday hour would show whether the end of the shadow of the vertical pin precisely touched the concentric circle that was indicative of the latitude the ship was following, or whether it fell within or outside of that circle.

The explorer Captain Bob Bartlett, who had made effective use of primitive methods of navigation as well as the most modern, told me that pre-Columbian navigators at sea could tell latitude within a distance of a degree or two, and on land, within half a degree, or about thirty miles.

When Henry's ship captains set out with him to the westward, their intended landfall was the great island of Estotiland (Newfoundland), which extends north-south for five degrees. From the returned fisherman they possessed fairly accurate knowledge of the height of the sun at Estotiland, and so after they were well out in the ocean, they would sail southwest until observations with the sun-shadow board showed they were within the latitudes covered by Estotiland, and then they would proceed west by holding as near as they could to that latitude until they made land.

The loadstone, the magnetic "travel stone," is mentioned in the fourteenth-century Icelandic *Hauksbók*. The floating needle had probably been used in the North Atlantic for several centuries.

Antonio Zeno used a compass, though his compass steering alone, if uncorrected by observations of the sun-shadow board, would not have kept him close to his course, since there were very large variations of the compass at the northern latitudes through which he sailed.[2] Compass steering would also be corrected by azimuths, or the directions of stars and sun.

If a ship was kept to the proper course or at the proper latitude, then speed and distance scarcely mattered. Because dead reckoning was largely guesswork, little attention need be paid it on a long voyage, and that is why the fisherman who had returned from Estotiland put the distance at "over 1,000 miles" when it was actually about 1,855 miles.

In crossing the open ocean there was no danger of running into land unexpectedly on a dark night; in the daytime the appearance of land birds many miles from shore was an advance warning of close approach to land. From their species, a mariner could form some estimate of his distance from the nearest shore. Captain Bob Bartlett, a native Newfoundlander, said that when navigating in fog he could tell by the birds he heard near the ship how near he was to the coast of Newfoundland, whether it was fifty miles or five miles or half a mile,

The story of the voyage was told in one of Antonio's letters:

Our great preparations for the voyage to Estotiland were begun in an unlucky hour; for exactly three days before our departure, the fisherman died who was to have been our guide: nevertheless, Zichmni would not give up the enterprise, but in lieu of the deceased fisherman, took some sailors that had come out with him from the island.

Steering westwards, we sighted some islands subject to Frislanda, and passing certain shoals, came to Ledovo [a place, it will be remembered, on the western side of the main island of Shetland], where we stayed seven days to refresh ourselves and to furnish the fleet with necessaries. Departing thence, we arrived on the first of July [April, not July. The "Ap" of the Italian "Aprile" in fourteenth-century script could have been easily misread as capital "J," and "rile" as "uli." This error was made in deciphering the manuscript of Antonio's letter; for, as we shall see, some weeks later it was not yet the first of June that the expedition made a landfall on the western side of the Atlantic.] at the island of Ilofe [an island in a Shetland bay]; and as the wind was full in our favor, pushed on. But not long thereafter, when on the open ocean, there arose so great a storm that for eight days we were continuously in toil, and driven we knew not where, and a considerable number of the vessels were lost to each other. At length, when the storm abated, we gathered together the scattered vessels, and sailing with a prosperous wind, we sighted land on the west.

Steering straight for it, we reached a quiet and safe harbor, in which we saw a very large number of armed people, who came running, prepared to defend the island. Zichmni now caused his men to make signs of peace to them, and they sent ten men to us who could speak ten languages,[3] but we could understand none of them, except one who was from Islanda [Iceland].

Being brought before our Prince and asked what was the name of the island, and what people inhabited it, and who was the governor, he answered that the island was called Icaria, and that all the kings that reigned there were called Icari, after the first king, who was the son of Daedalus, King of Scotland.

"Scot" was the ancient name for "Irish," and "Scotland" meant the land of Irishmen, from the many Irish who had in early times moved into it. The mythological notion that Icarus, the son of Daedalus, was the first king of Scotland was similar to the equally fascinating belief of Londoners that London had been founded by Aeneas of Troy.

The great island, called Icaria by some of its inhabitants who were Irish, was what the Fer Island fisherman had called Estotiland. Eugene Beauvois thought the original form of the name was "Escociland," from which each "c" was somehow changed to a "t." "Escociland" would mean land of Irishmen (Scots).

Antonio's narrative continues:

> Daedalus conquered that island, left his son there for king, and gave them those laws that they retain to the present time. After that, when going to sail farther, he was drowned in a great tempest; and in memory of his death that sea was called to this day the Icarian Sea, and the kings of the island were called Icari. They were contented with the state which God had given them, and would neither alter their laws nor admit any stranger.

> They therefore requested our Prince not to attempt to interfere with their laws, which they had received from that king of worthy memory, and observed up to the present time; that the attempt would lead to his own destruction, for they were all prepared to die rather than relax in any way the use of those laws. Nevertheless, that we might not think that they altogether refused intercourse with other men, they ended by saying that they would willingly receive one of our people, and give him an honorable position amongst them, if only for the sake of learning my language and gaining information as to our customs, in the same way as they had already received those other ten persons from ten different countries, who had come into their island.

> To all this our Prince made no reply, beyond inquiring where there was a good harbor, and making signs that he intended to depart.

> Accordingly, sailing round about [coasting] the island, he put in with all his fleet in full sail, into a harbor which he found on the eastern side. The sailors went ashore to take in wood and water, which they did as quickly as they could, for fear they might be attacked by the islanders and not without reason, for the inhabitants made signals to their neighbors with fire and smoke, and taking their arms, the others coming to their aid, they all came running down to the seaside upon our men with bows and arrows, so that many were slain and several wounded. Although we made

signs of peace to them, it was of no use, for their rage increased more and more, as though they were fighting for their own very existence.

Being thus compelled to depart, we sailed along in a great circuit about the island, being always followed on the hill tops and along the sea coasts by a great number of armed men. At length, doubling the north cape of the island, we came upon many shoals, amongst which we were for 10 days in continual danger of losing our whole fleet, but fortunately all that time the weather was very fine. All the way till we came to the east cape, we saw the inhabitants still on the hill tops and by the sea coast, howling and shooting at us from a distance to show their animosity towards us.

In all probability, the "north cape" was Cape Freels, with reefs and shoals beyond it, and the "east cape" was Cape Race.

We therefore resolved to put into some safe harbor, and see if we might once again speak with the Islando (Icelander); but we failed in our object; for the people more like beasts than men, stood constantly prepared to beat us back if we should attempt to come on land. Wherefore, Zichmni, seeing he could do nothing, and that if we were to persevere in his attempt, the fleet would fall short of provisions, took his departure with a fair wind and sailed 6 days to the westwards; but the wind afterwards shifting to the southwest, and the sea becoming rough, we sailed 4 days with the wind aft, and finally sighted land.

As the sea ran high and we did not know what country it was, we were afraid at first to approach it, but by God's blessing the wind lulled, and then there came on a great calm. Some of the crew pulled ashore and soon returned with great joy with news that they had found an excellent country and a still better harbor. We brought our barks and our boats to land, and on entering an excellent harbor, we saw in the distance a great hill (*monte*) that poured forth smoke, which gave us hope we should find some inhabitants in the island. Neither would Zichmni rest, though it [the hill] was a great way off, without sending 100 soldiers to explore the country, and bring us an account of what sort of people the inhabitants were.

Henry would not have dispatched inland more than half his force. We can safely conclude he had at least two hundred men in the expedition.

Meanwhile, we took in a store of wood and water, and caught a considerable quantity of fish and sea fowl. We also found such an abundance of birds' eggs, that our men, who were half famished, ate of them to repletion.

While we were at anchor here, the month of June came in, and the air in the island was mild and pleasant beyond description; but as we saw nobody, we began to suspect that this pleasant place was uninhabited. To the harbor we gave the name Trin, and the headland which stretched out into the sea we called Cape Trin.

A feudal lord's first reaction to such a wilderness must have been one of exhilaration. Here were no king's lands, no church lands, no earl's lands, no chartered lands, no privately owned lands, but free lands for all. Here were free hunting and fishing, with no one to challenge the exercise of such privileges.

When Prince Henry landed in Trin Harbor he no doubt, as was the custom, took formal possession of the land in the name of his principality. It is an entertaining thought that in what is today a Canadian province, he incorporated a new continent into his sea kingdom and by right of legal claim, annexed North America to the earldom of Orkney.

After eight days the 100 soldiers returned, and brought word that they had been through the island and up to the hill, and that the smoke was a natural thing proceeding from a great fire in the bottom of the hill, and that there was a spring from which issued a certain substance like pitch, which ran into the sea, and that thereabouts dwelt a great many people half wild, and living in caves. They were of small stature and very timid. They reported also that there was a large river, and a very good and safe harbor.

When Henry heard the report his soldiers gave of the "spring" with a black substance like pitch that flowed down like a brook, he could not fail to be reminded of the black oil swimming in St. Katherine's Holy Well near his birthplace, a well that had always been a symbol to him of special protection and good luck. He must have felt that St. Katherine, worker of miracles at brooks, and patron saint of his family, now in this western land had revealed to him her guiding hand. Obviously, she had led him across the ocean to this new world. Understandably, he was eager to see for himself the spring and the brook.

When Zichmni heard this, and noticed the wholesome and pure atmosphere, fertile soil, good rivers, and so many other

conveniences, he conceived the idea of founding a city [settlement].
But his people, fatigued, began to murmur, and say they wished
to return to their homes, for winter was not far off, and if they
allowed it once to set in, they would not be able to get away before
the following summer. He therefore retained only boats propelled
by oars, and such of his people as were willing to stay, and sent the
rest away in ships, appointing me, against my will, to be their
captain.

The boats propelled by oars were about the size of lifeboats or
whaleboats, and were carried on the decks of the ships when at sea.
Henry's retention of "only boats propelled by oars" indicates his serious
intention to explore coastlines, where the oars, like a modern auxiliary
engine, would be essential in harbors and rivers and small streams.

His retaining only the small undecked rowboats is positive evidence
that he planned to avail himself of the rich resources of timber in the
New World, and build a ship with which to return across the ocean, just
as the Fer Island fisherman had done before him. The new ship would
be an addition to his navy. For this purpose he must have kept with him
sufficient frieze-cloth to make sails, and also enough spare ropes, and
nails, rivets, and carpenter's tools.

There had been a shortage of food at the end of the westward
crossing, and it was practicable for only a portion of the large company
to remain in the wilderness over the winter, and certainly only those who
had a will to remain. The wooded country in the new land was far more
attractive than the treeless Orkneys and Shetlands. Antonio Zeno said
he himself would have preferred to remain there, though we know that
what he wanted most of all was permission to return to his home in
Venice.

Having no choice, therefore, I departed, and sailed 20 days
to the eastwards without sight of any land; then, turning my course
towards the southeast, in 5 days I lighted on land, and found
myself on the island of Neome [in the Shetlands?][4] and knowing
the country, I perceived I was past Islanda [Iceland]; and as the
inhabitants were subject to Zichmni, I took in fresh stores and
sailed with a fair wind in 3 days to Frislanda, where the people,
who thought they had lost their Prince, in consequence of his long
absence on the voyage we had made, received us with a hearty
welcome.

Antonio's eastbound voyage to "Neome" was "twenty days to the eastwards . . . then . . . toward the southeast . . . five." His actual distance out of sight of land from Trin Harbor to the Shetlands was about two thousand one hundred miles, at an average speed of about eighty-four miles a day, or better than three knots. His eastbound crossing was faster than the expedition's westbound crossing from the Shetlands to Newfoundland. From Ilofe on the first of April to the anchoring off Trin Harbor at the end of May were sixty days. Subtracting ten days spent among shoals off Newfoundland, and two or three days spent in foiled attempts to go ashore in Newfoundland, and ten days (six to westward and four with a southwest wind aft) somewhere to the west of that large island, we find about thirty-seven days were spent in the crossing of about 1,855 miles from the Shetlands to Newfoundland, at an average speed of fifty miles a day, or close to two knots.

We are fortunate in being able to make these computations. Antonio's crossings of the Atlantic are the earliest for which we have the written record of a participant. Since they are the only pre-Columbian crossings for which we have such a record, they are historically invaluable.

Chapter Thirteen

SMOKING HOLE AND SPRING OF PITCH

SIR NICOLO Zeno's description of the east coast of Greenland has been corroborated by geology and archaeology. Do those sciences bring any evidence to bear on Messire Antonio Zeno's account of a transatlantic voyage?

Antonio Zeno says that Prince Henry's westward-bound ships made their first landfall on an island so large that it took them days to coast its eastern side. There is no other island than Newfoundland that this could have been. They called that huge island Estotiland, and on the Zeno Map Estotiland is in the position of Newfoundland in relation to Greenland. Messire Antonio says they left that large island astern and sailed westward from it. Did they afterwards land on the North American Continent? Was it somewhere on that continent that the soldiers of the Prince of Orkney found a smoking hole at the bottom of a hill and a spring of pitch flowing down into the sea? If so, can we know in what particular region it was?

Not only do geography and ethnography give corroborating evidence that the Prince of Orkney landed on the continent of North America, but geology gives absolute proof that he did.

First, the geographical evidence:

Some have supposed that the country of the smoking hole and spring of pitch was Greenland. But it was definitely not Greenland; for this country grew trees ("they took in a store of wood"). It had fertile soil and good rivers, and air "mild and pleasant beyond description." It was a land that foot soldiers crossed, and therefore could not be Greenland with its interior of impassable ice fields. When we are told that the Prince of Orkney explored "the whole of the country" of the smoking hole, "as well as the coasts of Greenland," the "as well as" indicates that in Antonio's mind it was a different land from Greenland. He would not have used the phrase "his newly discovered island" in reference to Greenland, since Greenland was a land that had been known for generations and one with which Orkney had exchanged bishops.

The land of the smoking hole and spring of pitch was not Newfoundland; for the words "we did not know what land it was" tell us that the sailors among the crew, upon whom Prince Henry relied as guides because they had recently returned from Estotiland with the fisherman who died, did not recognize the newly discovered land.

The land of the smoking hole and spring of pitch was either a very large "island," or it was a peninsula, which the one hundred soldiers, coming out to a view of the sea on the other side of the land, assumed to be an island. Their assumption, however, was not verified during the time Antonio Zeno was there. In a few weeks, Messire Antonio was sailing back across the Atlantic. It was no doubt soon after his arrival in the Orkneys that he wrote the letter to Carlo in Venice in which he called the land of the smoking hole an "island." Prince Henry, returning home the next year, probably then told Antonio that the land where he had wintered was not an island; but as we know, most of the text of Antonio's later letter describing Prince Henry's explorations was destroyed before any portions of his letters were published.

We can estimate very closely the distance "across" the land from the fact that "after eight days the soldiers returned." In the "forest primeval" under tall trees there is little impeding undergrowth; explorers were able to travel through trackless woods much more rapidly than is possible through second growth and scrub. Charles W. K. McCurdy of Baddeck, Cape Breton, told me that he once walked through unbroken Canadian forests with a compass for nine hundred miles, most of the distance from Edmonton to Prince Rupert, and that he clocked his speed of walking at two and a half miles an hour.

It is reasonable to assume that Prince Henry's one hundred soldiers, even if they did not find an Indian trail, advanced fifteen miles a day. They reached the smoking hole at the bottom of a hill in about three and a half days, and presumably spent a day in the neighborhood of it. The distance to the smoking hole from where they started into the woods was therefore at least fifty miles. It could not have been much over sixty.

The larger islands on the western side of the North Atlantic: Nantucket, Martha's Vineyard, and Long Island, are none of them broad enough to have required eight days to march across and return. As for Cape Breton Island, broad waterways render a north-south or east-west overland march impossible.

Since the land of the smoking hole and spring of pitch was not any of the islands along the Atlantic seaboard of North America west of Newfoundland, we have the peninsular and continental portion of Nova Scotia to consider as the sole remaining possibility. Does this beautiful land of Old Acadia, with its entrancing vistas of indented shoreline and evergreens close to the sea, fit the geographical and geological requirements?

A geologist of the University of Michigan was the first to supply the answer. Dr. William H. Hobbs identified the Stellarton area in the Pictou region of Nova Scotia as the place that the soldiers described, because only there in all of the New World anywhere within one thousand miles of the Atlantic were the two phenomena in juxtaposition: "a great fire in the bottom of the hill," and "a spring from which issued a certain substance like pitch, which ran into the sea." The geological evidence is unique and incontrovertible. The identification is absolute, as we shall see.

There was an open deposit of viscous asphalt in the lake of pitch at Trinidad, at latitude $10°\ 14'$ N, and 2,300 miles southwest of St. John's, Newfoundland. This was clearly not the black brook of flowing pitch found by the Orkney Expedition, which came to land about two or three days' sailing distance beyond Newfoundland. Pitch Lake in Trinidad, covering 114 acres, almost $\frac{1}{2}$ mile in diameter, and 284 feet deep, does not fit the description of a "spring," though it is itself fed by subterranean springs. There is no "large river" near it.

Another open deposit of pitch, actually a pitchy swamp, was still further out of the question, since it was in Venezuela, up the Orinoco River.

In the United States of America, rock asphalts existed in Alabama, California, Kentucky, Missouri, Oklahoma, Texas, and Utah, all more than a thousand miles from where the Orkney Expedition could have landed.

In eastern Canada there were oil seepages in Ontario, in the Gaspé Peninsula, and in the Maritime Provinces, but the one at Stellarton in Nova Scotia is the only one of these that is associated with open coal seams and is in a geographical position to fit Antonio's description of a spring of viscous pitch flowing into the sea and close to a smoking hole at the bottom of a hill, and also close to a good harbor.[1]

Dr. Hobbs asserted authoritatively that such a spring of viscous pitch had existed in the Stellarton region. Since he did not say precisely where, I felt it was important to pinpoint it if possible. I therefore went to Pictou County, Nova Scotia. None of the local librarians or historians or public officials or coal mine directors had heard of it. All my inquiries in Stellarton drew a blank. When I presented my query to a prominent man in nearby New Glasgow, a man whose name happened to be Sinclair, he said of it in reference to the local authorities: "This will make them wrinkle their noses." In spite of the wrinkles, no information came.

On that first visit to Nova Scotia, I traveled by train. This was fortunate, since it led to acquaintance with the Canadian National Railways timetable, in which by chance I noticed the name of a flag stop called Asphalt, less than a mile from Stellarton Station. Since "asphalt," "pitch," and "bitumen" are three names for the same substance, this was a clue worth following.

The president of the railroad had no record as to the origin of the name of the flag stop. In the Public Archives of the Province of Nova Scotia, in Halifax, an assistant librarian found a reference on the strength of which he expressed the opinion that the flag stop on the hill above Stellarton had received its name from the fact that it was on the Asphalt Road. He guessed that this road was so named because it had been the first road in the province paved with asphalt. It seemed to me unlikely that the nature of a road's pavement would have given a name to a place through which the road ran.

It looked as though the road I was on had reached a dead end. However, in Stellarton I took a bus to the top of the hill, which has an elevation of one hundred and eighty feet, and got off where the road crossed the railroad tracks. The flag stop did not have any station building, but merely a level strip of gravel beside the tracks. It was at the corner of a community three blocks square, mostly of coal miners' houses. Two miners with whom I talked did not know why the place was called Asphalt, but they beckoned to an older man who they thought might know. The older man said he thought the name had a geological origin, since there was "oil shale" underneath it, but his knowledge seemed vague.

Mr. Roland H. Sherwood of Pictou thought my query as to the origin of "Asphalt" should be addressed to the readers of the *New Glasgow Evening News*, and he took action for me. The following explanation was received in reply:

> The "Asphalt" district of this town got its name from a deposit of asphalt or tar-like material which used to lie just above the present Receiving Home (Birch Hill) of the Children's Aid Society. That was the information conveyed to *The News* by Dan MacKenzie who came here in 1882 as a boy of ten. At that time the main road to Westville went along Bridge Street in Stellarton and was known as "the post road." The present route was the "Asphalt" road. The deposit of pitch was hardened and could be walked on, extending out about 100 yards. It was spongy and gave beneath a man's boots—but sprang back into place. It burned and a good many people in the neighborhood dug it up and used it in their stoves like the peat they knew in the old country.[2]

Here was the testimony of a surviving witness to the fact that at Asphalt on the top of Stellarton Hill there had been a spring of pitch. From that spring an asphalt stream had flowed down what is called Coal Brook, which remains black to this day. The brook of bitumen crossed the Foord coal seam at the bottom of the hill, a burning coal seam from which smoke poured forth. As Dr. Hobbs had already said, it was at Stellarton that there had been the two phenomena that existed in close proximity to each other, and nowhere else within a thousand miles of the North Atlantic. The Coal Brook from Asphalt and the burning Foord coal seam had been seen by the hundred soldiers of the Prince of Orkney in the fourteenth century.

Earl Henry's soldiers said the pitch "ran into the sea." The Coal Brook flowed into the East River, which is tidal to Stellarton. The bottom of the river exposed at low tide is black with oily wastes beginning at Stellarton and from there down the river. Below Stellarton, the East River is as broad as the River Thames above London, England, and would have seemed "large" indeed to men from the Orkneys and Shetlands. It is one of three rivers that flow into Pictou Harbor.

Pictou County contains more coalfields for its area than any other part of the world. In the Stellarton region there were exposed seams of coal rich in bituminous matter highly charged with inflammable gas. The fire Henry's soldiers found could have been started by a stroke of lightning, or by a forest fire, or from an Indian campfire. The Micmac Indians in Pictou County said that an opening in the ground there had burned and smoked for a long period of time.[3] At the bottom of Stellarton Hill, near the river, is an opening in the ground which in historic times has been a smoking hole. Three times between 1828 and 1830 a channel

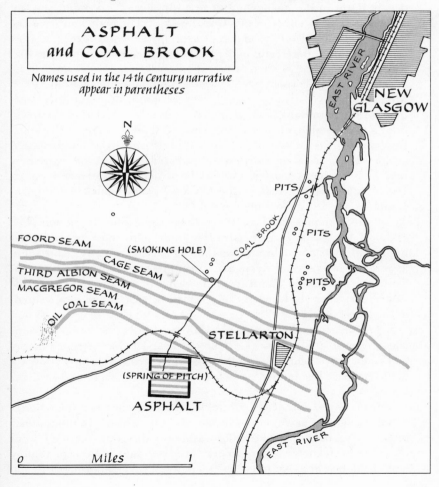

ASPHALT and COAL BROOK

Names used in the 14th Century narrative appear in parentheses

N

FOORD SEAM
(SMOKING HOLE)
CAGE SEAM
THIRD ALBION SEAM
MACGREGOR SEAM
OIL COAL SEAM

COAL BROOK

EAST RIVER

NEW GLASGOW

PITS
PITS
PITS

STELLARTON

(SPRING OF PITCH)

ASPHALT

EAST RIVER

0   Miles   1

had to be cut from the East River to pour water into the coal workings there to extinguish fires. A fire that started in 1832 burned for more than a year before the river quenched it. "Other fires after 1860 also required to be drowned out. In 1896 a commission was appointed by the Provincial Government to report on the Mine Fires of Pictou County, one of which had been burning since 1870, and continues to this day."[4]

The first discovery of coal in the Stellarton area was made on the MacGregor farm in 1798. It was made "on what is known as the Deep seam cropping out on the brook a little above where the main seam was deeply burnt in the unknown past to a distance of 1,000 and 500 feet along the crop on either side of Coal Brook."[5] The main seam was the Foord, the thickest bituminous coal seam in the world, over forty feet thick, with nine other seams under it. It takes its name from the fact that it once made a ford where it crosses the East River.

Stellarton, incorporated in 1889, had its name changed from Albion Mines. It received its new name (from the Latin *stella*, meaning star) because the material known as Stellar coal, which underlies the town, is an oil coal which when it burns, emits short bright flames like stars. Dawson says Stellar coal is "of the nature of an earthy bitumen, and geologically is to be regarded as an underclay or fossil soil, extremely rich in bituminous matter, derived from decayed and comminuted vegetable substances. It is, in short, a fossil swamp-muck or mud. . . . It yields 50 to 126 gallons of oil per ton."[6]

Picked samples of oil coal have given 190 gallons to the ton. The shales or bat yields 44 gallons to the ton.[7] "This most extensive and important collection of bituminous matter has been greatly disturbed in its original bed; several dykes and faults are known, which often confound the miner, and afford strong evidence of the former existence of subterranean fires, by which the substrata have been melted and elevated, or have produced faults."[8]

The oil coal is highly charged with gas. "Boys used to hold a puncheon over a small stream (Coal Brook) near Dr. MacGregor's house, and when the puncheon was full of gas, uprighted it and threw into it a lighted paper. The ignited gas would burn with a bright and brilliant blaze."[9]

Even in the East River,[10] bubbles of gas arising from the outcrop "could be lighted in winter by cutting a hole in the ice." In this manner miners' wives used to boil water for washing clothes. Gas from freshly cut coal "has been known to flow so pure as to put out the flame of a safety lamp held in it, and that too where there was a current passing of 10,000

cubic feet of air per minute. . . . Gas roared as a miner struck coal with
a pick; it would go off like the report of a pistol. The noise which the
gas and water made in issuing from the coal was like a hundred snakes
hissing at each other. . . . Putting flame to the firedamp at East River
on a calm day, it would spread over the river, like what is commonly
termed setting the Thames on fire."[11]

Pitch or bitumen or asphalt is a black or brownish black substance,
which melts at 90° to 100° C. It contains resins, nitrogenous compounds,
and oils vaporable at varying temperatures. From the heat of an under-
ground burning coal seam (which in one instance at Stellarton was so
intense it melted the iron chains used for hoisting coal out of a pit), pitch
might have been melted into a liquid and have flowed out of the ground
through a fissure, crevice, or fault, to form a superficial deposit. An earth
seepage of viscous pitch may also be induced by hydrostatic pressure or
by gas pressure. It is a very rare phenomenon. The ancient world knew
one at the Dead Sea in the Vale of Siddim (Genesis 14:10). There were
bitumen springs near Babylon at Hit, which according to ancient
superstition was "where the gods speak." Marco Polo described seepages
of liquid asphalt at Baku. Very few places in Europe had such seepages.

The Pictou region was well populated, being one of the five centers
where Indians lived in Nova Scotia. Antonio Zeno wrote: 'Thereabouts
dwelt great multitudes of people." We are told the same thing by the
earliest historical records of the province, and by archaeological studies.

> In a map accompanying Charlevoix's work, the mouth of the
> East River is marked as the site of an Indian village. This must have
> been situated on the east side, nearly opposite the loading ground.
> . . . There close by the river is a beautiful flat. . . . Here the land
> was clear when the English settlers arrived. . . . The opposite side
> of the river gives evidence of similar occupancy, in particular a
> field covered with oyster shells. . . . Fraser's Point and Middle
> River Point were also places of frequent resort.[12]

But where were the caves that the soldiers found to be human
habitations? Investigation revealed two caves in the neighborhood of
Stellarton; a limestone cave three and a half miles to the southeast, along
McLellan's Brook at the base of the north side of Irish Mountain; and
another cave near Bridgeville up the East River about ten miles to the
southwest. These were both on the route of Henry's one hundred soldiers
if they came to the site of Stellarton from the southeast. These two caves
are rightly placed, as will appear. And two caves suffice, for the soldiers
may have generalized. It brings to mind the story of the immigrant who

spent his first night in America in a farmhouse, where he saw the farmer's wife smoking. He wrote home to Europe that "in the United States the women smoke pipes," though after living in the United States for the next forty years he never saw another woman smoke a pipe. The soldiers may have found natives living or huddled in one or two caves and may have concluded that caves were the normal habitations for the people of the region.[13]

The one hundred soldiers reported to Prince Henry that they found the natives "of small stature." The Micmac Indians were of medium height, not so tall as Plains Indians.[14] They were short as compared with Orkneymen. The character of the natives described by the soldiers as "very timid" was quite different from that of the natives of Newfoundland as had been previously reported by the fisherman, and experienced by Prince Henry and his men when his ships attempted to land in Newfoundland.

The most important discovery that the hundred soldiers made was that near the black brook was "a very good and safe harbor." Pictou Harbor is one of the best. Indeed, there is no other harbor comparable to it on the north shore of Nova Scotia. It is completely landlocked.[15] No wonder the Orkney fishermen called it "safe."

Trin Harbor was eastward of Stellarton. Since the Orkney Expedition had approached the land from the southward, with "wind . . . southwest . . . aft," Trin Harbor was on the southern side of the Nova Scotia peninsula. Trin Harbor was therefore southeast of Stellarton. Its distance from Stellarton was about fifty to sixty miles.

Trin Harbor was near a single large cape. The words, "the headland which stretched out into the sea" suggest a long straight shore at the side of the cape, such as the northern side of Cape Canso. The Indian name Chedabucto (Chebuktook) duplicates the expression "stretched out" in the narrative; for Chedabucto means "deep extending" harbor or bay, or "running far back."

The words "the headland" indicate that there was only one cape near, and that it was a large cape. Trin Harbor could not have been one of the harbors like Country Harbor along the southern shoreline, since every one of those harbors is flanked on both sides by a small headland or cape. Drogio on the Zeno Map shows a large cape like Cape Canso.

From the fact that the ships were anchored at first outside the harbor without awareness that there was a harbor near, and some of the crew who "pulled ashore" returned "soon with great joy with news" that they had found a wonderful harbor, it seems that Trin Harbor could not have

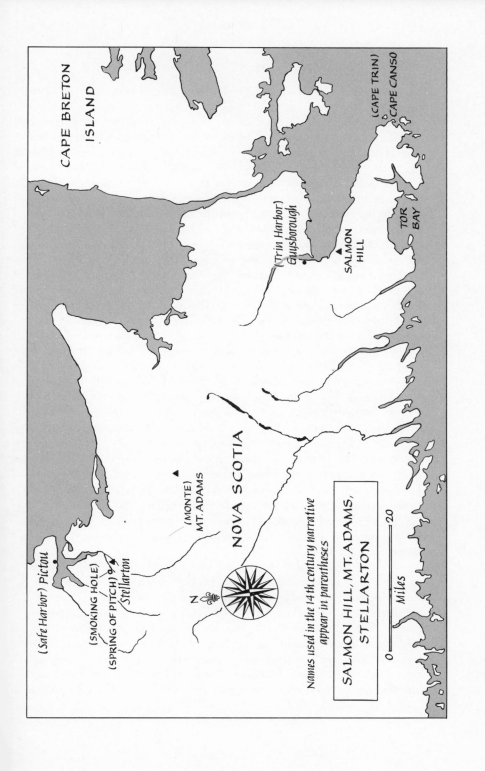

CAPE BRETON ISLAND

(Cape Trin)
CAPE CANSO

Trin Harbor)
Guysborough

SALMON
HILL

TOR
BAY

(Monte)
MT. ADAMS

NOVA SCOTIA

(Safe Harbor) Pictou

(SMOKING HOLE)

(SPRING OF PITCH) ?
Stellarton

N

Names used in the 14th century narrative
appear in parentheses

SALMON HILL, MT. ADAMS,
STELLARTON

0   20

Miles

been any harbor like Country Harbor, the mouth of which lies open and inviting and obvious.

At the head of the Bay of Canso is a wonderful harbor, the entrance to which is something special, deserving comment. In front of this harbor there is a gravel bar high enough to conceal the harbor, even at high tide, from men in the bay in rowboats. When such men in boats come to the west end of the bar, they meet with a surprise, for they find themselves abreast of the entrance to the harbor, the existence of which is revealed to them with astonishing suddenness. Earl Henry's men in a few moments ("soon") realized what a splendid harbor they had discovered. This was Guysborough Harbor, which satisfies every geographical requirement, and is the only harbor that does.[16]

Guysborough Harbor satisfies the description Antonio Zeno gives of Trin Harbor as "better" than "excellent," or from the point of view of Orkneymen, as close to perfection. It is completely landlocked, yet quickly accessible from the bay. Nicholas Denys thus described Guysborough Harbor (Chedabucto, as he called it): "A fine harbor is formed there by means of a dike of gravel 600 feet in length. This bars the mouth of this river, with the exception of the entrance which is a pistol shot wide, and makes inside a sort of basin. This dike still stands out five or six feet at high tide, so that the entrance thereto is very easy. A ship of 100 tons can enter there easily and remain always afloat."[17] Another writer says of the high point at the left of the harbor entrance: "The fort side is the best center for the cod-fishery in the vicinity, being within shelter of the harbor, though close to the fishing grounds outside, has an admirable landing beach just above the point, is very near the great bar which must have been very well adapted to the drying of fish, and in the immediate vicinity has ample fertile upland for cultivation."[18] Such were the advantages of Trin, the "better' than "excellent" harbor—advantages that Orkney fishermen could not have failed to observe.

Antonio Zeno tells of their going into Trin Harbor: "We brought our barks and our boats to land, and on entering an excellent harbor, we saw in the distance a great hill that poured forth smoke." They saw the hill and the smoke while they were far out in the bay at a considerable distance from the land. After they had landed in the harbor, they naturally wished to ascend the highest elevation in the vicinity. High ground was always a beacon to explorers, since it gave opportunity for inspecting the surrounding country. From the highest elevation near Trin Harbor the men of the Orkney Expedition saw the smoke again, rising from far inland. It seemed to come from a hill visible to them "in the distance," in the "middle" of the island.

Since Earl Henry knew that the Atlantic was to the east of him, he would not have sent the soldiers overland toward a smoking hill that lay anywhere to the east, at least not until after the exploring had been attempted by ship, as in that case it logically would have been. The smoking hill was somewhere to the west, northwest, or southwest of the harbor they called Trin.

Just south of Guysborough Harbor, only two miles from shore, is the top of Salmon Hill, the highest hill for forty miles, excluding hills on Cape Breton. Its elevation is 820 feet, and it affords an unobstructed view in all directions. It is the highest point on Cape Canso, and it reveals the fact that it is on a huge cape. From the shore, Earl Henry and his men could have reached its summit in two hours. There used to be an observatory at the top, but that was unnecessary, since there are extensive barrens, and no trees obscure the view. At no place along the south side of Nova Scotia is there any other such vantage point from which to see a great distance inland.

The highest hill to the northwest visible from the summit of Salmon Hill is at 315° true. All to the far westwards are hills. Of everything seen from the summit, the hill that appears to be the highest is one that looms in the distance back of nearer hills, looking as though it might be much loftier than it really is. This apparently highest hill, forty-two miles away, is at 295° true (NNW). It is the hill of 920 feet elevation now called Mount Adams, north of Lake Eden. Its summit is so close to being in a direct line between Salmon Hill and Stellarton that smoke rising at Stellarton would seem to be ascending from it. Another hill of the same height, called Blue Mountain, on which a fire lookout tower now stands, is so close to Mount Adams that from the distance of Salmon Hill it appears to be part of Mount Adams.

It was in a letter written after he had returned to the Orkneys that Messire Antonio wrote: "We saw in the distance a great hill that poured forth smoke." He had seen the smoke beyond various intervening hills. After the soldiers returned and told of the hill with smoke pouring from a hole at its base, it would have been natural for Messire Antonio to suppose that he had seen the actual smoking hill, not knowing that he could not have seen it from Salmon Hill. Mount Adams and Blue Mountain cut off the view of hills beyond them. The smoke, however, rose above all the hills.

In spite of the distance and the intervening hills, smoke at Stellarton would be visible from Salmon Hill. There are many summer days in that part of Nova Scotia when the atmosphere is of remarkable clearness. In the forenoon of a July day from the summit of Salmon Hill, I saw a moving column of smoke from far beyond the visible Mount Adams. I knew from its direction that the moving smoke was from a locomotive of a train traveling from New Glasgow to Stellarton, and when the train stopped at Stellarton, I photographed the smoke rising in a stationary column.

The distance from Salmon Hill to Stellarton is sixty miles. From the head of Guysborough Harbor to Stellarton is fifty-one miles.

After landing in Trin Harbor, the men of the Orkney Expedition, "half famished, ate . . . to repletion." Illustrative of the food resources they found there is the following description: "Towards the head of the Bay of Campeaux [Canso] . . . [is] a little river which I have named Rivière du Saumon. Having gone there to fish, I made a cast of the seine at its entrance, where it took so great a quantity of salmon that ten men could not haul it to land, and although it was new, had it not broken, the Salmon would have carried it off. We had still a boat full of them. The Salmon here are large; the smallest are three feet long."[19]

It seemed unfortunate, a frustrating omission, that Antonio's narrative did not mention the year of Henry Sinclair's voyage to Nova Scotia, a pre-Columbian crossing of the Atlantic that one feels he should have dated. While I was inspecting the harbor at Guysborough, I tried to fathom the significance of the name "Trin." It suggested something triple, and I wondered whether it could have been used in reference to three islands in the harbor, though I saw only two. There was nothing triple, however, about the cape to which the name Trin was also applied.

It then occurred to me that Henry Sinclair would have followed the custom of explorers from Christendom, which was to name a newly discovered harbor, cape, river, etc., from the day in the church calendar upon which he discovered or entered or formally took it into possession. The name Trin seemed to be an abbreviation of Trinity. This surmise becomes a certainty when we reexamine the context.

We read in one sentence: "While we were at anchor here, the month of June came in," and in the next sentence as a natural conclusion: "To the harbor we gave the name of Trin." Here was a hint of some connection between June and the name Trinity.

I did not know the church calendar, and while I was wondering how I might most quickly acquire the desired information, I saw in the village street of Guysborough the revealing collar of an Anglican rector.

I eagerly asked him whether there was in the church calendar a day devoted to the Trinity. "Yes," he replied, and added: "This year (1950) it was the first Sunday in June."

With the exhilarating prospect that I might be able to date the Orkney Expedition, I sought information as to Trinity Sunday, and learned that it was "a high principal feast in Holy Church." But had it found a place in the church calendar before the end of the fourteenth century? Yes, universal observance of Trinity Sunday was established by Pope John XXII in 1334.

Trinity is the eighth Sunday after Easter. Since Easter may occur as early as March 22 and as late as April 25, Trinity Sunday may be as early as May 17 and as late as June 20. The Orkney Expedition named Trin Harbor in a year when Trinity Sunday occurred on or immediately after the first of June.

Could I learn which year it was?

It was clear that the expedition came after 1394, in which year Sir Nicolò Zeno died. On the other hand, the expedition occurred before 1404, in which year Antonio Zeno returned to Venice. From 1395 to 1403 inclusive were nine years.

Would the dates of Trinity Sunday from 1395 to 1403 reveal the year of the expedition? When I read in the encyclopaedias of the formulas for ascertaining the calendar, involving solar equation and lunar cycle, complicated by the historical shift from the Julian to the Gregorian calendar, I realized that the computation of the dates of Easter in the fourteenth century presented a problem that I was unprepared to solve. I feared that if I did find the dates, I might learn that among the nine years there had been two years in which Trinity Sunday was on the first of June or so soon after the first of June as to render impossible any certainty of dating the expedition. Was there some way to get the information fast enough to satisfy my impatience? I sent an airmail letter to the Vatican Library inquiring for the dates of Easter in the critical nine years.

The very next day, however, in the New York Public Library I was happy to find reference tables in *The Book of Almanacs* by Augustus de Morgan, which give the calendars for the past two thousand years. The dates of Trinity Sunday according to this book were subsequently verified by the reply received from the Vatican.

Those dates are: June 6, 1395; May 28, 1396; June 17, 1397; June 2, 1398; May 25, 1399; June 13, 1400; May 29, 1401; May 21, 1402; and June 10, 1403.

These dates reveal the year of Henry Sinclair's Expedition to North America; for in only one of the nine years was Trinity Sunday immediately after June 1. Henry's ships were "at anchor" on the first of June, "when June came in," and he and his followers entered the harbor and landed and took formal possession the next day, on Trinity Sunday, the second of June, in the year 1398.

The landing of the Orkney Expedition on the continent of North America is as definitely dated as to year, month, and day, as the landing of Christopher Columbus on an island in the West Indies.

Curiosity irresistibly drew Earl Henry to the spring and flowing brook of pitch, and the perfect harbor.

There were material advantages in moving his camp from Trin Harbor, where he had met no natives, to the equally good Pictou Harbor where many people lived. He could obtain food supplies there by trade. It was reasonable to assume that the natives there resided where there was the best hunting, and that they would act as guides. The Micmac Indians of Pictou lived in an area where there were many animals in the forest: deer, moose, elk, bear, porcupine, squirrel, rabbit, wolverine, hedgehog, weasel, fox, beaver, otter, and muskrat. In the sea were hair seals and walrus. The inland waters were the homes of ducks, geese, loons, and cranes. Near Pictou Harbor there was a greater variety of trees than near Guysborough Harbor. Some of them were ideal for shipbuilding and some of them immensely tall. The trees there were oak, elm, ash, birch, maple, sycamore, pine, fir, spruce, hazel, willow, and bay. Above all, near the "safe harbor" was the invaluable pitch for caulking ship seams.

The one hundred soldiers who returned from the smoking hole and brook of pitch had passed over high ground from which they could not have failed to see the waters of Northumberland Strait which lies between the north shore of Nova Scotia and Prince Edward Island. They must have surmised that there was a water passage around from one harbor to the other. It did not take them long to discover the convenient and short water route through the Strait of Canso between continental Nova Scotia and Cape Breton Island, and thence to Pictou Harbor. Prince Henry, eager to see for himself the black brook and Pictou Harbor, would have traveled to see them as soon as he could.

This is as much as we can deduce from the descriptive letter of Antonio Zeno to Carlo Zeno. Without telling us the many additional things we would like to know, Antonio's narrative tantalizingly breaks off at the point where Antonio under orders sailed away from the new country with all the ships and most of the members of the expedition, and returned to the Orkneys. Would we perforce remain in ignorance of what happened to Prince Henry and the men who remained with him to face the winter in the "new world"?

Chapter Fourteen

THE BEGINNING OF
A LEGEND

ANTONIO'S EYEWITNESS account of Prince Henry's Expedition ceased with his return from Nova Scotia to the Orkney Islands. It seemed therefore that we could never hope to find out what Earl Henry experienced in the land on the western side of the Atlantic. If only Antonio Zeno had told where the Prince spent the winter, whether at Pictou Harbor or in some other region!

Two brief passages in Antonio's later letters looked appetizing. His sixteenth-century descendant wrote of one of the letter fragments: "What happened subsequently to the contents of this letter I know not beyond what I gather from conjecture from a piece of another letter, which is to the effect that Zichmni settled down in the harbor of his newly discovered island, and explored the whole of the country with great diligence." The harbor was presumably Pictou Harbor. Another provocative fragment hinting at Prince Henry's activity in the new country spoke of "the city [settlement] that he founded." These two statements seemed to offer bait without chance of hooking further facts.

The Province of Nova Scotia is three hundred and fifty miles long, and it covers an area of so many square miles that to search for Earl Henry's winter campsite in that great expanse of territory seemed futile. Believing that the place where the Prince of Orkney wintered could never be located, unless by accident, I gave up looking for it.

Two years later and by what seemed quite by chance, I came upon a clue. In order to be able to describe the natives Henry Sinclair encountered, I was rereading everything that had been published about the Micmac Indians of Nova Scotia. I mention the authors I read, since I shall frequently quote from them. They were S. T. Rand, A. L. Alger, A. G. Bailey, W. R. Bird, D. G. Brinton, J. B. Clark, H. Piers, C. G. Leland, and J. D. Prince. The studies of the Micmac Indians by these writers and translators had all been published before Dr. W. H. Hobbs identified Nova Scotia as the land that Henry Sinclair explored. Therefore, the geographical details these writers mentioned, having been recorded directly from the lips of the Indians, were entirely objective, and not colored or warped by any theory bearing on Prince Henry Sinclair.

In all that had been written about the Indians of Nova Scotia, there loomed large the Micmac telling of a "culture hero" who came among them as a visitor. This tradition or legend was in the form of songs or chants preserved in tribal memory and handed down by oral transmission. How the details of the legend were collected by missionaries and other observers is vividly described by A. L. Alger:

> This story was told to me by an old man whom I had always thought dull and almost in his dotage; but one day, after I had told him some Indian legends, his whole face changed, he threw back his head, closed his eyes, and without the slightest warning or preliminary began to relate, almost to chant this myth in a most extraordinary way, which so startled me that I could not at the time take any notes of it, and was obliged to have it repeated later.

Several passages in the Micmac chants are of a higher order of poetry than we have generally credited to American Indians, as we judge from the songs translated into English poetry by C. G. Leland of Harvard, and revised for strict literalness by J. D. Prince, Amerindian linguistic scholar at Columbia University. The first translator, the famous missionary to the Micmacs, Silas Tertius Rand, apparently had failed to recognize that the tales he heard chanted were poetry and deserved a metrical translation. Perhaps Rand was put off by the fact that, to use Professor Leland's words, the primitive rhythms of the chants were "quite irregular, following only a general cadence rather than observing any fixed number of beats in each line. . . . Amerindian metres are not all like that of *Hiawatha*."[2]

Bailey said this legendary hero was "involved, in a number of tales, with the encroachments of Europeans."[3] All the scholars agreed that the legend had been initiated by the visit of a European. While none of them had any opinion as to when that European crossed the Atlantic, they assumed it was after Columbus.

Quotations hereafter are from Rand, except as otherwise specified.

The Indians had added mythological elements to the historical tale of the hero, enlarging him to the dimensions of a Paul Bunyan, who could do anything and everything. Supernatural feats and conversations with birds and animals were interwoven with what seemed to shine through as the original realistic narrative. Clark said: "Of the 87 stories in Dr. Rand's collection [*Legends of the Micmacs*], many are pure and simple myths; some are mythical with an evident purpose to teach some practical lesson, and so may be considered fables or parables; while still others are merely records of history, somewhat mythical perhaps, and yet no doubt largely the record of facts."[4]

In the stories that Rand first "charmed from the unlettered past," the legendary hero was described by the Indians as a leader who "came from the east, far across the great sea."[5] It seemed that he might have been the leader of any European expedition, until I read that he was a "prince,"[6] and that his first meeting with the Micmacs was at Pictou.[7] Here was an arresting fact, that the legendary hero's first meeting with the Micmacs occurred at the same place where the Prince of Orkney's one hundred soldiers first apprized the natives of his existence, and where he soon afterwards in person first met them.

Was the geographical repetition a mere coincidence? Or had the Prince of Orkney actually been the visiting prince of the Indian tradition?

When a comparison of the facts concerning the prince of the Micmac legend and those concerning the Prince of Orkney showed seventeen identical details, it became obvious that so many parallels could not be coincidences. We might allow two or even three coincidences, but not seventeen. The numerical chances are so astronomical that the equating of the Prince of Orkney with the prince of the Micmac legend is incontrovertible." Prince Henry Sinclair and the hero of the Micmac tales surely are one and the same person.

Here, brought into one paragraph, are twelve of the seventeen parallels: The visiting hero was a "prince." He was a "king,"[8] who had often sailed the seas. His home was in a "town" on an "island,"[9] and he came with many men and soldiers. He came across the ocean via Newfoundland, and first met the Micmacs at Pictou.[10] His principal weapon was "a sword of sharpness."[11] (Since a sword was his principal weapon, it is to be assumed that he came before the advent of firearms.) He had "three daughters."[12] His character was unusual, and was precisely that which biographical study of Henry Sinclair reveals. He explored Nova Scotia extensively. He slept for six months in the wigwam of a giant named Winter.[13] He remained in the country only from the sailing season of the year of his arrival to the next sailing season.

These and other parallels will be discussed in due course.

The prince had "made long trips across the ocean with his feet on the backs of whales."[14] (From the context of the Indian tradition, we know that the "whales" were decked ships.) He was entertained by the playing of "flutes."[15] He possessed "money, iron, and a store."[16]

The Micmac chief became ambitious to become a son-in-law of the handsome powerful visitor, and inquiry revealed the information that the prince had three daughters. The number of the prince's daughters was of greater interest to the chief than the number of his sons.[17]

The prince and his men were not accustomed to building a small fire, Indian fashion, to warm themselves. The Micmacs observed critically: "They built up a roaring fire, and at midnight it is all out."[18] This was the white man's faulty way of making a fire.

The arrival of a man like the Prince of Orkney, leading a large expedition, and his dwelling among the Indians of Nova Scotia for nearly a year, could not fail to make a tremendous impression on the natives. Such an extraordinary event would inevitably become a legend. The essential facts would be fixed in tribal tales. We feel so certain of this that it is fair to ask this question: If Earl Henry Sinclair was not the prince of the Micmac legend, where else in Indian legends is the story of Earl Henry's visit?

The Indians would transmit by word of mouth to succeeding generations the geography of the visit of the stranger. They would especially retain in memory the place where the white chief first appeared. They would keep alive the story of his travels while among them, where he spent the winter of his sojourn, and by what route he departed. They would remember his activities. A significant feature of the legend would be his parting words to them, in their prophetic aspect.

All these details were clearly stated in the Micmac narrative of the visiting hero. The story of the prince grew through generations of re-telling. It appropriated many elements, most of them the product of Indian imagination. But the realistic and basic facts were not difficult to distinguish from the supernatural and mythological overlay.

The Micmac name for the prince was "Glooscap." Variant spellings are "Glūs-Kabé" and "Kulóskap."

In *Kulóskap the Master and Other Algonkin Poems*, translated by Leland and Prince, we are told in the Introduction: "Among the poems are selections taken from the Passamaquoddies, Penobscots, Abenakis, Micmacs, and Delawares—all of the Wabanaki branch of Algonkin." Although the Glooscap legend had spread for a thousand miles and was treasured by several branches of the tribe, appearing "in the legends of the entire Algonkin family, though often under another name," the geography of it was all in Nova Scotia.

Here is a factual passage from the above-named translation:

> Kulóskap was first,
> First and greatest,
> To come into our land—
> Into Nova Scotia . . .
> When the Master left Ukâkumkùk,
> Called by the English Newfoundland,
> He went to Piktook or Pictou,
> Which means "the rising of bubbles,"
> Because at that place the water
> Is ever strangely moving.
> There he found an Indian village,
> A town of a hundred wigwams.
> Kulóskap being a handsome
> And very stately warrior
> With the air of a great chief,
> Was greatly admired by all,
> Especially the women;
> So that everyone felt honored
> Whose wigwam he deigned to enter.

The Micmacs described Glooscap as "sober, grave, and good." Alger gives us the rules of personal behavior that Glooscap treasured: "You must never speak in praise of yourself, but pay attention to all that is said to you. Always control your temper. The Law is: Mind your own business."[19]

The Indians observed that Glooscap was a man of great experience in dealing with others:

> He read the thoughts of men
> As though they were strings of wampum—
> Seeing deep into every heart.

Rand says of Glooscap: "He seems to have been, on the whole, a noble-minded, generous sort of personage. You do not often meet with any mischievous exercise of his power. Strangers were always welcome to his wigwam, and the necessitous never failed to share in his hospitality, until some act of treachery on their part, or some distrust of his ability, called for castigation."[20]

All these qualities were in the character of Henry Sinclair. It is persuasive evidence that the prince who visited the Micmacs was not one of the vikings, since the vikings never got on well with the Indians, but fought them on the slightest provocation, or on none.

The supernatural elements in the Glooscap legend misled some readers into assuming that the visiting prince was a religious personality like Quetzalcoatl. Bird expressed the opinion that the Micmac conception of him as "their man-god, was very near the form of Christian belief."[21] It is true that in some of the poems he had become so magnified that he was called the Creator of the World. Analysis of the legend, however, as will be demonstrated, indicates that such a view of him was a mythological overlay. While the prince did speak of angels and the devil, and possessed a prayer book, the Micmacs said of Glooscap: "He looked and lived like other men. He ate, drank, smoked, slept, and danced along with them."[22] They initiated him into the use of a pipe, so that we may say that the Prince of Orkney was the first European to smoke tobacco.

> He was ever a boon companion
> And a right valiant smoker.
> In all the world was no man

Who loved a well-filled pipe
Of good and fragrant tobacco
So heartily as he did.

The visiting prince was a secular individual, not a divine personality.[23] Geoffrey Ashe, in *Land to the West*, names "Glooscap" as one of the American heroes,[24] and says: "In a few cases where modern anthropology has been able to anatomise the creation of a divine figure comparable to the American heroes, the figure has turned out to derive from real human beings and not from mythopoeic imagination."[25]

The Micmacs built into a tradition what the visitors had told them of the distant sighting of a smoking hill and of the eight-days' march to it by the soldiers. In the following passage the details are unmistakable: "Morning came. Glooscap puts on his belt and leads off. About the middle of the forenoon they reach the top of the high mountain. From thence they can discern another mountain away in the distance— its blue outlines just in sight above the horizon. The men conclude it will take them at least a week to reach it."[26] Only in the forenoon, when the sun is behind one, can an observer on Salmon Hill get a clear view of the hill in the distance to the westwards in line with Stellarton, the hill from which the smoke seemed to come. And the "eight days" and "at least a week"—if there were nothing else, the circumstantial parallel with Antonio Zeno's narrative would be sufficient to equate Glooscap with Prince Henry.

The character of Glooscap, we are told by Professor Prince, "in spite of his name, was essentially benevolent. His name means 'the liar.' This appellation, uncomplimentary as it sounds to our ears, was not meant in this sense by the Indians."[27] Glooscap "is called the deceiver, not because he deceives man, but because he is clever enough to lead his enemies astray, the highest possible virtue to the early American mind."[28] His enemies were night, darkness, and a serpent that represented storm, rains, and the water. These he "conquers not by brute force but by craft and ruses," and in this respect he is like the "wily Ulysses."[29] His victories are those of mind over matter. It should indeed be pointed out that his triumphs over darkness, storm, and the water are precisely what must have most deeply impressed the Micmacs when they learned of what was to their minds his magic power, his ability to create a decked ship and to navigate it by night as well as by day, through storms and "the current's swirling waves"[30] that would have swamped their canoes. On one occasion, the Micmacs noted, he "withdrew far up the rushing stream where no canoe may pass,"[31] except for a large decked canoe like his.

Without trepidation, but with willingness to be shown error, I offer a linguistic suggestion. The Micmac tongue, Rand tells us, could not negotiate a combination of "r" with other consonants without greatly distorting the sound. Rand says there is no sound of "r" in the Micmac language, and that the sound of "l" substitutes for it. The Micmacs heard the visitors refer to their prince as the "Jarl" (Earl), pronounced with an initial guttural. To a Micmac tongue the word as sounded presented insuperable difficulties. The guttural became "G" or "K" and the "r" became "l" and strengthened the other "l," leaving as a result "Gl" or "Kl." The Micmacs did not know that proper usage in Europe forbade applying a title like "Prince" or "Jarl" to its holder's family name. They could well have ignorantly put "Jarl" and "Sinclair" together, and come up with a combination of "Gl" with the sounds of the initial consonants of the two syllables of "Sinclair," an "s" and a hard "c" (sound of "k"). This combination was "Gloosc" ("Kulosk"). The change from "Jarl Sinclair" to "Glooscap" is phonetically reasonable. It is as credible as the change effected by the Micmacs in attempting to pronounce "Jesus Christ," which on their lips became "Sasoo Goole."[32]

Whether the linguistic equation I have suggested is correct or not, there can be no doubt that Earl Henry Sinclair, the Prince of Orkney, was Glooscap.

The Micmac Indians did not cultivate corn, but lived by hunting and fishing. Glooscap helped them in both. In words that may refer to the Orkney fisherman whose description of the "new world as it were" stirred Prince Henry to undertake his transatlantic expedition, we are told:

> Before he came they knew not
> How to make nets.[33]

The costume of the Micmacs was a skin breechcloth attached to a leather girdle, with a cloak of otter, beaver, moose, stag, bear, or lynx, tied with a leather thong, and one arm usually thrust out. They had moccasins of moose hide, and long leggings tied to the belt. Most of the Micmacs had black hair, but some of them auburn. They wore no headdress. They greased their bodies to defend themselves against flies.

Their weapons were strong bows and Stone Age arrows, and clubs of wood. They played a game called *cumugesjokouk* ("to play with little sticks"), which was "almost the counterpart of jackstraws, maybe of European origin."[34] Perhaps Sinclair's men taught it to them. They had another game called "altestakun" or "woltestakun." This was "a dice game, undoubtedly of pre-Columbian origin. . . . It was played on a circular wooden dish about one foot in diameter. . . . Mr. Hagar states that this game was taught by Glooscap."[35]

Antonio Zeno wrote that "Zichmni explored the whole of the country with great diligence." This statement is paralleled by the Micmac account of the extensive exploring of Nova Scotia accomplished by Glooscap. After having come to meet the Indians first at Pictou, Glooscap, led by Micmac guides, went northwestward by small boat along the shore, and "came to Baie Verte and crossed the portage to Cumberland Bay."[36] The airline distance across the neck of land that makes Nova Scotia part of the continent of North America is sixteen miles, but the carry for small boats is only three miles.

From Cumberland Bay, Glooscap went south to Parrsboro, which the Indians thereafter called "Glooscapweek," meaning "Home of Glooscap." In this traveling he followed the canoe route from River Hebert, a route that runs parallel to the "Boar's Back," a north-south ridge in Cumberland County.[37] In this comparatively straight passage of about twenty-two miles, the only portage is less than a quarter of a mile.

Glooscap then crossed Minas Basin and visited Cape Blomidon, which thereafter was also called "Home of Glooscap."[38] Presumably, he wished to ascertain the distance from Minas Basin to the ocean, and so from there he crossed the peninsula of Nova Scotia to the site of the town of Liverpool on the south shore, where the Micmacs said he met an adventure with the "Sorceress of the Atlantic."[39] To accomplish this crossing of the peninsula he probably followed the shore from the south side of Minas Basin westward to Digby, and to the site of Annapolis and thence up the Lequille stream. A short but rugged portage then put the canoes into Liverpool Head Lake, whence the Mersey River carried them through a series of lakes to the ocean at the site of Liverpool. South of Liverpool is a hill three hundred and seventy feet high, which gives a horizon visibility of twenty-nine miles. From its summit, Prince Henry could have acquired an accurate notion of the trend of the southern coast, knowledge that would be useful to him in setting his course when he sailed home to Orkney.

He returned to the north shore of Minas Basin, and visited places between Partridge Island (near Parrsboro) and the shores of Cumber-

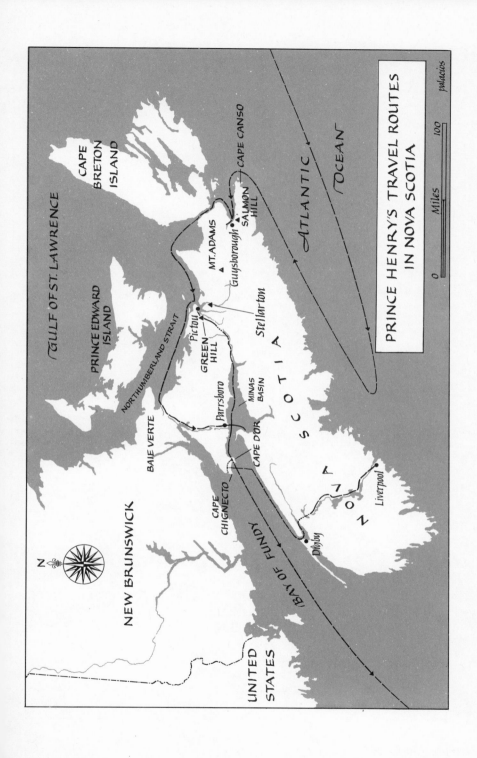

PRINCE HENRY'S TRAVEL ROUTES
IN NOVA SCOTIA

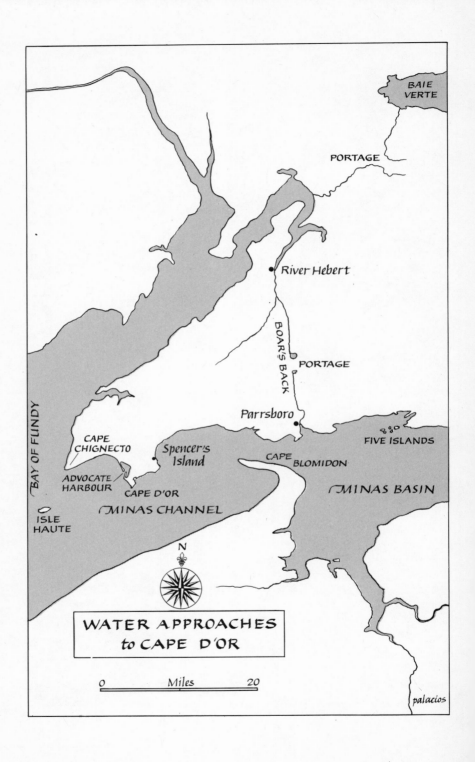

BAIE VERTE

PORTAGE

River Hebert

BOAR'S BACK

PORTAGE

Parrsboro

CAPE CHIGNECTO

Spencer's Island

CAPE BLOMIDON

FIVE ISLANDS

BAY OF FUNDY

ADVOCATE HARBOUR

CAPE D'OR

MINAS CHANNEL

MINAS BASIN

ISLE HAUTE

N

WATER APPROACHES to CAPE D'OR

0   Miles   20

palacios

land Bay. He also traveled along the north shore of Minas Basin, which the Micmacs picturesquely called his "beaverpond."[40] He attended the gathering of Micmacs from all over Nova Scotia held in October on Green Hill, a few miles west of Pictou Harbor, when "'twas the time for holding the great and yearly feast with dancing and merry games."[41]

After the above-mentioned traveling, the Micmacs said of Glooscap: "His next halt was at Spencer's Island."[42] This was at the site of the present village of that name. "There Glooscap engaged in a hunting expedition on a somewhat large scale. A large drove of animals was surrounded and driven to the shore, slaughtered, and their flesh sliced up and dried. All the bones were afterwards chopped up fine, placed in a large kettle, and boiled so as to extract the marrow, which was carefully stored away for future use."[43] Glooscap was obviously preparing to winter in the vicinity.

Where did he camp for the winter? If it had been at Spencer's Island, the Indians would have said so. Instead, they specifically said it was farther to the west: "He remained all winter near Cape D'Or, and that place still bears the name of his wigwam." They said the name of the place where he wintered was "Owokun," which means "Crossing Over Place," or "Portage." They also said of his winter campsite: "He resided near salt water, on a high bank, against which the deep sea dashed."[44]

Where "near Cape D'Or" was a portage, or any need of a portage? There was a "high bank" there, yes. Any bank only fifty feet in height such as one finds at or near Spencer's Island, would not have occasioned the comment "high," for there are banks higher than that at many places for miles along the shore of Minas Basin. But near Cape D'Or, from near Horseshoe Cove around to the point of the cape, the bank is from one hundred to one hundred and fifty feet high, and on the west side of the promontory it is two hundred to three hundred and fifty feet high.

One detail, however, in the Micmac statement as to the location of Glooscap's winter campsite seemed incompatible with the actual geography, and I confess that, at the time, I wished I could ignore it, or shunt it off to some other connection. For what at first seemed a valid reason, I could not accredit the Micmac description of the bank upon which Glooscap set up his winter wigwam as a bank "against which the deep sea dashed." This detail, "the deep sea dashed," seemed quite inapplicable to any coastline near Cape D'Ôr. That cape is on the shore of an inland body of water, many miles from the ocean. I could not see how in proximity to that cape "the deep sea" could be accurately said to have "dashed," until the memorable day when I approached the Cape D'Or lighthouse and witnessed a phenomenon that made all clear. From the road high above the lighthouse I beheld a thrilling and stupendous sight.

It was the greatest tidal rip in the world. The tides of the Bay of Fundy are twenty-eight feet. In certain places in the Minas Basin where incoming tides are funneled into estuaries, the tidal rise is fifty feet. At every tide into and out of the Minas Basin, more than two cubic miles of water pass through Minas Channel, around Cape D'Or. Meeting the obstruction of the western side of the Cape D'Or promontory, which lies

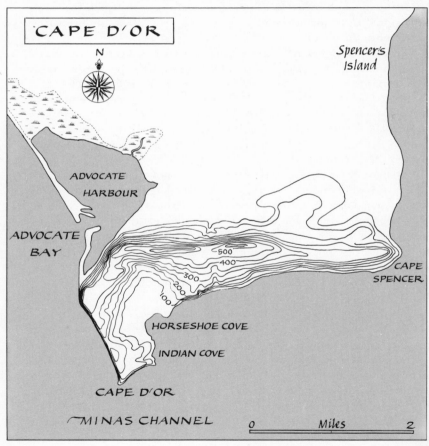

obliquely athwart its path, the incoming tide is forced sideways toward the point. It there churns up waves six to eight feet in height. A semicircle of swiftly racing white foaming water is flung out from the point for two miles. When asked how fast the tidal rip tears around the point, the lighthouse keeper said: "Twelve to fourteen knots." A speed of fourteen to sixteen miles an hour! Perfectly descriptive of it was the Micmac phrase, "the deep sea dashed," especially the apt word "dashed."

What I had been tempted to discard as inapplicable to the Cape D'Or promontory is strikingly corroborative of the geographical identification of the locale of Glooscap's winter campsite. Now in the Leland and Prince translation of the Glooscap legend, I found phrases descriptive of the tidal rip at Cape D'Or: "in the current's swirling waves" and "the rushing stream where no canoe may pass, save only stone ones."[45] As we shall see, the Micmacs applied the term "stone canoe" to a ship with a deck on which, as on a rock, a man could walk.

Of course there was a portage at Cape D'Or! There had to be.

Cape D'Or Looking North

Canoes could not make headway against the tides, or stay afloat in the rip. The Indians would never attempt to round that cape. When desirous of passing it, they would put into a cove on the east side of the promontory, where the shore is sheltered from the tidal currents, and there cache their canoes. They would carry their belongings up a trail to a height of three hundred and fifty feet, and down on the west side to the near end of Advocate Harbour. With other canoes cached at the harbor, they would paddle for two miles inside the harbor to its western end, and there carry their canoes over a narrow bar less than two hundred feet wide (it is narrowest at the west end), and so to the shore of Advocate Bay. Thence they would hug the coast to the west unhampered by any current, and when far enough to the west to be safe from being caught in the Cape D'Or tidal rip, would cross the open water to the south shore and follow the coast to Digby.

Somewhere along the portage on the Cape D'Or promontory was Prince Henry Sinclair's fourteenth-century campsite.

After landing on the promontory, Prince Henry and his men would have explored the whole of it in a few hours, up to the five-hundred-foot ridge that walls it off along the north side, a mile and a quarter from the point of the cape. They would have been apprized of the most important geographical fact of the region, the great harbor to the west below the ridge, the best harbor for fifty miles. The Zeno Narrative shows Prince Henry very harbor-conscious, and he certainly knew of the existence of Advocate Harbour since he was acquainted with the coastline west of Cape D'Or; for the Micmacs said: "In the spring, Glooscap went hunting to the west as far as to Cape Chignecto."[46]

We can be reasonably certain that Prince Henry decided to build his ship on the shore of Advocate Harbour. After its launching, it was undoubtedly anchored in the harbor, where his men could step the masts. The high bank on the western side of the promontory, only twelve to fifteen minutes from Horseshoe Cove by trail, and only a half-mile to one mile from the near end of Advocate Harbour, was an ideal site for his residence, whence he could quickly descend to inspect his men's activities. Fresh water at his campsite was no problem, since it is available everywhere within a very short distance, even on the high ground, and was still more so when there was a primeval forest coverage. The earl, as a hunter, would have considered the whole promontory as a hunting field. The autumn roundup of animals at Spencer's Island left undisturbed the animals on the Cape D'Or promontory for hunting during the winter. Deer come to the promontory to winter in the milder areas near salt water. Snows usually cover the ground in that part of Nova Scotia from November to about the middle, sometimes the first, of March.

From under the tall trees of the unbroken forest, Prince Henry would have enjoyed magnificent views, eastward down into Horseshoe Cove and off to Cape Spencer and Cape Blomidon; southward across nine miles of water to the shore of Minas Channel and the high ridge that shelters Grand Pré and the Annapolis Valley; westward to Isle Haute in the Bay of Fundy, and the bold cliffs toward Cape Chignecto, reminiscent of cliffs in the Orkneys.

The Indians said Glooscap was "guarded by sentinels."[47] With soldiers stationed in or near Horseshoe Cove and at Advocate Harbour, the whole promontory was a mighty fortress, with unscalable cliffs on the south and west, and the five-hundred-foot ridge curtaining it off in a larger horseshoe around at the north and northeast. It was a lordly demesne, fit for a king, a residential area as grand as that possessed by any monarch in Europe.

As an amateur archaeologist, I sought to identify the Sinclair-Glooscap winter house site. From the Micmac description, it seemed most likely at the outset that the house must have been somewhere on the high bank along the western side of the promontory,[48] and so I looked there for house sites and for a portage trail. There on the heights I found a trail that for long distances has no vegetation growing in it. In its width of eight to ten inches, the earth has been too hard-trodden to catch and hold seeds. There is further evidence that the trail is a very old one; for in a comparatively level place where it lies straight and visible for several hundred feet, it touches the trunk of a large tree, the huge roots of which have grown across and over it. Anyone sticking to the trail would bump his shoulder against the trunk of the tree, since the trail does not swing out around the tree as a properly behaving trail should. The tree obviously started its growth long after the trail had been established. The tree is a black spruce twenty-two inches in diameter, and from the number of rings revealed by a corer is close to one hundred years old. The trail follows the edge of the cliff along the west side of the promontory from two hundred to three hundred and fifty feet above the water, except that in two places a fallout of the cliff caused by erosion has removed several hundred feet of the trail. This is evidence of the trail's great age—of its having existed before those fallouts occurred.

This ancient trail begins in a small cove only two hundred feet wide, a quarter of a mile south of Horseshoe Cove. My first assumption

had been that the principal Indian portage trail began at Horseshoe
Cove and climbed directly toward Advocate Harbour. The Micmacs
may have used such a trail in bad weather, especially when it was foggy.
But when it was fair, they would have much preferred the slightly longer

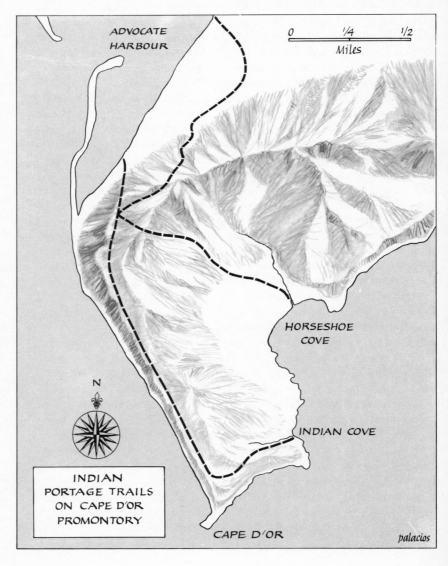

trail in more easy gradient. Corroborative of this is the answer given to the question whether the tiny cove where the cliff-edge trail started had a name. "Oh! Yes," the old-timers said, "We don't know why, but that has always been called 'Injun Cove.'" The Indians would have been attracted to the cliff-edge trail because the views it afforded were exhilarating and gave them a sense of supremacy over their environment, something primitive man craved.

Extensive search of the whole promontory revealed nine or ten house sites. These were visibly ridged rectangles, locally miscalled cellar holes. There was a definite pattern in the location of several. They were less than two hundred feet from the cliff edge along the western side of the promontory, too close to the cliff, it appeared, for shelter from the winter winds from the west and northwest. The persistence or unanimity with which early settlers had built their houses near the cliff edge seemed somehow lacking in good sense. Failing to understand, I turned from them and investigated the four-acre plateau one hundred feet above and immediately to the south of Indian Cove at the southeast point of the promontory, where the ebbing tide dashed.

That plateau is sheltered by higher ground on every side except to the east. Being enamored of the idea that Prince Henry's winter house site must have been there and that he had therefore built his ship in the gully at Indian Cove, I went there in 1957 with a professional archaeologist, Edward V. McMichael, and made a preliminary investigation of the plateau and gully. An archaeological expedition in 1959 completed the search of gully and plateau. The expedition included three men from the University of Maine: Dr. Harold W. Borns, a professor of geology, and Lamont W. Curtis and Forrest W. Meader. Funds were provided by the Kermit Fischer Foundation through the generosity of Kermit Fischer of Hatboro, Pennsylvania. Negative results in gully and plateau forced the positive conclusion that the Sinclair-Glooscap house site must have been on the bank on the western side of the promontory.

I returned to the cliff-edge house sites. There, Ronald Barkhouse and I made a significant meteorological discovery. Throughout our digging one morning at a site one hundred and seventy-five feet from the cliff edge, we had suffered stifling heat with no breath of moving air. When we stopped for lunch and went to sit down one hundred feet farther away from the edge, we were amazed to encounter a good breeze from the west.

We thus were brought to realize that the wind from off the Bay of Fundy when it hits the cliff, since it cannot pass under nor to the right or left, rushes upward, and the updraft passes over the first two hundred feet of upland before it descends to ground level up on the promontory. The house sites near the western cliff edge were in a windless zone.

We found that the loam inside each ridged rectangle had been formed since the house was abandoned, and was invariably of less depth than the loam in test holes outside the rectangle. The houses at all of these sites, except for one that had been a cabin with floor at ground level, were of half-sod construction with the floors three or three and a half feet below the surrounding surface, and with the walls built up of loam and gravel (hardpan) dug from the interior excavation. Each house was built with a shovel, and only the roof had timbers or tree trunks, now collapsed and turned to loam. A trench through the highest (west-side) ridge of each rectangle revealed a ton or more of flat field-stones, showing where the chimney had stood. A typical finding was several feet of loam in the ridge from the decayed wall, under which were pockets of hardpan mixed with flowed clay that had formerly mortared the chimney stones; then below the hardpan pockets more loam that had originally been laid up in the wall, and finally basic hardpan at the level of which, or two or three inches above it, we found the charcoal bed of the fireplace. Artifacts were seventeenth-century (French Acadian) or eighteenth-century (English) ceramic pieces, some rusted iron, bones, and so forth.

These house sites were too far from the lighthouse point to answer the Micmac description of Glooscap's winter residence; for only along the first three hundred yards of cliff edge nearest the point does one have immediately below one the dashing visible race of water toward the point.

In 1951 a road for a subsequently abandoned copper mining operation was bulldozed parallel to and about two hundred feet from the straight cliff edge. Local men, Ronald Barkhouse of East Advocate, and Morton Morris, Assistant Lighthouse Keeper, testify to there having been a rectangular hollow and what seemed to them to have been a house site ("cellar hole") before the bulldozed road altered three-quarters of it. The location of this is only one hundred yards from the south end of the road and only two hundred yards north of the lighthouse point. It is where the cliff edge is about two hundred feet high, and whence one looks down on the "rushing stream" of dashing tidal rip. It is only one hundred and twenty-five yards from the spring from which the lighthouse gets its water. With a background of experience with other sites when we investigated this site in August 1960, it was obvious to us from the flow of soil at the remaining northwest corner of it, or what we believed to be a remaining corner of it, that this was very much older than any of the other house sites, and if it was older than the Acadian French, what have we? I believe it may have been the Sinclair-Glooscap winter house site. There is an absence of large fieldstones, and it may be that some early Acadian settler removed the fieldstones for his own chimney, or it may be that the Sinclair chimney was built in primitive Orkney fashion with "sticks and clay."

Whether or not we have found the precise location of the Sinclair-Glooscap winter house site, the Province of Nova Scotia, in view of the specific geographical details given by the Micmacs, should name the extraordinarily scenic road from Parrsboro to Advocate Harbour the "Sinclair Trail." It would be a worthy mate to the "Cabot Trail." Someday there should be a road paved and made passable for passenger autos out to the point of Cape D'Or promontory. The phenomenon of the greatest tidal rip in the world would justify it as a tourist attraction.

The Micmac story supports the theory that Sinclair appropriated the entire promontory. In the rigorous season, the Micmacs could not use their canoes and did not travel, but remained in their wigwams, which they lined inside and covered outside with spruce boughs against the cold. They did not visit the Sinclair-Glooscap camp during the winter months and so they did not witness the shipbuilding. When, coming from the east, they returned to the promontory in the spring, one of the first things they were told was that they would be shown the prince's "canoe." In other words, the ship that had been built was at the moment not visible to them, as it would have been were it in Horseshoe Cove or Indian Cove. This tells us that it was in Advocate Harbour on the other side of the promontory. When the Indians ascended the portage trail past Glooscap's dwelling to where they could look down into Advocate Harbour, they were amazed at the sight of the completed ship, unlike anything they had ever seen, and they interpreted what they saw in terms of what was familiar to them.

Not understanding what it is, the Indians "look for his canoe, but near the shore there is a small rocky island with trees growing on it. This, Glooscap tells them, is his canoe."[49] This is what his ship looked like to them from three hundred and fifty feet above it.

The ship was motionless like an island, and out in the harbor where no island had ever been. It was either moored off shore, or stranded there at low tide. The prince courteously invited the Indians to visit his ship.

"They go on board, set sail, and find the floating island very manageable as a canoe. It goes like magic."[50]

F

This was the impression made on the imagination of the Micmacs, in whose experience the only means of transportation over water was a craft of birchbark, or skin covering, fragile and open. Glooscap's "canoe" had a hard top on which men could walk. They aptly described it as a floating island. The "trees" on it were obviously masts. With masts, plural, probably two masts, the ship would have been about forty to fifty feet in length.

There is a passage in the Micmac legend of Glooscap which says that "when about to go away and leave the Indians, he called up a whale to carry him off on its back. The sound of the words and the chanting tone of voice he used as his men set the sails are still handed down. The words were these, repeated thrice: "Nemajeechk numeedich."[51]

Was there some sea chantey of the Orkney sailors, one that Prince Henry would have used when raising sail or anchor, the refrain of which might have suggested to Indian ears the words they gave to it in their own language? I handed the question to my Scandinavian friends. William Williamson, curator of the Marine Museum of the City of New York, found equivalent Norse words dug from memory of chanteys he heard sailors sing in the Norwegian seaport where he spent his boyhood. These words of Old Icelandic mean: "Now must I, now must you." I am setting the Micmac words immediately below them so that the close parallel may be the more readily observed:

"Nu mo jag, nu mo deg"
"Nemajeechk numeedich"

With the transposable guttural "g" becoming "chk" and "ch," the consonants of the expressions from both languages are the same.

Rand says the Micmac words mean: "Let the small fish look at me."[52] A literary friend has questioned whether the equating would not be more certain were the Micmac words gibberish. On the other hand, is it likely that aborigines would use, or retain for centuries, phonetic syllables which to them had no meaning? Primitive men closely imitated bird and animal cries, but in doing so did they not tend to modify those sounds into recognizable words, like our "Whip poor Will" or "Weep poor Will"?

In the chantey refrain offered by Mr. Williamson, and in the Micmac version of what they heard from Glooscap's lips, we seem to have a direct phonetic equation, a pre-Columbian linguistic bridge between Europeans and North American Indians.

Clark tells us that the Micmacs said that Glooscap sailed away out through the Bay of Fundy, "on Fundy's ebbing tide."[53] With an ebbing tide certainly, but he must have sailed also with a following wind. While the ebbing tide from Advocate Harbour into the Bay of Fundy would carry a ship for twenty miles without benefit of wind, the incoming tide, if there were no wind, would bring the ship back again.

The Bay of Fundy seen to the west from Cape D'Or looks like open ocean, on either side of Isle Haute. The tides indicated to Prince Henry and his men that its waters led to, if they were not part of, the ocean. There could be no doubt as to the way to the open ocean from Advocate Harbour.

The Micmacs remembered as one of the final statements the visiting prince made to them: "From now on, if there should ever be a war between you and any other people, I shall be back to help you."[54]

After the winter had passed, when it became time for Glooscap to depart, he said to the group of Micmacs who were present: "I shall not return to rule over you."[55] This was the sort of statement which no one less than a nobleman of princely rank would have made. The hero of the Micmac legend was obviously accustomed to being in the position of ruler.

Glooscap is said to have added: "Sometime men will come to teach you religion."[56] This prophecy seems to be conclusive evidence that Glooscap himself was not a teacher of religion. It is also obvious that he came from a civilization in which a missionary impulse existed. In his recognition that the natives of Nova Scotia did not yet have what he recognized as "religion," the original person about whom the Glooscap legend grew is thus clearly dated as before the coming of the first Jesuits.

Missionaries in the nineteenth century in Nova Scotia believed that the Micmacs had learned something of Christianity previous to the arrival of the Jesuits. They assumed that this knowledge had been brought to the Micmacs by the Norsemen, or by the Basques who for centuries before Columbus had presumably come to the fishing banks of Newfoundland. In Yarmouth County, Nova Scotia, in an inlet north of Cape Fourchu, Samuel de Champlain, in the early seventeenth century, discovered a moss-covered decayed cross that points to a knowledge of Christianity long before his time.

It is improbable that Earl Henry Sinclair had been motivated even in part by a missionary impulse. His prophecy in 1399 that missionaries would come to teach the Micmacs religion implies that so far as he had observed they had not yet received any instruction in the religion that he valued. It is therefore deducible that the Micmacs first learned of Christianity, not from the early Norsemen, but from European contacts in the early fifteenth century.

Prince Henry Sinclair represented the finest flower of Norman culture. That some of the Indians of North America were exposed to it is of great historical interest. The deep impression it made on them is recorded in the Glooscap epic.

The equating of Glooscap with Sinclair reveals what may be a unique instance of a full-blown legend in which it is possible to pry apart the historic facts that gave rise to it, from concretions added to it by the myth-making imagination of primitive tribesmen. It illustrates how a legend started and to what extravagances it ran.

At his departure from Nova Scotia, according to Leland's metrical translation of the Micmac chant that recounted the event, Glooscap

> *Invited all to a parting banquet*
> *By the great Lake Minas shore*
> *On the silver water's edge.*
> *And when the feast was over,*
> *Entered his great canoe*
> *And sailed away over the water,*
> *The shining waves of Minas;*
> *And they looked in silence at him*
> *Until they could see him no more,*
> *Yet, after they ceased to behold him*
> *They still heard his voice in song,*
> *The wonderful voice of the Master,*
> *But the sounds grew fainter and fainter,*
> *And softer in the distance,*
> *Till at last they died away.*[57]

Chapter Fifteen

A BROKEN SWORD

PRINCE HENRY sailed out to the southwest through the Bay of Fundy. To do that he had to have a following wind, a northeaster. A northeaster is a blow that usually lasts from forty-eight to seventy-two hours. Such a wind carried his ship to the New England coast.

In New England he waited for a prevailing westerly before beginning his homeward crossing of the ocean. Knowing from his visit to the site of Liverpool in Nova Scotia approximately how far south from Minas Basin the land of Nova Scotia extended, he would have wanted to follow the New England shore far enough south so that he would clear Nova Scotia when he set his course eastward. He knew there was open ocean south of Nova Scotia, for he most certainly had not forgotten that he had sailed in that part of the ocean for "six days to the westward" and "four days" back toward the northeast previous to his sighting the land in which he had wintered.

While waiting in southern New England for a fair wind from the west, he naturally improved the time by exploring the new region in which he now found himself. To explore it quickly, he sought the summit of a hill that would give him a wide view over the terrain. The highest lookout hill in eastern Massachusetts is the one originally called "Tad-muck Hill," and now "Prospect Hill," at Westford. Prospect Hill is four hundred and sixty-five feet in altitude, and affords a view of thirty to sixty miles in all directions. Indians for centuries used it for smudge-fire signaling. Sea captains coming into Boston Harbor used to sight an elm tree on Prospect Hill, twenty-five miles from Boston and ten miles northwest of Concord. Several Indian trails led to it, one of them directly from Boston Harbor, a trail that later became a road, the historic road through Lexington to Concord. Prince Henry, however, probably reached Prospect Hill by boat up the Merrimac River to a little above Lowell, and thence up Stony Brook to the ford where a trail from Tyngsboro to Prospect Hill crossed the brook.

The Algonkin Indians preserved in their legend an association of Glooscap with hills in eastern Massachusetts in the Boston area. Charles G. Leland in his Preface to *Kul skap the Master* testifies: "A Penobscot woman once told me that it was Klûs-kâbe [her pronunciation of Kulóskap] who divided the great mountain of which Boston originally consisted into three hills."[1]

One of the knights attendant on Prince Henry died on this hill-climbing trip. Whether his death was caused by an Indian arrow, a heart attack or other illness, or a bite of a rattlesnake, we can only guess. The name "Snake Meadow" on a hill a little to the northwest is suggestive. Prince Henry had his most loyal friends with him over the winter, and the death of one of his knights rated a permanent memorial. He had his armorer make a representation of the deceased knight on a ledge, a gently sloping rock surface on which one walks.

It had long been known at Westford that there were man-made markings on a ledge of fine-grained gneiss on the old Tyngsboro trail, now the Tyngsboro road. A local historian tells us: "A broad ledge which crops out near the house of William Kittredge has upon its surface grooves made by glaciers. [Professor Gunning, who once visited the spot, said it was a remarkably well defined instance of glacial action.] Rude outlines of the human face have been traced upon it, and the figure is said to be the work of Indians."[2]

The parallel glacial striations on the ledge are indeed most remark-able. They are more than one to an inch (fifteen of them in one foot), as though the surface of the gneiss had been subjected to a giant comb. The

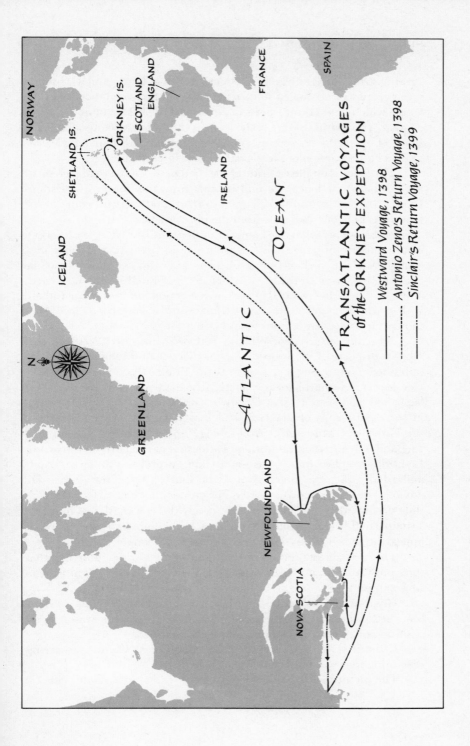

TRANSATLANTIC VOYAGES
of the ORKNEY EXPEDITION

Westward Voyage, 1398
Antonio Zeno's Return Voyage, 1398
Sinclair's Return Voyage, 1399

NORWAY

SHETLAND IS.

ORKNEY IS.

SCOTLAND
ENGLAND

FRANCE

SPAIN

IRELAND

ATLANTIC OCEAN

ICELAND

GREENLAND

N

NEWFOUNDLAND

NOVA SCOTIA

striations run from 12° west of north to 12° east of south, and were made when glacial ice advanced southward and ground across the face of the ledge, which is tilted up from the horizontal by a slant of about seven degrees. The southern edge of the ledge is thus slightly higher. Since the slope of the ledge raised the mile-thick southward-moving ice, the groove-cutting action of the glacial ice was intensified.

The ledge is on the east side of the road between the road pavement and an old stone fence. To find it, start from the library at Westford Center, drive north on the Tyngsboro road, and you will come to the ledge precisely one-half mile from the library.

One sees only what one knows or understands, or what one has been conditioned to observe. Some Westford residents had seen what they thought was the work of Indians, because they did not know of anyone else who had been in the area before the first English settlers arrived. They assumed that what they saw was a representation of an Indian, with or without a pipe. Others saw a long sword. Some saw a "face," but thought it was separate from the other markings.

Sometime after 1940, William B. Goodwin visited Westford and made a drawing of the sword, which is more than fifty inches long. He published this drawing in a book in 1946.[3] Frank Glynn, president of the Connecticut Archaeological Society, who had not seen the Westford ledge and who assumed that Goodwin's drawing was of a viking sword, in 1950 sent a copy of Goodwin's book to T. C. Lethbridge, curator of the University Museum of Archaeology and Ethnology, Cambridge, England. Glynn called Lethbridge's attention particularly to the sword. Lethbridge replied that it was not a viking sword, but a "large, hand-and-a-half wheel pommel sword" of fourteenth-century type. He advised Glynn to go to Westford and examine the rock surface that was thus decorated. From his acquaintance with rock markings in Great Britain, Lethbridge wrote Glynn that he should find the sword as appearing to be held in the hands of a medieval knight in armor.

This was an astounding assumption for Lethbridge to make, that such pre-Columbian evidence associated with feudalism might exist in Massachusetts!

Glynn went to Westford in May of 1954, got local people to show him the location of the ledge, and behold! There upon it was a representation of an armored knight holding the sword!

Lethbridge had not hypnotically conditioned Glynn into seeing something that was not actually on the ledge.

The picture on the ledge is of the type called a "military effigy."

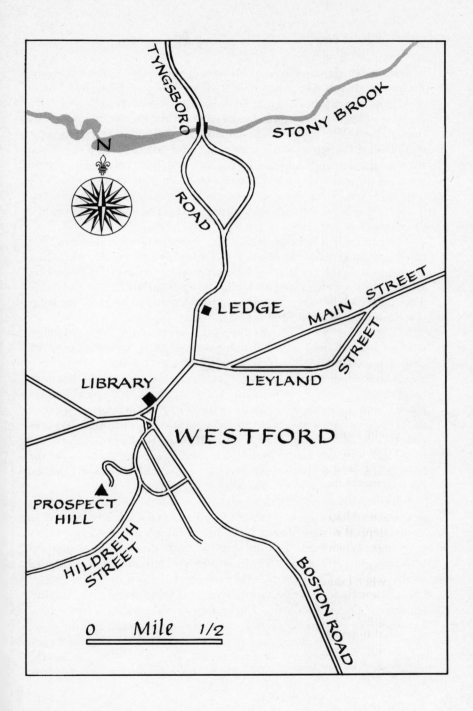

The markings for the most part consist of punch holes made by some sharp tool, driven with a hammer or stone. The punch-hole method of making a pattern is not unique; for Arhus runestone 6, listed as No. 68 in *Danmarks Runeinskrifter* by Lis Jacobsen and Erik Moltke, was made by that method. The figure of the knight at Westford incorporates some marks made by nature along with those made by man. Where colored streaks and patches and parallel glacial scratches in the gneiss would serve his purpose, the patternmaker, obviously with limited time at his disposal, saved labor by accepting them. Enough of the pattern was made by human workings to establish that it is not a mistake for us also to accept those natural ones.

Glynn made a drawing of the effigy and sent it to Lethbridge. Then came a most sensational revelation. Lethbridge wrote that the arms, armor, and heraldic emblems were those of a late fourteenth-century knight, North Scottish, and "a kin to the first Sinclair Earl of Orkney"! Thus before I had heard a word of it, the pattern on the Westford ledge was brought into my field of interest.

The next step was Frank Glynn's telling me of the Westford ledge, which I immediately visited. I made a close study, prone on the rock with a magnifying glass, which revealed the punch holes.

The following are undeniably man-made workings: the pommel, handle, and guard of the sword; below the guard the break across the blade that is indicative of the death of the sword's owner; the crest above the pommel; a few holes at the sword's point; the punch-hole jess lines attached to the legs of the falcon; the bell-shaped hollows; the corner of the shield touching the pommel; the crescent on the shield; and the holes that form a decorative pattern on the pommel. Some will question the face or head with raised basinet.

Remarks that have been made by various scientists should help us to visualize the problem of seeing. A college classmate, Dr. Donnell B. Young, who had studied rock markings in the United States for many years, stepped with me upon the ledge, to study the sword and adjacent workings. When I said: "There is also the knight's face," Donnell swiftly replied: "I saw the face the moment I stepped upon the ledge." Later, when I said to him: "Frank Glynn sees a falcon above the knight's left hand," Donnell replied: "I have seen the falcon for the last hour." On another occasion, when a curator and an assistant curator of an armorial museum had for some time been studying the pattern on the ledge, one of them was overheard asking the other: "Do you see the lion?" and the other responded: "Sure, I see the lion." Though these armorial specialists were conditioned by their knowledge that the most frequently appearing decoration on a sword pommel is a rampant lion, their seeing a rampant lion with natural lighter coloration in the rock suggesting the body of the animal and unquestionable punch holes forming the animal's legs and upcurving tail has made it practically impossible for other observers to avoid seeing or imagining that they see the lion when it is pointed out to them.

My technique for bringing out the pattern, since a stick of chalk is too thick to enter the holes, has been to touch the bottom of each hole with a fine artist's brush and white watercolor paint that the first rain would wash away. With the holes thus marked, I indicated the position of each hole on tracing paper, from which I transferred the pattern to graph paper. My drawing shows all the punch holes the magnifying glass revealed, each in its precise location in respect to the others.

Many hours of study on five separate visits have convinced me that not only the crescent, but the galley and buckle are on the shield. I feel less certain of the five-pointed mullet. Of all the heraldic emblems the mullet, as Frank Glynn wrote me, is "the most difficult to be sure of."

As for the various sizes of the punch holes, there are some places where the tips of four fingers close together will fit into four adjacent holes. Other holes are weathered down so that very small depressions remain, but where these are in straight or curved lines, there is no likelihood that the lines were not man-made. Gradations in size and depth and visibility of the holes indicate that the patternmaker's spike or punch or whatever tool he used got blunted, as sharp steel quickly does when cutting into rock as hard as that ledge, and he could not make all the holes as large and deep as the first ones he had made. This is one of the decisive evidences of genuineness. A hoaxer would have provided himself with means for keeping the tool he used sharp and pointed, but Sinclair's man had a limited time and no effective tool sharpener at hand on the trail twenty-five miles from the ship. Presumably, the sword and the eyes and mouth of the face were first delineated, and the edges of the shield near the pommel. These were most important, since their positioning determined the positions of everything else in the pattern. The heraldic emblems on the shield, and the falcon and whatever the knight is holding in his right hand, were put in with the blunted tool.

Here is a conservative statement of some of the things in the pattern: The pommel, hilt, guard, and break in the blade of the sword are outlined with large punch holes. Two parallel glacial striae form the edges of the blade. The hilt is eight inches long, and the length of the guard is

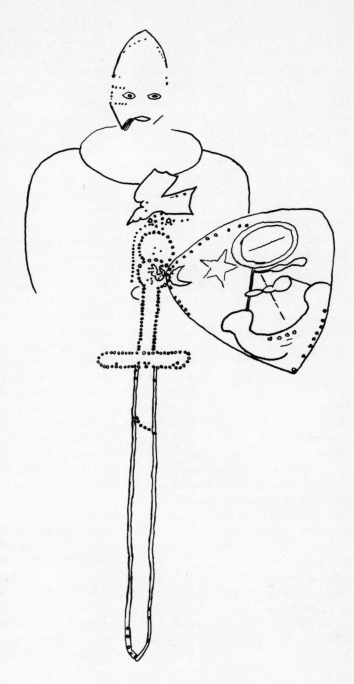

Military Effigy on Westford Ledge

about ten and a half inches. The length of the sword, which was no doubt measured off by the knight's actual sword laid on the rock, is fifty-two and a half inches from the top of the pommel to the tip of the blade. The blade itself is thirty-nine inches long, and its greatest width is between two and a quarter and two and a half inches. The head of the effigy, with eyeballs formed by elevations in the middle of hollows that represent eyesockets, with mouth and drooping moustache, but nose area eroded or broken out, is surmounted by a raised, pointed basinet, the eyeholes of which are represented by natural dark spots in the gneiss. On the armor just to the right of the knight's right eye is a rectangular hinge to fasten the basinet when lowered over the face. The knight seems to be wearing a great surcoat. I use "seems" in order to express some degree of question. At the right armpit there is a lance rest in the form of a rosette, and there may be a dagger in the right hand, of which four fingers seem to be indicated, with the thumb behind the handle. Being uncertain of these, I have omitted them from my drawing. The left hand resting upon the pommel of the sword is concealed behind the base of a falcon crest. Suspended from the left arm is a convex-curved triangular shield, an upper corner of which overlaps part of the wheel pommel. As Glynn and I see it, the heraldic emblems on the shield "in the chief" (across the top) are a crescent, a mullet (five-pointed, it seems, and not a star, which would be six-pointed), and a buckle; and in the base, a boat with high ends like a galley, or lymphad, possibly without a mast, though there is a natural line in the gneiss which the patternmaker apparently accepted as a mast, and which I therefore think we should accept.

All the evidences support the identification and dating by Lethbridge.

1.   The long sword with large wheel pommel is of a late fourteenth-century type. It is a Scottish claymore of 1350–1400.

2.   Armorial scholars say that the basinet is of a form that was in fashion for only twenty-five years, from 1375 to 1400.

3.   Observers who have had much experience with rock markings and who have made comparisons with the oldest gravestone letterings in the vicinity of Westford agree in estimating that the weathering of the human markings on the Westford ledge indicates an age of decidedly more than four hundred years. Their estimate takes into account the fact that gneiss weathers more slowly than granite, and that the ledge lying horizontal and only slightly inclined is somewhat protected from wind erosion, and is exposed to a very gentle flow of runoff from rainwater and snow.

Iain Moncrieffe in *The Highland Clans* identifies the heraldic emblems of the military effigy on the ledge at Westford as those of the Gunn Clan, a family associated with Orkney and with Caithness in Scotland.[4] Moncrieffe discusses the discovery of the military effigy and presents a drawing of Rosslyn Castle, since he associates the effigy with the Sinclair Expedition.[5] Here is what he says of the heraldic emblems on the shield of the effigy:

> Burke's *General Armory*, which lists a number of officially un-recorded coats-of-arms, attributes to Gunn (Sutherland) a three-masted galley, and on a red "chief" a bear's head between two stars; while for Gunne (Caithness) it has a ship under sail on the sea, and three stars on a red "chief" above the ship. Basically, therefore, the Gunn coat is obviously the Ship of Caithness (derived from the Galley of Orkney) with a "chief" of Sutherland (golden stars on red) on which another device is usually also incorporated. Considering the changes in coats-of-arms brought in by various marriages, Moncrieffe says: "It therefore falls to be considered what was the earlier device borne by the Gunns in their "chief": and the obvious answer is, their famous silver brooch (heraldically a "buckle") as Crowners of Caithness.
>
> Startlingly enough, the earliest surviving example of the Gunn chief's coat-of-arms appears to have been punch-marked by a medieval armourer-smith on a rock in Massachusetts. . . . The heater-shaped shield there, borne by what appears to be the effigy of a fourteenth century knight, appears to show a distinctively Norse-Scottish character: a galley, and in chief a star between two large buckles. As with many Scandinavian heraldic boats, no mast appears to be shewn: but the oars are crossed in saltire at the blades, as in some Highland coats. The dexter [right-hand] buckle is badly eroded, but part of its outer curve remains, and heraldically the star would always be placed between two similar objects. The rest of the shield seems too clear to be a mistracing of any natural rock formation or of some redskin inscription, the more especially considering the circumstances attending its discovery by someone without specialist and mediaevalist heraldic knowledge. . . . The mode in which the Galley of Caithness is depicted . . . makes it possible that it is not oars but mast-ropes that are punch-marked on the Westford rock.[6]

In the final hours before setting sail for home from North America, Sinclair's men filled the freshwater casks and from their last days' hunting replenished the food stocks on board to replace what they had eaten since leaving Advocate Harbour; for the chief hazard in an ocean crossing was the length of time it might take, during which water and food might fail. The men had arrived in Nova Scotia almost starved when they came westward, and they would have been most concerned about avoiding a repetition of that hardship.

In view of what has been demonstrated as to Prince Henry's departure from Nova Scotia toward the west, and the evidence that a knight of the Gunn family died on Prospect Hill in Massachusetts, the following passages from the Micmac legends of Glooscap suggest several possibilities that the reader may now find entertaining. These passages suggest that "Kuhkw" may have been the Micmac pronunciation of "Gunn." They suggest that several of the Micmacs had accompanied the departing prince across the Bay of Fundy, and with him had ascended Prospect Hill and were witnesses to the death of the "important personage" near the prince. They further suggest that some Micmacs from the Pictou area had accompanied the one hundred soldiers when they returned to Trin Harbor with their report on the smoking hill and spring of pitch; and that these same Micmacs climbed with the prince to the summit of Salmon Hill; and on their return homeward after they "reached the top of this second mountain" suddenly saw their native village. In a statement as to the time it took them to get home, there appears to be a confusion with the coming of the prince and the duration of his visit.

He came from the east; went away toward the west. There he is still tented; and two important personages are near him, who are called Kuhkw and Coolpujōt. . . .

Kuhkw means Earthquake; this mighty personage can pass along under the surface of the ground. . . . One of these seven visitors was wonderfully enamoured of a fine country; and expressed a desire to remain there; and to live long; whereupon, at Glooscap's direction, Earthquake took him and stood him up and he became a cedar-tree . . . seeds producing all the cedar-groves that exist in New Brunswick, Nova Scotia, and elsewhere. . . .

The other men started, and reached home in a short time. . . .

The next day they prepare a festival, and all four are feasted and sumptuously entertained. They are then taken to the top of a hill which is very high and difficult of access. The ground is rocky, broken, and totally unfit for cultivation. On the very apex of this hill, where the sun would shine from morning until night, they halt; and Glooscap takes the man who had desired to live for a long time, clasps him round the loins, lifts him from the ground, and then puts him down again, passing his clasped hands upon the man's head, and giving him a twist or two as he moves his hands upwards, transforms him into an old gnarled cedar-tree, with limbs growing out rough and ugly all the way from the bottom. "There," he says to the cedar-tree, "I cannot say exactly how long you will live—the Great Spirit alone can tell that. But I think you will not be likely to be disturbed for a good while, as no one can have any object in cutting you down; . . . I think you will stand there for a good long while. . . ."

He now inquires of them when they intend to go home, and in what direction their home lies; they inform him that they wish to return immediately, but they are utterly ignorant of the way . . . their home must be very far away, and the prospect of ever again finding it is small. He smiles, and tells them that he knows the way well, having often traveled it. They request him to be their guide; he agrees to do so, and bright and early the next morning they prepare to start. Morning dawns; Glooscap puts on his belt and leads off. About the middle of the forenoon they reach the top of the high mountain. From thence they can discern another mountain away in the distance—its blue outlines just in sight above the horizon. The men conclude it will take them at least a week to reach it. They push on; and to their astonishment, at about the middle of the afternoon they have reached the top of this second mountain. From the top of this they are directed to look around, and lo! all is familiar to them. They are perfectly acquainted with hill and forest, lake and river; and Glooscap says to them, "There is your own native village." Then he leaves them, and returns. They go on, and before sunset are home.[7]

The Sinclair Expedition to North America left its mark both in Canada and in the United States, in Canada as a legend; in the United States, on a Massachusetts rock in the form of a punched-hole pattern of a military effigy, with a broken sword.

The Sinclair Expedition to North America is unique among pre-Columbian transatlantic crossings in that two records of it have survived, one on each side of the ocean. We have seen how the story told by the letters of Antonio Zeno in Europe and the record handed down by oral transmission among the Indians in America dovetail together and corroborate each other.

In conclusion it is fair to say that Henry Sinclair was the first to place "really civilized foot" on North America, the continent that Columbus never saw. It has been well said of him: "He is destined to bulk more and more largely to future Americans."[8] And to Britishers also, one should add: The honor of having produced Henry Sinclair belongs to Great Britain. This makes his accomplishment, as a discoverer of America before the Great Age of Exploration, a matter of extraordinary interest and pride to all the English-speaking world, and especially to Scotsmen and to citizens of Canada and the United States, which countries have a culture stemming in large part from British traditions.

Portions of the story have been lost. Nevertheless, this is a unique case in pre-Columbian history where it has been possible to fill in enough of the gaps to give the story life by force of logic and geography, and by scientific proof which persuasively establishes as fact the Sinclair Expedition to the "new world" in the fourteenth century. This is the more gratifying in that it brings to his proper place a great man, whose name belongs on the roll of the leading figures in discovery and exploration and adventure.

Chapter Sixteen

BURIED IN ARMOR

WHY DID Prince Henry's expedition to North America have no immediate repercussions in Europe?

One reason is that in his day there was no means for quick and wide publicity. Printing with movable type had not yet been introduced into Europe, and publishing by hand-copied manuscripts was a slow process. Henry himself was not a writer. Antonio Zeno's letters told the story of the ocean crossing, but they were sent to Carlo Zeno in Venice. Why did Carlo not appreciate at once the importance of that crossing?

However assiduous Carlo Zeno may have been in telling his fellow Venetians about the discoveries and explorations in which Antonio in the Far North was interested, Carlo, like everyone else in Mediterranean countries, had no clear idea as to the geographical relationships of Scotland, the Orkneys, the Shetlands, Iceland, Greenland, Estotiland, and the reported "new world." Accurate maps did not exist. The map Antonio sent home or brought home with him a few years later may have been in some particulars the most accurate up to that time, but no one then in Venice had any means of knowing that it was.

Also, the great land that seemed to be "a new world" was reported as lying far to the west from the extreme north. The thought that it might be accessible directly to the west from the Mediterranean may not have occurred to anyone in Venice at that time. If it did, it could be no more than mere conjecture. The new land lay somewhere beyond Greenland; and Greenland, by all reports, was a grim, forbidding land in an isolated region.

But why did Prince Henry's expedition lead to no permanent colony of Orkneymen in the land he had explored?

Even if extensive publicity had been possible, it would have failed to start an emigration to the new world at the end of the fourteenth century. The ideas which were then astir and dominant in men's minds were those that later convulsed Europe and impelled the Church of Rome to initiate its great heresy persecution against reformers. Men's minds in the fourteenth century were directed toward the necessity of curbing the swollen wealth of the clergy and of solving the pressing problem of church ownership of land.

At the end of the fifteenth century when Columbus in 1493 returned as he said from the "Indies" in the West, it was not the idea of a "new world," a great wilderness peopled by savages, that immediately stirred in Europeans a desire to cross the Atlantic. It was the misinformation that Columbus disseminated, that he had found a short, quick route to Asia. Europeans were seeking to acquire wealth from "Eastern" lands, not to reside in a new Western continent. The only adventurers who followed Columbus in the first decade were those who sought jewels and gold and spices from the Columbus-juggled "East." It was not until nearly a hundred years after Columbus that the real significance and value of the "New World," by that time spelled in capitals, penetrated the minds of Europeans, and only then did large numbers of them begin to migrate to it.

Hitherto, historians of the discoveries of America have pointed to a contrast between the discoveries made by the early Norsemen and those made by the Italian navigators who served the Spanish, Portuguese, French, and English. But the Sinclair Expedition in 1398 included men of the North and of the Mediterranean, Orkneymen and Shetlanders and perhaps some Scotsmen, along with Italians—Antonio Zeno and some of his Venetian sailors.

Henry came home to his island earldom in 1399. He told his wife,

Janet, and all his family about the fabulous land to the west, of which they had heard from Messire Antonio. He said it was richer than Scotland in forests and game and natural resources. He told them of the marvelous black brook of flowing pitch that their patron St. Katherine had revealed to him. But his eldest son, little disposed toward sea adventures, had no wish to visit a region so inconveniently distant. The young man, unlike his father, was disposed to look upon the islands of Orkney and Shetland as merely a means of enhancing the luxury in which the family could live in Roslin.

Henry had only a few months left to pick up the threads of his manifold duties as earl. This is the final reason why his discovery was temporarily forgotten.

In August 1400, King Henry IV, invading Scotland, reached Edinburgh. His fleet must have been there the same month, or possibly earlier. In any case, sometime that year, "the English invaded, burnt, and spoiled certain islands of Orkney."[1] They came into Scapa Flow, where their ships would be safe from sudden storms, and where they could land within a short mile and a half from Kirkwall. They no doubt came swiftly, under cover of darkness or thick weather.

Awakened by the watcher who brought the news, Henry felt an indignant fury at the imminent invasion. There was a scurrying to put on armor and to saddle horses. Prudence would have counseled remaining inside the castle and defying the English. It was not Henry's way. His duty was to repulse the enemy's landing and prevent their ravishing the land. He and his men rode agallop and flung themselves against overwhelming odds.

Father Hay describes Earl Henry's battle against them:

> Henry Sainclaire was advertised of ane armie of Southerns that came to invade the Orcade Isles, who resisting them with his forces, through his too great negligence and contempt of his unfriendly forces left breathless, by blows battered so fast upon him, that no man was able to resist—[2]

As he was forced down by his besetting foes, did he regret that he had scorned protection behind the walls of Kirkwall Castle? As he struck his last defensive blow, did his thoughts leap from the battlefield to the safety of the fort in Bres in Shetland? Perhaps, in his last moment of consciousness, as he lay prone on the earth, he had a fleeting vision of that distant, unspoiled land, unknown to his enemies, far across the wide ocean, where he would have been beyond their reach.

The Diploma of 1446 says: "Henry Sinclair deit Eirle of Orchadie, and for the defense of the countrie was sclane thair crowellie be his innimiis."

Thus perished the man who, had he been spared a few years, could and no doubt would have brought the "new world" to the attention of many in the Orkney earldom and in Scotland, and so might have antedated Amerigo Vespucci in announcing that there was a new continent to be added to the map of the world. So near North America was to becoming known ninety or more years before Columbus! But the chance of it was ended by Henry's death. He left no one to carry on the work of exploration and settlement; for his son Henry, captivated by luxury, was not the man to do it.

Henry's family took his body to St. Matthew's Church in Roslin, where he was buried in armor without a coffin.

The site of the obscure skirmish in which he was killed is unknown. There has been some question as to the year. Holinshed states that in 1404 an English fleet "landed on some of the Orkneys and spoiled them," and some historians in consequence have accepted 1404 as the date of Henry's death. But the absence of any record of Henry in the four years from 1401 to 1404, though we have records of his activities in every year for thirty years preceding, support the view that he died in 1400. All we know is that in that year English ships from Lynn, approaching the Scottish coast, beat off an attack by Sir Robert Logan, who was captured. The English then sacked some of the Orkney Islands. The most reasonable conjecture is that 1400 was the year in which Prince Henry fell fighting his foes.

In the course of time, the national records of Scotland were taken to England, and later when being returned, a hogshead of these papers was lost by shipwreck. Orkney records were stolen and taken out of the islands and lost. The records of Shetland, being taken to England, were lost at sea off Orkney. The sea was kind to Henry living, but, to Henry dead, it was merciless, swallowing all it could of the memory of him.

An argument advanced for 1404 as the date of Henry's death is that in that year Antonio Zeno went back to Venice. It might appear that Antonio, who had been eager to return home but for years had not been free to do so, left the islands immediately after Earl Henry died. But Henry's heir may have insisted that Antonio remain as captain of the fleet for several years until he himself was completely master of the earldom.

Antonio wrote in his last letter to Carlo from Orkney:

> Concerning those things that you desire to know of me, as to the people and their habits, the animals, and the countries adjoining, I have written about it all in a separate book, which please God, I shall bring with me. In it I have described the country, the monstrous fishes, the customs and laws of Frislanda, of Islanda [Iceland], of Estlanda [Shetland], the kingdom of Norway, Estotiland, and Drogio; and lastly, I have written . . . the life and exploits of Zichmni, a prince as worthy of immortal memory as any that ever lived, for his great bravery and remarkable goodness. In it I have described the exploration of Greenland on both sides, and the settlement that he founded. But of this I will say no more in this letter, and hope to be with you very shortly, and to satisfy your curiosity on other subjects by word of mouth.

This letter, with its reference to Antonio's biography of Henry and Henry's deserving "immortal memory," obviously was written after Henry's death. If Antonio, at Henry's death, suddenly found himself free to return to Venice, he would not have written and sent the letter but would have started home at once by the first available ship. The conclusion seems reasonable that Henry died, not in 1404 but in 1400, the same year as the poet Chaucer.

Antonio Zeno in Venice had no time to have manuscript copies made for distribution of the biographies and geographical descriptive works he had written. He died a few months after he reached home, in 1405. Carlo Zeno was interested in Antonio's manuscripts, but failed to realize their importance and did nothing about them.

In one of his highly individual pronouncements, John Ruskin said: "I date the commencement of the Fall of Venice from the death of Carlo Zeno, 8th of May, 1418."[3]

The portions of the letters of Antonio Zeno that survived leave us with regret that we do not have the descriptions of Frislanda, Iceland, Shetland, and the Kingdom of Norway, the exploration of Greenland on both sides, Antonio's biography of Sir Nicolò, and his biography of the Prince of Orkney. The last of these would have been a great prize.

A few words should be given to the family of Henry Sinclair.

> Efter the decess of this Henrie, first Erile of Orkney, in the parts of Orkney, cam be chans the modir of the said Erile Henrie the First, and baid continuallie thair after the decess of hir son Henrie, the first erile, and brukit lyfe after the decess of all his sisters sonnis and dowchtters.[4]

The extramarital attachment of Henry's niece and Sir William, first Earl of Douglas, had been a true love affair, which triumphed over convention, in that the couple remained lovers until death parted them. A monument in St. Magnus Cathedral in Kirkwall has a carved shield bearing for the female in the second and third quarters a symbol of the Orkney earldom, a galley with sails; with an overall engrailed cross of the Roslin Sinclairs; and in the male first quarter, a heart, symbol of Douglas, and in the fourth quarter, a buckle signifying victorious fidelity. Was this monument, which would have been in accordance with the wishes of Henry's niece, erected in memory of her son, George de Douglas?[5]

> The vicissitudes of great families form a curious chapter in the general history of mankind. . . . The interest attaching to individual fortunes excites more human sympathy than the fate of kingdoms. But such details are not on the surface. They must be dug up from buried documents, disinterred and the dust swept off. . . . Greatness [in a family] is built up by well-directed energy. . . . There is little stability in the highest gifts of fortune. Family trees, like all other trees, must eventually perish. The most lasting houses have their seasons: their spring, summer sunshine glare, wane, decline and death. . . . No family in Europe beneath the rank of royalty boasts a higher antiquity, a nobler illustration, or a more romantic interest than that of St. Clair.[6]

In the family of the Sinclair Earls of Orkney, our Henry was the colorful and energetic spring. His son Henry was the summer; his grandson William, earl from 1420 to 1479, was the full-harvested autumn; his great-grandson William, the last Sinclair Earl of Orkney, was the inevitable winter.

Henry, the second earl, was a valiant prince and good-looking, and he continued our Henry's work of building the family fortunes. He enlarged the donjon of Roslin Castle. He made parks for fallow and red deer. He was the guardian of the Crown Prince of Scotland. When King Robert III's eldest son died in the hands of murderous enemies, the king decided to send his young son James to France, to secure his safety, and for this purpose put him under the care of Earl Henry. The prince and the earl took ship together, but were captured by the English in February 1405–6. Prince James, whose father died of grief when he heard the news of his capture, became King James I. Earl Henry soon escaped from the English, but King James was held prisoner in England for eighteen years, during which incarceration he wrote the famous poem *The King's Quair*. Scotland ultimately paid £40,000 ransom for his release.

William, the third Sinclair earl, was "well-proportioned, of middle stature, broad-bodied, fair in face, yellow-haired, hardy and stern."[7] When he visited Orkney, he was met by three hundred men with red scarlet gowns and coats of black velvet. When he resided in Roslin, "he had all his victuals [fish and mutton] brought by sea from the north."[8] Like a king in fear of poisoning, he had his dainties tasted before him. He obtained great lands in Scotland, the wardency of the three marches between England and Scotland and many baronies. He had eight brothers and sisters who all made prominent marriages. In Roslin, where he dwelt in luxury, he kept an almost regal court, with three hundred riding gentlemen continually in his house, and fifty-five gentlewomen, of whom thirty-five were noble ladies. He had a greater number of retainers than any feudal baron of his time.[9] He built the chapel at Roslin, which became famous for its unique architectural features. It was intended to be a great collegiate church to take the place of the old Church of St. Matthew, which was in decay. It became the burial chapel of the Sinclairs. When the old church at Roslin was torn down, our Henry's armored skeleton was laid to final rest in the chapel.

The Norse tradition of tomb-fire and fire-boat burial haunts the chapel; for that building is said to appear to be on fire just before the death of any of Henry's descendants. Sir Walter Scott thus phrased the superstition:

> *Seemed all on fire that chapel proud*
> *   Where Roslin's chiefs uncoffined lie,*
> *Each baron for a sable shroud*
> *   Sheathed in his iron panoply.*
>
> *Seem'd all on fire within, around,*
> *   Deep sacristy and altar's pale;*
> *Shone every pillar foliage-bound,*
> *   And glimmer'd all the dead men's mail.*
>
> *Blaz'd battlement and pinnet high,*
> *   Blaz'd every rose-carved buttress fair—*
> *So still they blaze when fate is nigh*
> *   The lordly line of high St. Clair.*[10]

But the coming of winter to the Sinclair family was written in the book of fate. King Christian I of Norway arranged the marriage of his daughter to the King of Scotland, and having nothing for her dowry, he very unwisely mortgaged Orkney and Shetland to the Scottish king in 1468. Norway never redeemed the islands. Eventually, Henry's great-grandson, called "William the Waster," was "induced" (a euphemism for compelled) by King James III to renounce his title and right to the Earldom of Orkney, and to accept in exchange "the more lucrative [!] lands of the Castle of Ravenscraig, near Dysart in Fife."[11]

The castle in Kirkwall had fallen into the hands of Stewart earls who were cruel despots.[12] One of these earls finally raised a rebellion against the king, who ordered the earl's capture and death, and the razing of Kirkwall castle.

The ordnance brought against the castle in 1614 consisted of "ane great cannon callit Thrawn Mouthe, markit with the porcupine, and ane battering piece, markit with the salamander." The ammunition consisted of "three-score bullets for each of the two battering pieces, four score and two stones of gunpowder, and two barrellis with cuttit iron for hail-shot." The besieger planted his pieces "within one half-quarter of a mile of the Castle." At the second shot one of the turrets upon the head of the house was pierced and almost beaten down. The Earl of Caithness reported: "It is one of the strongest houses in Britain, for I will bring with me to your lordship cannon bullets broken like golf balls upon the Castle, and cloven in twa haffis."[13]

The castle was beleaguered for three months, but might have held out for as many years had not treachery led to its surrender.[14]

It was demolished at the king's command in 1615. The only thing now left of it is a red stone set in the wall of a building at the site, bearing the heraldic coat-of-arms, the galleys of "the Erle of Orkney of auld," and the engrailed cross.

Roslin Castle was bombarded by King Henry VIII in 1554, and many apartments of it were laid in ruins by Oliver Cromwell in 1650. An immense collection of rare literary and historic treasure was destroyed.

Father Hay, who had access to the charter room of Roslin Castle, said that room had had many secrets to tell before fire reduced its records. There is a local legend that precious manuscripts are in a sealed-up room in the cellar of the castle, and that they will be discovered by a blind person. An attempt to find manuscripts was made by "General Count Poli, an Italian descendant of the prevost of Roslin Castle, who came in 1834 with an ancient volume" which supposedly directed their finding.[15] The Italian count did not find the treasure of manuscripts in the Roslin Castle cellar, or at least none that have ever been heard about. Perhaps it was because he was not blind. Long before him and in another place, another Italian, a boy who was blind in another sense, as to what he found, came upon documents that are a true treasure, because they have enabled us to reconstruct the story of the Prince of Orkney's Expedition to North America.

Chapter Seventeen

A PARCEL OF OLD LETTERS

THE NARRATIVES of the Orkney fisherman's discovery of land in the West and of the Earl of Orkney's exploration of it long lay buried. There is romantic treasure in the tale of how the facts were throughout the centuries gradually uncovered and finally confirmed. It is a chronicle of happy chances, extraordinary accidents, patient labor, and well-directed guesses. The first step in the long unveiling was the following incident that occurred nearly a century and a half after the main events.

About the year 1520 in a palace in Venice, a small boy one day escaped from the eyes of his mother or nurse. He wandered alone into a room where curiosity led him to an unlocked chest. Looking for something to play with, he came upon a pile of old letters and ancient maps. With a child's instinct for destruction, and before he was stopped, he tore up most of the letters.

This boy, Nicolò, whom we shall call "Junior" to distinguish him from the fourteenth-century Nicolò, was born in 1515, a son of the prominent Zeno family. The letters he had mutilated were written between 1390 and 1404, by Sir Nicolò and Antonio Zeno. Antonio was Nicolò Junior's great-great-great-grandfather.

As the boy grew into maturity, an interest in geography and exploration was awakened in him. He read those pieces of the letters that he had not completely destroyed, and as a man he bitterly regretted what his childish hands had done. Those fragments of letters became his most prized possession, for they told of sensational voyages made by his ancestors. They got more and more worn with repeated handling as he milled over them and reassembled what he could. He did not find it easy to read the old handwriting in faded ink. Where there was nothing in the context to help him to proper names of persons and places, he failed to decipher them correctly.

In those fragmented Zeno letters, the lucky chance by which enough survived to start us on the trail of Henry Sinclair makes us wonder how many records of important discoveries in the distant past have been totally lost through accident, ignorance, or carelessness.

Nicolò Junior's father showed the old letters to a relative, Marco Barbaro, who was writing biographical notes on distinguished Venetians. Barbaro's book, *Discendenza Patrizie* [Patrician Ancestors], dated 1536, mentioned the fourteenth-century voyages of Sir Nicolò and Antonio Zeno. The work is a manuscript in several volumes, now in the Correr Museum in Venice. In Volume S–Z we read on page 200:

> Nicolò the Chevalier, of the Holy Apostles Parish, called the Old— in 1379 captain of a galley against the Genoese. Wrote with brother Antonio the voyage to Frislanda, where he died.
>
> Antonio wrote with his brother Nicolò the Chevalier the voyage to the islands near the Arctic Pole, and of their discoveries of 1390 by order of Zichno, King of Frislanda. He reached the continent of Estotiland in North America. He remained fourteen years in Frislanda; that is, four with his brother, and ten alone.

This unsupported claim that Antonio Zeno of the fourteenth century had reached the continent of North America was seen by only a few readers. No one knew what to make of it, except to feel pride in Venetian prowess.

At the death of his father, Nicolò Junior acquired ownership of the torn letters. A year later he prepared a narrative in which he quoted the surviving portions of the letters. He published it with this title: THE DISCOVERY OF THE ISLANDS OF FRISLANDA, ESLANDA,

ENGRONELANDA, ESTOTILANDA, AND ICARIA: MADE BY TWO BROTHERS OF THE ZENO FAMILY, NAMELY, MESSIRE NICOLO, THE CHEVALIER, AND MESSIRE ANTONIO. WITH A SPECIAL DRAWING OF THE WHOLE REGION OF THEIR DISCOVERY IN THE NORTH. Venice, 1558.[1]

In the concluding paragraph of the narrative, Nicolò Junior mentions his manuscript sources and what he had done with them in his childhood:

> These letters were written by Messire Nicolò (and Antonio) to Messire Carlo his brother; and I am grieved that the book[2] and many other writings on these subjects, I don't know how, came easily to ruin; for, being but a child when they fell into my hands, I, not knowing what they were, tore them in pieces, as children will do, and sent them all to ruin; a circumstance which I cannot now recall without the greatest sorrow. Notwithstanding, in order that such an important memorial should not be lost, I have put the whole in order, as well as I could, in the above narrative; so that the present age may, more than its predecessors have done, in some measure derive pleasure from the great discoveries made in those parts where they were least expected; for it is an age that takes a great interest in new narratives and in the discoveries which have been made in countries hitherto unknown, by the high courage and great energy of our ancestors.

For more than two centuries the published Zeno Narrative was regarded as a mere curiosity. No one understood how it could fit in with actual persons and places and events. The narrative involved a "Prince" (*"un principe"*) who ruled over islands, but the spelling of his name as printed, "Zichmni", did not resemble that of any lord of the isles of historical record. This inevitably gave the impression of falsity to those who sought to ascertain whether the narrative was based upon facts. The idea that the narrative was a factual account of an expedition that reached the continent of North America a century before Columbus seemed fantastic to all who bowed to consensus. Most scholars were skeptical about all claims of pre-Columbian crossings of the Atlantic.

Some even questioned whether a fourteenth-century Venetian would or could have voyaged to Northern Europe via the Atlantic. However, one scholar who was completely skeptical as to the genuineness of the Zeno Narrative wrote: "There is no reason to doubt the probability of a voyage into the North Sea by the brothers. An annual voyage to England and Flanders was made under the auspices of the Venetian Senate, in most ordinary years, from 1313 to 1533."[3]

The Zeno publication of 1558 continued to fascinate historians, and its study persisted.

Valid attacks were made on the Zeno Map. The "special drawing" (*disegno particolare*) is a separate feature mentioned in what amounts to a subtitle. The illustrative map has latitude and longitude lines, but latitude and longitude lines had not been invented in the fourteenth century, and were therefore additions by its sixteenth-century maker. The map has some imaginary islands and place names that were probably copied from other maps, notably, as Erik Wilhelm Dahlgren, a scholar in the field of cartography, pointed out, from the Claus Magnus Map of 1529. The form of Greenland on the Zeno Map appears to have been copied from the Claudius Clavus Map of 1556. These objections to the Zeno Map were repeated by many scholars, including Eugene Beauvois in 1889, Fred W. Lucas in 1898, and Richard Hennig in 1953.

Nicolò Junior apparently believed that copying from other maps into his map of the Far North would be helpful. To the contrary, what he produced was a botchwork that for many years confused everyone. His map has been a disservice to the narrative he prepared from the letters. Without his map, it is likely that the narrative would have been sooner recognized as factual. His map, as pointed out by the skeptics, was not based upon the narrative. There seem to be few original details in it.

Though the errors in the Zeno Map are numerous, the map is significant for several reasons. It tells us that its maker believed that southwest of Greenland was a land called Estotiland; and that southwest of Estotiland, there was another land called Drogio. His drawing of the north and east sides or ends of Estotiland has the conformation of the north and east sides or ends of Newfoundland, with more than a dozen points of comparison.[4] Drogio is in a position to represent Nova Scotia. Patently, questions as to the origins and meanings of the names of those two lands, or as to whether they originated with the Zeni, cannot upset the fact of the positioning of both and the conformation of one.

In view of what has been discovered since 1949, discrediting of the Zeno Map is a side issue that has no essential bearing on the question of the veracity of the Zeno Narrative. On the showing of all the evidences in hand, the Zeno Map is to be dissociated from the Zeno Narrative.

In the Zeno Narrative errors are few, and such as there are have been satisfactorily disposed of. For example, the year in which the fourteenth-century Nicolò Zeno was shipwrecked was not 1380, as printed. It has been generally accepted that the error was caused by the omission of one "X" by the typesetter. Marco Barbaro in *Discendenza Patrizie*, in 1536, having drawn material from the same manuscript letters as Nicolò Junior did twenty years later, gave the correct date of Nicolò Zeno's voyage from Venice as 1390.[5]

Charges that the narrative presented by Nicolò Junior was a preposterous hoax were countered by D. Placido Zurla, who defended the Zeno family against imputations of fraud on the ground of the exemplary character of its members. Even though Zurla was as partial in favor of the Zeni as the skeptics were against, the characters of Sir Nicolò and Antonio Zeno stand clear in rebuttal of the aspersions cast upon them by the skeptic who has had the widest hearing, Fred W. Lucas. In view of the fact that Earl Henry Sinclair always stood as a loyal vassal to the Norwegian Crown, the charge by Lucas that if Earl Henry Sinclair were "Zichmni", he was "a perjured rebel and traitor" is unscholarly and foul slander. 'See Chapter 9, Note 4.)

With expansion of knowledge of geography and history, the authenticity of the Zeno Narrative has been accepted by general consensus.[6] In the past two hundred years a fascinating work of reconstruction has been undertaken. Essential features of the story have been substantiated by geology.[7] Geographical detective work has solved problems of time and place. The story of the Orkney Expedition to North America has been corroborated and amplified in Nova Scotia by an Indian legend, and in the United States by a fourteenth-century memorial on rock. Now we know how the brave deeds of Henry Sinclair, Earl of Orkney, made him, as Antonio Zeno said most aptly, a man "as worthy of immortal memory as any that ever lived."

Sources and Notes

Introduction · THE DETECTIVE SPEAKS

1. Jacques Cartier, *The Voyages of Jacques Cartier*, pp. 238, 239.

2. Samuel de Champlain, *The Works of Samuel de Champlain*, vol. I, p. 463. Also, Marc Lescarbot, *History of New France*, vol. II, pp. 362, 363.

3. Alfred G. Bailey, *The Conflict of European and Eastern Algonkian Cultures*, pp. 4, 5. Bailey says that the Breton Pizigani Map, 1367, suggestively depicts a Breton disaster in the region of "les îles fantastiques". In 1514 it was stated that the French had for sixty years been accustomed to pay a tax on fish caught "tant en la cost de Bretaigne, la Terre Neuf, Islands que ailleurs." (Quoted from La Roncière, *Histoire de la marine française*, vol. 3, Paris, 1906.) Bailey's comment is: "It is difficult to know whether the "sixty years" clause applies to Newfoundland as well as to the coast of Brittany, but La Roncière and Harris appear to have considered it not beyond the scope of reasonable possibility. On the other hand, J. Winsor and La Roncière reject the Basque contention."

4. Frederick J. Pohl, *The Sinclair Expedition to Nova Scotia in 1398*.

Chapter One :   BOY

1. When Roslin Chapel was built as the beginning of a great church, the old St. Matthew's Church of our hero's day was razed, and the contents of the burial ground were removed to the chapel.

2. Sir Walter Scott, *The Lay of the Last Minstrel*, Canto VI, xxiii, 25–46.

3. Lines from Scott's *The Lord of the Isles*, Canto III, xxvii, 3–8, are applicable to Henry Sinclair:

> *His was the patriot's burning thought,*
> *Of Freedom's battle bravely fought,*
> *Of castles storm'd, of cities freed,*
> *Of deep design and daring deed,*
> *Of England's roses reft and torn,*
> *And Scotland's cross in triumph worn.*

4. R. W. Saint-Clair, *The Saint-Clairs of the Isles*, p. 481, quotes lines that describe the critical moment of the hunt:

> *Light down! Light down! thou St. Clair bold!*
> *Or never go hunting more;*
> *Now have at her, Help! Now hang to her, Hold!*
> *And they turn her back to the shore.*

5. The site of the Church of St. Katherine in the Hopes is at the lower end of what is now the Glenmore Reservoir. A "hope" is a bay.

Chapter Two :   MAN

1. Young people in the fourteenth century learned Latin from the text of Donatus, studied *De Arithmetica* of Boethius and the history written by Orosius; they also read Isidore of Seville and other authors.

2. Scott, *The Lay of the Last Minstrel*, Canto VI, xxiii, 44.

3. The St. Clairs, Hubert and Walderne, were first cousins of the father of William the Conqueror, and the children of Walderne through their mother were first cousins of the Conqueror. When no one else in Normandy would risk his life to go to England on an embassy, Hubert de St. Clair volunteered, and "brought back the mandates and symbols which made Duke William master heir of the crown of England." Nine St. Clairs in armor fought at the Battle of Hastings (Senlac). They were Hubert with four sons, and his brother Walderne with three sons. The St. Clairs were rewarded with estates in England, except for Walderne's son William, who had a falling out with the Conqueror and went to Scotland. The advantage

of having a family name, as this William did, appealed so much to King Malcolm that the king had his parliament confer surnames and titles on all the Scottish nobility. It has been said of the Norman Conquest that England (and because William St. Clair went to Scotland we may with reservations include that country) "had the unspeakable good fortune of being taken in hand, for high training, by a nation of cultivated masters of the best life then existent" (Thomas Sinclair, *The Sinclairs of England*). The Norman nobles were "born rulers with civil capacity. They knew when to use fire and sword, but when peace gave opportunity, they eagerly sought to shape happy policies." There are some good arguments for believing it.

4.   The Stewart family genealogy is problematical and unconvincing until long after the time of William, the "seemly St. Clair," who was high steward to the royal court in the eleventh century. If the Stewart family, as is claimed, took its name from having a steward ancestor, that ancestor may have been a St. Clair. Actually, there seems to be good evidence that only one Stewart was ever a king, for the queen mother of the second so-called Stewart king confessed on her deathbed that his father was not her husband the king. However, we shall not, for these interesting but heretical reasons, rewrite the history books.

5.   Henry's great-great-grandfather, Sir William, born in 1266, was guardian to Alexander, Crown Prince of Scotland, who as king granted him a charter of the lands and barony of Roslin in 1280. Sir Henry, second Lord of Roslin, was the Royal Baxter, or chief baker, the "panetarium Scotiae," or Governor of the Corn Trade. Sir William, our hero's grandfather, married a sister of the first queen of King Robert the Bruce.

6.   Father Hay, a priest who had access to the then existent Sinclair family archives in the cellar of Roslin Castle, tells us (*Genealogie*, p. 15) that Henry's grandfather had "sent a priest to the grave of St. Katherine in which there is a precious oyle that issueth from her bones, to bring him thereof, that he might carry it to his new-builded chapell. The priest goeing and returning with the oyle, he became so weary he was forced to rest at a place a mile distant from Libertoune Church, where falling asleep upon a rush bush near by, he lost his oyle. The news thereof comeing to Sir William St. Clair, he made workmen to digge the place where the oyle was spilt, and presentlie up sprung a fountaine or well, which to this day hath a black oyle swimming upon it."

7.   J. Russel Walker, '*Holy Wells*' *in Scotland*, pp. 172–75, gives the quaint translation by Bellendon into some sort of Scotch-English from the Latin of Hector Boece: "Nocht two miles fra Edinburgh is ane fontane dedicat to Sanct Katrine, quhair sternis of oulie springis ithandlie with sic abundance that howbeit the samin be gaderit away, it springis incontinent with gret abundance. This fontane rais throw ane drop of Sanct Katrine's oulie, quhilk was brocht out of Monte Sinai, fra her sepulture, to Sanct Margaret, the blissit Quene of Scotland. Als sone as Sanct Margaret saw the oulie spring ithandlie, by divine miracle, in the said place, sche gart big ane

chapell thair in the honour of Sanct Katrine. This oulie has ane singulare virteu agains all manner of kankir and skawis."

8. George Algernon Fothergill, *Curiosities of Edinburgh and Neighborhood*, p. 57 *passim*, gives several references to St. Katherine's Oily Well. Peder Swave of Lubeck mentions "a spot where oil flows out of the ground" (*Early Travelers in Scotland*, ed. by P. Hume Brown). Bishop Leslie in 1578 in his *Historie of Scotland* wrote: "A fontane, quhair gret drapis of oyle perpetuallie so spring upe, atht nathir gif ye take mony sal they appeir the fewar, nather gif ye take nocht ane, sal thay seim the mae." Matthew Mackaile in *Moffet-Well*, 1664, wrote: "Its profundity equalleth the length of a Pike, and is alwaies replet with water, and at the bottom of it there remaineth a great quantity of black Oyl, in some veins of the earth." The actual depth of the well is 8 feet 6 inches. The "foetid smell" of the well was "like unto smell of smoke of Coals and their Oyl."

9. The region south of Edinburgh in which the well exists is geologically a carboniferous limestone with "productive coal measures." These coal strata explain the phenomenon of the "black oyle," a bituminous substance consisting of "tarry matters, more or less fluid," with "a smell of Coals." South of Liberton on the map of Lothian in the Blaeu Atlas of 1654 appears the name "Oylywel."

Chapter Three: CHECKMATE

1. The marriage dowry of Henry's mother was the right of inheritance to the Earldom of Orkney. The other daughters of Earl Malise were not unfairly deprived of inheriting from his estate, for he had three other earldoms. The record applying to Henry's mother is in the "Diploma" or "Deduction concerning the genealogies of the Ancient Counts of Orkney, from their First Creation to the Fifteenth century, Drawn up from the most authentic Records by Thomas, Bishop of Orkney, with the assistance of his Clergy and others"—issued at Kirkwall, June 1, 1446.

3. The "John Sincler" who witnessed the agreement between the Bishop of Orkney and Haakon Jonsson may have been Sir John St. Clair of Herd-mannston, who became the second husband of Henry's sister Margaret.

3. The Royal Archives of Sweden have no records of a Florentia. The Royal Archives of Denmark say that "a tradition attributes three sisters to King Haakon VI, but as to their names or lives nothing reliable seems to be known."

4. There are more confusions and careless errors in genealogy than in any other field. Many births, marriages, and deaths do not appear in surviving records.

5. "I care not," wrote Logan of Restalrig, "for all else I have in this kingdom, in case I get a grip of Dirleton, for I esteem it the pleasantest dwelling in Scotland."

Chapter Four: EARL

1.   The Installation reads: "To all who shall see or hear the present letters Henry Earl of the Orkneys, Lord of Roslin, wishes salvation in the Lord. Because the very serene prince in Christ, my most clement lord, Haquin, by the grace of God the king of the kingdoms of Norway and Sweden, has set us by his favor over the Orcadian lands and islands, and has raised us into the rank of jarl over the beforesaid lands and islands, and since this is required by the dignity, we make well known to all, as well to posterity as to contemporaries, that we have made homage of fidelity to our lord the king himself, at the kiss of his hand and mouth, and have given to him a true and due oath of fidelity, as far as counsels and aids to our same lord the king, his heirs, and successors, and to his kingdom of Norway, must be observed. And so, let it be open to all that we and our friends, whose names are expressed lower, have firmly promised in faith and with our honour to our same lord the king, and to his men and councillors, that we must faithfully fulfill all agreements, conditions, promises and articles which are contained in the present letters to our beforesaid lord the king, his heirs and successors, and to his kingdom of Norway.

1st term   "In the first place, therefore, we freely oblige us to serve our lord the king outside of the lands and islands of the Orkneys, with 100 good men or more, equipped in complete arms, for the conveniences and use of our same lord the king, whenever we shall have been sufficiently requisitioned by his messengers or his letters, and forewarned within Orkney three months. But when the men shall have arrived in the presence of our lord the king, from that time he will provide about victuals for us and ours.

2   "Again, if any may wish to attack or hostily to invade, in whatsoever manner, the lands and islands of the Orkneys, or the land of Zetland (Shetland), then we promise and oblige us to defend the lands named, with men in good condition whom we may be able to collect for this solely, from the lands and islands themselves, yea, with all the force of relatives, friends, and servants.

3   "Also, if it shall be necessary that our lord the king attack any lands of any kingdom, by right or from any other reason or necessity, then we shall be to him in help and service with all our force.

4   "Moreover, we promise in good faith that we must not build or construct castles or any fortifications within the lands and islands beforesaid, unless we shall have obtained the favour, good-pleasure, and consent of our same lord the king.

5   "We also shall be bound to hold and to cherish the said lands and islands of the Orkneys, and all their inhabitants, clergymen and laity, rich and poor, in their rights.

6   "Further, we promise in good faith that we must not at any time sell or alienate that beforesaid county and that lordship, whether lands or islands, belonging to the earldom, or our right which we obtain now to the earldom, the lands, and islands, by the grace of God and of the king our lord, from our lord the king himself, or his heirs, and successors, or from

the kingdom, nor to deliver these or any of these for surety and for pledge to any one, or to expose them otherwise, against the will and good-pleasure of him and his successors.

7　"In addition, if it happen that our lord the king, his heirs, or successors wish to approach those lands and islands for their defence, or from other reasonable cause, or to direct thither his councillors or men, then we shall be held to be for help to our same lord the king, and his heirs, to his councillors and men, with all our force, and to minister to our lord the king, and his heirs, his men and councillors, those things of which they may be in need for their due expenses, and as necessity then requires, at least to ordain so from the lands and islands.

8　"Moreover, we promise that we must begin or rouse no war, law suit, or dissension with any strangers or natives, by reason of which war, law suit or dissension the king my lord, his heirs or successors, or their kingdom of Norway, or the beforesaid lands and islands, may receive any damage.

9　"Again, if it happen, but may this be absent, that we notably and unjustly do wrong against any within the beforesaid lands and islands, or inflict some notable injury upon any one, as the loss of life, or mutilation of limbs, or depredation of goods, then we shall answer to the pursuer of a cause of that kind in the presence of our lord the king himself, and his councillors, and satisfy for the wrongs according to the laws of the kingdom.

10　"Also, whenever our lord the king shall have summoned us, on account of any causes, to his presence, where and when he shall have wished to hold his general assembly, then we are bound to go to him, to give him advice and assistance.

11　"Further, we promise that we shall not break the truces and security of our same lord the king, nor his peace, which he shall have made or confirmed with foreigners or natives, or with whomsoever others, in any manner whatever, to violate them, nay defend them all as far as our strength, and hold those as federated to us whom the king of Norway himself, our Lord, may wish to treat as his favourers and friends.

12　"We promise also that we must make no league with the Orcadian bishop, nor enter into or establish any friendship with him, unless from the good-pleasure and consent of our lord the king himself; but we must be for help to him against that bishop, until he shall have done to him what is of right, or shall be bound to do so for that special reason, upon those things in which my lord the king may wish or be able reasonably to accuse that bishop.

13　"Besides, when God may have willed to call us from life, then that earldom and that lordship, with the lands and the islands, and with all the jurisdiction, must return to our lord the king, his heirs and successors freely; and if we shall have children after us, procreated from our body, male, one or more, then he of them who shall claim the abovesaid earldom and lordship must demand, with regard to this, the favour, good-pleasure, and consent of our lord the king himself, his heirs, and successors.

14　"Further, we promise in good faith that we shall be bound to pay to our abovesaid lord the king, or to his official at Tunisberg, on the next festival of St. Martin the bishop and confessor, a thousand golden pieces, which are called nobles, of English money in which we acknowledge us to be bound to him by just payment.

15 "Also, we promise, because we have been now promoted to the earldom and lordship oftensaid by our lord the king himself, that our cousin Malise Sparre must cease from his claim and dismiss altogether his right, if it be discernible that he has any, to those lands and islands; so that my lord the king, his heirs, and successors shall sustain no vexation or trouble from him or from his heirs.

16 "Again, if we have made any agreement or any understanding with our cousin Alexander Ard, or have wished to enter into any treaty with him, in that case we will do similarly on our part and on the part of the king my lord to whatever was done in precaution about Malise Sparre.

"Further, we, Henry, earl abovesaid, and our friends and relatives within-written, namely Simon Rodde (Ard), William Daniels, knights, Malise Sparre, William Chrichton, David Chrichton, Adam Byketon, Thomas Bennine, and Andrew Haldaniston, armsbearers, conjunctly promise in good faith to our oftensaid lord the king, Haquin, and to his first-born lord the king, Olaf, and to his councillors and men within-written, namely, to the lords Siguard, Haffthorsen, Ogmund Findersen, Eric Ketelsen, Narvo Ingnaldisen, John Oddosen, Ulpho Johnsen, Ginther de Vedhousen; John Danisen, Haquin Evidassen, knights of the same lord the king; Haquin Jonssen, Alver Hardlessen, Hantho Ericson, Erland Phillippsen, and Otto Remer, armsbearers; and for this, under preservation of our honour, we bind ourselves and each of us in a body to the aforesaid lords, that we must truly and firmly fulfil all the agreements and conditions and articles which are expressed above to our lord the king, within the above-written feast of St. Martin the bishop and confessor, so far as one particular business was declared by itself above.

"That all these things now promised may have the greater strength for this, and may be fulfilled the sooner, we the aforesaid Henry, Earl of the Orkneys, place and leave behind us our cousins and friends Lord William Daniels, knight, Malise Sparre, David Chrichton, and the lawful son of the said Simon, by name Lord Alexander, here in the kingdom hostages. Upon this faith they oblige and promise themselves to this, that from our lord the king of Norway, or from that place in which he shall have wished to have them within his kingdom of Norway they in nowise may go away, publicly or secretely, before all the abovesaid things be totally fulfilled with entire integrity to our lord the king; and particularly and specially, the conditions and articles for whose observation the within-written reverend fathers, bishops, and prelates of the churches of the kingdom of Scotland, and the other nobles within-written of the same kingdom, Lord William, Bishop of St. Andrews; Lord Walter, Bishop of Glasgow; Lord William, Earl of Douglas; Lord George, Earl of March; Lord Patrick Hepburn, Lord Alexander Haliburton, Lord George Abernethy, Lord William Ramsay, knights, must promise in good faith, and upon this remit their open letters to our same king the lord, with their true seals, in the before-noted time, as in our other letters written upon this is declared more fully.

"Also, we promise in good faith that we must assume in no direction to us the lands of our lord the king, or any other rights of his which his progenitors and the king our lord are known to have reserved to themselves; and concerning those lands or jurisdictions not to intromit in any manner whatsoever. They have reserved those laws, indeed, and those pleas within the Orcadian earldom, as is before said, and the lands and pleas of that kind will remain in all cases safe for them; but if, upon this, we shall have his special letters, then we ought to be specially bound thereafter to our same lord the king.

"Besides, but may it be absent, if all those aforesaid things shall not have been brought to conclusion, and totally fulfilled to the same my lord the king as it has been expressed above, or if we should have attempted anything in the contrary of any of the premises, then the promotion and favour which we have experienced from the king our lord, and of his grace, ought to be of no strength; yea, the promotion and favour of that kind done to us must be broken down altogether, and in their forces be totally empty and inane, so that we and our heirs for the rest shall have no right of speaking for the beforesaid county or for the lands or beforesaid islands, or we of acting about those lands and islands in any way whatsoever, that it may be manifest to all that the promotion and grace of this kind was given by no force of law or justice.

"And so we append our seal, together with the seals of our said friends, to our present letters, in testimony and the firmer evidence of all the premises.

"These things were done at Marstrand, in the year of the Lord 1379, the 2nd day of August." [The original Latin of Henry's Installation is in Torfaeus's *Orcades*, and the English translation is in Sinclair's *Caithness Events*.]

2. A thousand English nobles were equivalent in modern purchasing power to more than $20,000.

3. *Diplomatarium Norvegicum*. Translated extracts in Sinclair, *Caithness Events*.

4. *Ibid*.

5. "The right to coin money was never exercised by any of the Orcadian earls." Saint-Clair, *The Saint-Clairs of the Isles*, p. 551.

6. The statement as to the powers exercised by the Sinclair Earls of Orkney was made by Father Hay, *Genealogie*, p. 16.

7. Ingeborg, whom Henry's son John married, was probably born about 1375 or 1376. King Waldemar, her father, died in 1375. She was perhaps his last child, born about the same time as Henry's son John, assuming that Henry married Janet Halyburton about 1374, had his eldest son Henry about 1375, and son John about 1376.

8. The stanza is from "Orcadia, Land of the Engrailed Cross," a poem by David Vedder given in Saint-Clair, p. 476.

Chapter Five: CASTLE

1. Fred W. Lucas, *The Annals of the Voyages of the Brothers Zeno*, assumed that in building a castle in Kirkwall in 1380, and a fort in Shetland in 1390, Earl Henry violated his oath of fealty. But the argument of Lucas crumbles with a careful reading of the 4th term (fifth paragraph) of the Installation of Earl Henry.

2. The words from King Robert's Resignation of Orkney are quoted by Alexander Nisbet in *A System of Heraldry*. The full text of the resignation would be welcome. The Lord Lyon, King-at-Arms, writing me from Edinburgh on May 1, 1968, expresses uncertainty as to the present whereabouts of the original document.

3. Torfaeus, *Orcades*, p. 177; *Diplomatarium Norvegicum*, vol. 55, no. 460, p. 358; translated extracts in Sinclair, *Caithness Events*, p. 157. A copy of the letter of Earl Henry issued September 1, 1379, is in the Norwegian Riksarkiv.

4. Hugh Marwick, *Orkney*, p. 87.

5. Rytger Hermannides (*R.H. Britannia Magna*) had a description of Kirkwall: "Church Bay has a good many buildings of brick and stone. There was a royal castle fortified with machines of war. The walls of this castle were so thick that the soldiers of the garrison had their barracks in them" (translated from the Latin by George E. McCracken of Des Moines, Iowa).

6. Evidence that there were broad sands appeared in the *Orkney Herald*, March 7, 1865. "The Earl of Caithness came with ordnance. The Cathedral tower and the Earl's [Bishop's] Palace were first besieged and captured. Robert Stewart, however, and several of his associates escaped across the broad sands to the Castle."

7. On the wall above the shop of W. T. Sinclair, General Draper, is this inscription: "Near this spot, facing Broad Street, stood in the year 1864 the last remaining fragments of the ruins of the Castle of Kirkwall. A royal fortress of great antiquity and originally of great strength, but of which, from the ravages of war and time, nearly every vestige had long previously disappeared. Its remains, consisting of a wall 55 feet long by 11 feet thick, and of irregular height, were removed by permission of the Earl of Zetland, on application of the trustees acting in execution of the Kirkwall Harbour Act, 1859, in order to improve the access to the harbour, and this stone was erected to mark the site. MDCCCLXVI." The stone bearing Earl Henry's Orkney coat-of-arms is set in the same wall.

8. J. S. Clouston, *A History of Orkney*, p. 236.

9. In his *Vindication*, given in *Harleian Miscellany*, vol. 1, p. 88, Machiavelli said of ecclesiastics: "These by their temporalities have almost a third part of all the land in Europe, given them by the blind zeal, or rather folly of the northern people. . . . They exempt themselves, their lands and goods, from all secular jurisdiction, from all courts of justice and magistracy, and will

be judges in their own causes. . . . If the ordinary justice, nay the sovereign power, do proceed against such offenders, they thunder out their ex-communications, cut off from the body of Christ not the prince only but the whole nation and people, shutting church doors and commanding divine offices to cease, and sometimes even authorizing the people to rise up in arms, and constrain their government to a submission."

10.   The opposition to grasping prelates led to an antipapal movement. Wycliffe's preaching expressed the ferment of the time. In a pamphlet "De Officio Regis" (1379), Wycliffe said: "All men are tenants-in-chief under God, and hold from him all that they are and possess; the Pope claims to be our mesne-lord, and to interfere between us and our divine suzerain, and therein he grievously errs." In the year of Henry's Investiture, Wycliffe had said that the State must act as guardian over the Church. The Church should be under the secular power in each country. In England, he would have a separate English Church. This meant the abolition of the papacy, and in 1382 Wycliffe said: "After Urban VI, no one ought to be received as Pope, but men should live, after the manner of the Greek Church, under their own laws." If anything in the continuous evolution of humanity can be pointed to as a beginning, Wycliffe's preaching was the origin of the Protestant Reformation. He planted the seeds of it. In England, Anne of Bohemia, King Richard's Queen, was sympathetic with Wycliffe, and she had his pamphlets carried to Bohemia where they gave rise to the Hussite Movement, which in turn inspired Martin Luther.

But how in the years 1378–1382 could the sermons of Wycliffe delivered in Oxford and London have any effect upon Earl Henry in his far-off castle of Roslin and during the building of his castle in Kirkwall? Did Scotsmen as well as Englishmen know what Wycliffe was saying? Most assuredly. The ideas of Wycliffe were brought to Scotland by no less a person than John of Gaunt, the great Duke of Lancaster, who had befriended Wycliffe, and had urged him to preach the stripping of lands from the Church. The duke, richer and more powerful than the king in England, had incurred jealousies, and had aroused political resentment. In November 1380, he took refuge in Edinburgh, where he was hospitably received and where he remained until July 1381. It is therefore more than probable that Henry Sinclair met and talked with John of Gaunt. If Henry was at Roslin during John of Gaunt's visit nearby, he almost certainly did talk with him. In any case, Henry's friends and relatives picked up the latest ideas from London from the distinguished Englishman in their midst. John of Gaunt remained in agreement with Wycliffe's preaching against prelates and clerical corruption, though he opposed Wycliffe's heresies. John of Gaunt advo-cated the expulsion of the clergy from all secular offices, and the destruction of their political power. This bore directly on Henry's fight against the Bishop of Orkney, and was a theme that Henry would have wished to discuss with the duke. Henry was unquestionably receptive to the view that outward observances without the inward grace of religion were hollow shows, mockeries, and hypocrisies. Furthermore, there is evidence in Henry's career that unlike most nobles he believed that a lord should be judged primarily by his real worth as a man. With no respect for churchmen merely because they were churchmen, it was only one step further to believe as Wycliffe did that reason and conscience are the guides of the self-directed soul. We cannot tell how completely Henry took that step, but it is clear that to some extent he was leavened by the new yeast.

11.   *Icelandic Annals*.

Chapter Six: FLEET

1.   Sir Walter Scott in *The Pirate*.

2.   The hardy folk of the Northern Isles feasted on "made-dishes." They had strubba—coagulated milk whipped to consistency of cream. Klokks was new milk simmered until clotted, and flavored with cinnamon and sugar. Kirn mill was a curd of buttermilk with mill-gruel. Blaund was whey of bleddik or buttermilk. Hungmill was cream hung in a bag, like cream cheese. Klabba was junket set thick by action of "yearmin" (rennet). Eusteen was hot milk reduced by sherry to curd and whey. Pramm was cold milk mixed with meal, a dish for a bairn or beggar. Eggaloorie was salt, eggs, and milk boiled. Da pukkle was oats, called "bursteen" when ground. Virpa was a brew made of corn husks. A very popular dish was knocket corn, cracked wheat or groats boiled with kail and pork. At Christmas they had Yule-brünies or rye cakes. Ploy-skonn was a short-bread. The dairy and vegetable products were enhanced with slott, fish roe beaten to cream, with flour and salt added, or with stapp, a mixture of fish heads with liver. Special palates were pleased with kiossed heeds, fish heads which had become gamey. At Christmas and at embarking on perilous voyages, they had whipkull, egg yolks with sugar beaten with cream and enforced with potent spirit. (*Orkney and Shetland Miscellany*, p. 70.)

3.   An old Orkney impression of the hum of a spinning wheel.

4.   It is a fair estimate that the building of a ship of the lightweight viking type, of average length, say sixty-five feet, required cutting down at least sixty oak trees. Yet the register of Norwegian battleships built from 995 to 1263 lists sixteen ships of one hundred and seventy or more feet in length. One of them, the *Kristsuden*, completed in 1263, had been two hundred feet in length. The king of Norway, that same year, in an attempt to restore Norwegian sovereignty in the islands west of Scotland, had conducted an expedition of one hundred and sixty ships. Considering the size and number of ships in the records of early Norwegian history, it is a wonder that the oak forests of Norway lasted as long as they did. Because of the exhaustion of available timber, Norwegian sea power declined. In 1382 King Olaf the Young ordered the building of one "ship for defence" which was to be thirty-six feet in length, and an old ship was to be burned to get out the metal rivets to be used in the new ship. The specifications required the completion of the new ship in three years. Contrasting this with the great days of Norwegian shipbuilding, when a ship of twice the size was

completed always in one season, we see the real situation to which Norway had been reduced. Ten years before King Olaf's feeble gesture, a treaty with the Hanseatic League had renewed to the Germans all the "freedom, rights, privileges and old usages that they had ever enjoyed." The Hanseatic merchants, with plenty of timber available in Germany, had established almost a monopoly of trade with English ports and had a practical stranglehold on Norwegian trade. They forbade competitive shipbuilding in Bergen. The building of ships required also the construction of sheds to cover the ships in winter. A ship that lay in water all winter would be "sodden and heavy-rowing" and would have to have her bottom scraped. Orkneymen advised Earl Henry along the lines which had been written in a thirteenth-century book of advice to Norse shipowners, the *King's Mirror*: "Tar your ship well in the autumn and let it stand so through the winter. If the ship comes so late under a roof that it may not be tarred in autumn, do it in early spring and let it dry well after. Seek to have your ship clear by summer, and fare out in the best of the summer season. Take heed that all is in good order on your ship. Never be long upon the sea in autumn by your own will. . . . Whenever you fare out to sea, have with you in the ship two or three hundred ells of frieze cloth such as is fit to mend the sails at need. And many needles and abundance of yard and reefbands. Though these be little things to talk of, yet it is often one shall need the like. Nails, also, you shall have good store of in the ship, and of that size that is convenient for the ship, both spikes and rivets, and all such tools as shipbuilding requires" (translated by Brögger in *The Viking Ships*).

5.   The size of Henry's Orkney fleet, thirteen ships, compares interestingly with the number of warships in the Orkneys and Shetlands together in viking times, when an arrangement existed by which a long ship was provided by every two parishes; that is, thirty-two parishes maintaining sixteen ships. Henry's fleet, to which he continued to add ships, is impressive in light of a naval agreement between the king and his Norwegian enemies in 1309 that attempted to put a stop to an armament race, the king and his enemy agreeing that neither of them should muster more than fifteen ships. Henry's fleet in 1390 gave him greater striking force at sea than was possessed by his liege lord, the king of Norway. But with it Henry continued to serve Norway. In his naval activities he established a family tradition, so that centuries later it was a descendant of his, Admiral Alexander Sinclair, who fired the first shot and the last in a North Sea battle called Jutland.

Chapter Seven :   POLITICS

1.   On the twenty-second of June, 1384, Earl Henry infefted his cousin James St. Clair, Baron of Longformacus, with a twenty markland (land area), the witnesses being Thomas Erskine of Dun, George Abernethy of Soulston, Walter Halyburton of that Ilk, and John Halyburton of Dirleton.

2.   *Diplomatarium Norvegicum*, vol. II, no. 515, p. 396.

3. Henry's cousin Malise Sparre had taken advantage of what might be called a power vacuum in the Shetlands and had seized lands there that had belonged to a lady named Herdis Thorvaldsdatter. He did this on a claim of a right to them, and so it was necessary for the case to be brought before King Olaf in council at Bergen. The lands were adjudicated to the proper heirs of Herdis. On October 8, 1386, at Bergen, John, canon of the Church of the Twelve Apostles, and the Lawman Arnulf, son of Funnar, declared that they had examined a charter by Ogmund, the son of Fin, Royal Steward of Norway, by which, in the king's name, is adjudicated to John and Sigurd Hafthorsson and their children the estates in Shetland that belonged to the deceased lady whose first name was Herdis. Malise Sparre refused to accept the decision of Olaf's court. He defied the king's authority. In 1387, soon after King Olaf died, Earl Henry persuaded Malise to sign a friendly agreement that was intended to put an end to their quarrel, and should have done so. The tone of it shows that Henry was disposed to conciliation. The so-called Amends of Malise Sparre, given in Sinclair, *Caithness Events*, p. 163, and also in Saint-Clair, *The Saint-Clairs of the Isles*, p. 511, read as follows:

> To all to whose knowledge the present letters shall have arrived, Malise Sper, Lord of Skuldale, salvation in the Savior of all! Let all men know that I have made, in the presence of a magnificent lord, James, Earl of Douglas, firm friendship with Henry Sinclair, Earl of Orkney and Baron of Roslin, and have condoned and remitted finally all actions of injuries and offences, by him, his men, or whomsoever in his name, to my men, lands, and possessions whatsoever, and as to his universal goods, acquired by him or his. Further, I firmly promise to restore, pay and satisfy, with my men whomsoever, concerning all injuries, offences and things acquired, as to the beforesaid Lord Earl, or whomsoever in his name, up to the present day, with lands and possessions excepted, if there are any to which my men have the right of claiming according to the laws of the country. In testimony of this transaction my seal was appended to the presents at Edinburgh, 18th of November 1387.

Earl Henry's negotiating of this settlement with Malise Sparre illustrates the aptness of the description of the Sinclair family by the Reverend J. B. Craven (*History of the Church in Orkney*): "the nobility, refinement, justice, and kindly manners of that family appear in all its traditional history."

Chapter Eight: THE RESCUED CAPTAIN

1. The man Earl Henry met on Fer Island always called the Lord of the Isles the "Prince," as did Antonio Zeno also. Since both narrators of the subsequent career of our Henry were themselves noblemen, it is safe to assume that they were correct in giving him that title.

2. Catherine Sinclair, *Shetland and the Shetlanders*, p. 101.

3. The conversations in this chapter are not fictional but are what must have been Earl Henry Sinclair's questions and Nicolò Zeno's answers, according to the letter Nicolò wrote, which forms part of the Zeno Narrative.

4. Sinclair, *Caithness Events*, p. 142.

Chapter Nine: THE WINNING OF SHETLAND

1. There may have been an easterly variation of the compass in 1390. There was such a variation in 1580 in Paris and London when the first records were made.

2. Ledovo was not Little Dimon Island, as the present writer in a previous study carelessly repeated from someone else's assertion. The cliff sides of Little Dimon are so precipitous that no one can land on it.

3. Sir Nicolò seems to have used "Frislanda" to mean two different things, or else he used two slightly different names that later were read as one. He used Frislanda to mean the small island upon which he had been shipwrecked. He used it also to mean the great fishing port in Shetland. Antonio Zeno later used, or was understood to have used, Frislanda for the entire Orkney earldom. Lucas, p. 115, says: "Luigi Bossi (*Vita de Cristoforo Colombo*) believed that the name Frislanda was a corruption of Fixlanda, which he held to have been a Teutonic word signifying 'the land of fish' or 'the land abounding in fish,' and that it was given originally not only to Iceland, but to the Orkneys, the Shetlands, the Faeroes, etc.— in short, that it signifies a maritime region rather than a single island." J. R. Forster, *History of the Voyages and Discoveries made in the North*, p. 262, said that Frislanda is Fair Isle, "the island of Faire or Fera which is also called Ferasland."

4. The main argument of Lucas against equating "Sinclair" with "Zichmni" was this: "Is it possible to believe that two Venetian nobles, educated, or at least able to write their own language, should have been holding high office, the one for four or five years, the other for fourteen years, under a man whose name, Sinclair, was not only of Latin origin but was frequently used in its Latin form, 'de Sancto Claro,' without being able to approach nearer to the true form than the fearful and wonderful bejugglement (as Fiske calls it), 'Zichmni'?" Lucas suggests that "the true name and proceedings of Zichmni more closely resemble those of the Vitalian pirate Wichmannus, than those of Sinclair. Lucas called the Zeno Narrative "a contemptible literary fraud—one of the most successful and obnoxious on record." He charged that it was motivated by Venetian jealousy of Genoa, which had given the world Columbus.

   In answer to Lucas we ask: Is it likely that the vertical curves of a capital "W" of Wichmannus would be or could be misread as a capital "Z"? Is it likely that two wealthy members of the Zeno family could have served a pirate for four to fourteen years without detection? In an age when nobles were intensely proud of rank and jealous of titles, can we believe that two Venetians of a noble family, living under a chieftain to whom they referred as "a prince" (*un Principe*), would have applied this high title to a pirate? Did they not say of the prince they served that "this man was a great lord" (*era costui gran Signore*)? Messire Nicolò was knighted by "Zichmni" and was thereafter "the Chevalier." Could anyone with a title less than that of a prince "make a belted knight"? The *Encyclopaedia Britannica* says: "It has been the general opinion, as expressed by Sainte Palaye and Mills, that formerly all knights were qualified to confer knighthood. But it may be questioned whether the privilege was thus indiscriminately enjoyed even in the earlier days of chivalry; the sounder conclusion appears to be that the right was always restricted to sovereign princes, to those acting under their authority or sanction, and to a few other personages of exalted rank and station."

Zichmni was active among the Orkneys ("in the direction of Scotland") and "to the northwards"—among the Shetlands. Lucas himself says that "Bres" in the Zeno Narrative is the island Bressay in the Shetlands. In the Orkney and Shetland islands at that time, who but the Prince of Orkney qualifies as a knight-maker? The Zeno Narrative indicates that the Prince "Zichmni" was a man of the Prince of Orkney's actual dimensions. The argument of Lucas that to accept Sinclair would be tantamount to accusing Sinclair of being a perjured rebel has no validity in the presence of the biographical facts. Sinclair's activities need no apology. Strongly corroborative of the authenticity of the Zeno letters is the admiration Sir Nicolò and Antonio Zeno expressed for their prince, and their ascribing to him, almost to the point of self-effacement, credit for valor and judgment, and the initiating of daring explorations.

5.   Andrea D. Capelli, *Lexicon Abbreviaturarum. Dizionario di abbreviature latine ed italiane, usate nelle arte e codici specialmente del medio-evo, riprodotto con oltre 14,000 segni incisi* . . . Milan, 1949.

6.   Pohl, "Prince 'Zichmni' of the Zeno Narrative," pp. 78–80.

7.   The witnesses to Henry's charter to his half-brother David were Lord Walter of Buchan, the Archbishop of Shetland, the Reverend Simon from Papa, the Reverend Thomas from Kirkness, the Reverend John Punkyn, the Reverend Michael from Westray, the Reverend Hakon; and the military men: Richard Sinclair, Thomas Leask, Alexander Clapham, Thomas Leith, and others." *Regesta Dip. Hist. Danicae*, April 23, 1391.

8.   Brøgger, *Ancient Emigrants*, p. 144.

9.   Saint-Clair, *The Saint-Clairs of the Isles*, p. 98.

10. *Ibid*, p. 98.

11. John R. Tudor, *The Orkneys and Shetland*, p. 58.

12. "They went out to attack Estlanda [Faeroe Islands?], which lies off the coast between Frislanda and Norway; there they did much damage, but hearing that the king of Norway was coming against them with a great fleet to draw them off from this attack, they departed under a terrible gale of wind, so that they were driven upon certain shoals, and a good many of

their ships were wrecked. The remainder took shelter in Grislanda [Gross-ey in Orkney?], a large island, but uninhabited. The king of Norway's fleet being caught in the same storm, was utterly wrecked and lost in those seas. When Earl Henry received tidings of this from one of the enemy's ships that was driven by chance upon Grislanda, he repaired the fleet, and perceiving that Islanda (Iceland) lay not far off to the northward, determined to make an attack upon Islanda, which together with the rest was subject to the king of Norway. Here, however, he found the country so well fortified and defended, that his fleet being but small and very ill-appointed, he was fain to give up that enterprise, but removed his attack to the other islands in those channels which are called Islande [Shetlands] which are seven in number: Talas, Broas, Iscant, Trans, Mimant, Bambere, and Bres; and having taken them all he built a fort in Bres, where he left Messire Nicolò, with some small vessels and men and stores. For himself, thinking that he had done enough for the present, he returned with those few ships that remained to him, in all safety to Frislanda."

13. George W. Longmuir, Librarian of Zetland County, correctly says no evidence has ever been uncovered of a fortification erected at Lerwick prior to the construction of Fort Charlotte there in 1665. There may have been such a previous fort, with all records of it lost. Thomas Sinclair in *The Sinclairs of England*, p. 194, says: "There is knowledge of Spere [Sparre] building a fort at Bressay before Lerwick had existence," but this may be merely an echo of the Zeno Narrative. I have searched the shore of the island of Bressay across the harbor from Lerwick, on the Guester farm and near the ferry landing, and a half mile south of it, but I did not find or hear of anything that might be the foundation of a fourteenth-century fort.

Chapter Ten: VOYAGES TO GREENLAND

1. A Catholic writer, Dr. Luka Jelić, says that a "complicated financial reckoning shows that about 10,000 persons paid Peter's pence in 1327 in Greenland. This statement gives an exaggerated idea of the size of the population of the Greenland Colonies, since only 6,912 Peter's pence, or their equivalent, were actually paid in 1327. And this payment may have covered two or more years."

2. The word "resolved" implies that the plan for Sir Nicolò's voyage to Greenland was independently conceived. Nevertheless, as Admiral of the Fleet, Sir Nicolò certainly reported his intention to Earl Henry. "Discovering" meant exploring of land known to exist but not known in intimate detail.

3. The Friars Preachers, Dominicans, formerly known as Black Friars, from the black cappa, or mantle, worn over their white habit, were assigned to eight provinces, one of them Dacia (Denmark and Scandinavia). These friars were very evangelical, and their province of England or that of Dacia carried its missions as far as the east coast of Greenland (*Catholic Encyclopedia*).

4. The map published with the Zeno Narrative was called a sea chart or
    sailing chart. It was intended to show the islands and lands mentioned in
    the Zeno letters. It was a fantastic mixture of fact and fiction, and in this
    respect it was no exception to all early sea charts. The only real help the
    Zeno Map could give a pilot was the information that there were islands
    north of Scotland, that Scandinavia lay to the east of those islands, Iceland
    to the north, Greenland to the north and west of Iceland, Estotiland far to
    the west, and Drogio southwest of Estotiland. Nicolò Junior, who copied
    and tried to improve the sea chart, thought he was creating a map that
    would illuminate the narrative. He expressed his motive in these words:
    "Of these northern parts I thought good to draw the copy of a sea chart
    which among other antiquities I have in my house, which although it be
    rotten through many years, yet it falleth out indifferent well, and to those
    who take delight in these things, it may serve for more light to the under-
    standing of that which without it cannot so easily be conceived." Sea charts
    were fun to a man who, while he did his exploring, kept his feet under a
    table at home, and Nicolò Junior wanted to share with his readers his
    "delight in these things." Since the chart made by his ancestor Antonio did
    not enable him to follow in all details the geography of the story told by the
    letters, he in all innocence borrowed from other sea charts, and made
    additions to it. He did not know that many elements in sea charts had been
    introduced to conceal ignorance. The maker of a chart that had large
    empty spaces would not gain a reputation for knowledge. Spaces had to be
    filled. The ocean must be dotted with islands. Nicolò Junior acquired a
    great reputation as a cartographer. In the sixteenth century his sea chart
    was valued more highly than the narrative. The original copy of his map
    was preserved, whereas the original worn and torn letters were not. Zurla
    tells us in 1808 that "the map is still possessed in the house of the editor
    Marcolino." More study was given to the map than to the narrative,
    because there were other maps with which to make comparisons. The text
    of the narrative was unique in its period, and no one knew how to evaluate
    it. Errors in the map were susceptible of demonstration as soon as geo-
    graphical explorations gave scholars sufficient information.

5. According to Sir Nicolò's report, the friars in Greenland heat the church
    of the monastery and their own living quarters by using a spring of boiling
    hot water, and they also use it in their kitchen to cook. They put bread into
    closed brass pots and it is baked as though it were in a hot oven. They have
    small gardens covered over in the winter to protect them from the snow
    and severe cold of a region "far under the pole." In these gardens they
    produce flowers and fruits and herbs in their seasons. The "rude and
    savage" natives there "seeing these supernatural effects, take those friars
    for gods." Their building material is supplied them by the fire; "for they
    take the burning stones that are cast out like cinders from the fiery mouth
    of the hill, and when they are at their hottest they throw water on them
    and dissolve them, so that they become an excellent white lime which is
    extremely tenacious, and when used in building never decays. These
    clinkers when cold are very serviceable in place of stones for making walls

and arches; for when once chilled they will never yield or break unless they be cut with some iron tool." The roofs of their houses are for the most part arched. When the first snow falls, "it does not thaw again for nine months, which is the duration of their winter. They live on wild fowl and fish; for, where the warm water falls into the sea, there is a large harbor, which, from the heat of the boiling water, never freezes, and the consequence is, that there is such an attraction for sea-fowl and fish that they are caught in unlimited quantity, and prove the support of a large population in the neighborhood." On every side of the hill which vomits fire, the natives live in round houses "about twenty-five feet broad, narrowing toward the top, having at the summit a little hole for air and light. The ground below is so warm that those within feel no cold. Hither in summer come many vessels from the islands thereabouts, and from the Cape above Norway, and from Trondjheim, and bring the friars all sorts of comforts, taking in exchange fish, either dried or frozen, and skins of various kinds of animals. By this means they obtain wood for burning, and admirable carved timber, and corn [wheat], and cloth for clothes. To this monastery come friars of Norway, of Sweden and of other countries, but the most part are of Islande [Iceland]. There are continually in the harbor many barks, which are kept there by reason of the sea being frozen, waiting for the spring of the year to dissolve the ice.

"The native fishermen's boats are made like unto a weaver's shuttle. Taking the skins of fishes [walrus hides], they fashion them with bones [bone needles] of the self-same fish, and sewing them together and doubling them over, they make them so sure and substantial that it is wonderful to see how, in bad weather, they will shut themselves close inside and expose themselves to the sea and wind without the slightest fear of coming to mischief. If they happen to be driven on any rocks, they can stand a good many bumps without receiving any injury. In the bottom of the boats they have a kind of sleeve, which is tied fast in the middle, and when any water comes into the boat, they put it into one half of the sleeve, then closing it above with two pieces of wood and opening the band underneath, they drive the water out of the boat; and this they do as often as they have occasion.

"The water of the monastery being sulphurous, it is conveyed into the apartments of the principal friars in vessels of brass, or tin, or stone, so hot it heats the place like a stove, and without carrying with it any stench or offensive odor whatsoever. They also convey hot water by a conduit under the ground, so that it should not freeze. It is then conveyed into the middle of the court, where it falls into a large vessel of brass that stands in the middle of a boiling fountain. This is to heat their water for drinking and for watering their gardens.

"These good friars do not lack for ingenious and painstaking workmen; for they are very liberal in their payments, and in their gifts to those who bring them fruits and seeds they are unlimited in their generosity. The consequence is that workmen and masters in various handicrafts resort there in plenty.

"Most of them speak the Latin language, and especially the superiors

H

and principals of the monastery." At this point the account of what Sir Nicolò had seen in Greenland breaks off.

6. W. H. Hobbs, "Zeno and the Cartography of Greenland," pp. 15–19. Hobbs speaks of the geological and archaeological description of the east coast of Greenland between 70° and 75° north, given by Koch, Johnson, and Larsen. These writers tell of many sites of previous Eskimo habitation and of a series of ancient volcanoes. There was a large volcano in Sofia Sound. There are hot springs on either side of the entrance to Scoresby Sound a little north of 70° N. The temperatures of the hot springs are very variable. One at Cape Tobin, on the north side of the entrance to Scoresby Sound, has the highest temperature, 62°C (140°F). There are extensive volcanic ash beds in various places. The precise location of the monastery Sir Nicolò visited has probably not been ascertained, but the geology and archaeology appear to leave no room for doubt as to its onetime existence.

7. Of the biography ("life and exploits") of the prince that Antonio had written, and that Nicolò Junior had destroyed, Antonio wrote: "In it I have described the exploration of Greenland on both sides." These words were on the piece of a letter to which Nicolò Junior refers in the following: "What happened subsequently to the contents of this letter [in which Antonio described the transatlantic expedition] I know not, beyond what I gather from conjecture from a piece of another letter, which is to the effect: That Zichmni settled down in the harbor of his newly discovered island and explored the whole of the country with great diligence, as well as the coasts of both sides of Greenland, because I find this particularly delineated in the sea charts [plural]; but the description is lost."

The Zeno Map shows that whoever drew the map of Greenland was following a compass in a region where there were, as now, very large variations of the compass. The compass points not to the true north but to the magnetic pole. From Greenland, the magnetic needle points considerably to the west of true north. The Zeno Map gives a close-to-accurate outline of Greenland, but one that is turned clockwise. This clockwise shift is more pronounced on the western coast, as mapped, than on the eastern coast, as mapped, and is progressively greater in higher latitudes. Columbus in the course of his voyage in 1492 was the first to observe the fact that the compass varies from the true north. The fact that the discovery of the variation of the compass came in the time of Columbus is persuasive evidence that the Zeno Chart's mapping of Greenland was done before the variation of the compass was known. It is the effective argument of Hobbs that the clockwise shift of Enroneland and Estotiland on the Zeno Chart indicates its pre-Columbian origin.

8. Erik W. Dahlgren, *Map of the World 1542*, with explanations by Dahlgren, Stockholm, 1892.

9. D. Placido Zurla, *Dissertazione intorno ai viaggi e scoperte settentrionali di Nicolo ed Antonio Fratelli Zeni.*

10. Lucas, *Annals of the Voyages of the Brothers Zeno*, p. 59, says there were three persons of name Nicolò Zeno in Venice in 1379.

Chapter Eleven: FISHERMAN'S TALE

1. "Many interpreters." The banks of Newfoundland apparently attracted fishermen from various countries before Columbus, and indeed before the days of Sinclair. Along the shores of Newfoundland the fishermen dried their fish and their nets, and picked up words of each others' speech. The native Indians along those shores became polylingual; that is, they could talk "pidgin" in several tongues. Records from the early sixteenth century picture Newfoundland as a land where "the Indians understood any language, French, English, Gascon, and their own tongue."—Robert Lefant of Bayonne, quoted by Bernard G. Hoffman in *Cabot to Cartier*, p. 146. In and around Newfoundland, Cartier picked up words "derived from various seafaring groups (that is, Old French, Breton and Norman, West Coast, Provençaux, Catalan, and Italian)" (Hoffman, p. 151).

2. The fisherman's report of Latin books in Newfoundland indicates that Christian priests had formerly labored in that island.

3. The "gold" was probably pyrites.

4. The Indians of Newfoundland and of Nova Scotia knew of each others' existence, and there was undoubtedly some trade between them. Trade between Newfoundland and Greenland may have been a link in the exchange of some goods from both sides of the Atlantic. The furs (*pellerecie*) probably included buffalo hides from the North American continent, some of which are said to have been sold in Florence a century before Columbus. The sulphur was used for tanning hides, as well as for other purposes. The "pitch" (*pegola*—liquid tar) may have been resin from conifers in Newfoundland, and would have been used in treeless Greenland for caulking ships.

5. The fisherman said his life had been spared by the natives along the coast of the great country southwest of Estotiland, because he had been able to teach them how to fish with nets. Was there any way of finding out whether American Indians began to use nets in the fourteenth century along that seacoast? This question was in my mind when I attended a meeting of the Eastern States Archaeological Federation held in Rochester in November 1953, where a paper was read by Dr. William S. Fowler, Curator of the Bronson Museum of the Massachusetts Archaeological Society. Dr. Fowler described Indian sites he had uncovered in New England, and among the objects he had found were stone sinkers of the size used with a hook and line, and also a larger side-notched stone used for a net sinker. I asked Dr. Fowler whether the strata at which he had found the line sinkers and the net sinker indicated any difference in the times when they were used. "Yes, indeed," he replied. "Line sinkers are found all the way up from the lowest strata, while the net sinkers first appear much later." Here was a possibility that archaeology might shake hands with history. I told Dr. Fowler the tale of the Orkney fisherman. On April 8, 1954, Dr. Fowler wrote me: "You will be pleased to hear that our net sinker evidence at Green Pt. site proved to be of such a kind as to make it possible for me to link it with your

Zeno narrative within a fairly close tolerance." His study of net sinkers was published in July 1954 in the *Bulletin* of the Massachusetts Archaeological Society, pp. 78, 80. It is important enough to quote at some length: "It has been customary in the past to assign the introduction of net fishing to the Ceramic-Agricultural Age. However, the appearance of a net sinker in refuse pit No. 18 with shell content leads to interesting speculations. As good luck would have it, this pit lay near the wood in the strip of land first excavated at a spot where former plowing had cut to a depth of only 5″. Consequently, the pit's level of origin could be traced as high as 4″ above junction in humus leaving 5″ above of disturbed humus. However, since its top had been sheared off by the plow, it seems only fair that an estimated $2\frac{1}{2}$″ might be added to compensate for the destroyed area. This would make the restored level of origin $6\frac{1}{2}$″ above junction, leaving $2\frac{1}{2}$″ of humus above. Now since the total depth of humus is 8″ which represents a span of 2,200 years, approximately, then elapsed time as represented by the $2\frac{1}{2}$″ distance from pit's level of origin to the top of the ground would equal $2\frac{5}{8}$ of 2,200 or 611 years. Deducting this from today's date of 1954 gives a date of 1343 A.D. for the origin of the pit, of the net sinker, and presumably of net fishing. However, since this is subject to error, add or subtract 50 years, whichever lends itself best to any given situation. While this result is somewhat speculative, it seems to have enough validity to link native net-fishing to the authenticated historical account."

Explorers after Columbus found the Micmac Indians of Nova Scotia using nets up to fifty yards in length, made of intertwined branches of birch, elder, or other trees and bushes. Dr. Fowler believes Indian nets in New England, like fishlines there, were made of native hemp.

The fisherman said that the great land beyond Estotiland to the southwest had been named by the people he met in Estotiland. It was "a country which they call Drogio." Since the Zeno Narrative implies that the people in Newfoundland whom the Sinclair Expedition met were Celtic (Irish or Scottish), we have a hint as to the possible meaning of the name given to the continent of North America in the fourteenth century. "Drogio" may have come from the Celtic word *droighionn* meaning thorn or bramble. Since vines of the Vinland of the vikings were probably the thorny *Smilax rotundifolia*, we may here have an Italianization of the Celtic equivalent to "Vineland." A second possibility is that the Celtic *droch* (evil) was the basis for Drogio, which would mean Land of Evil (cannibals?). But Drogio may be derived from the Gaelic *drogha*, with the last two letters misread by young Nicolò. The context suggests support for this interpretation; for drogha was a hand line for fishing, and Drogio most likely may have been a fisherman's name for a coastal country where hook and line were used for fishing, and no nets. We are told in the second sentence following the first use of the name, almost as though it were a reason for the name, that Drogio was a land where the lives of the fishermen were saved because they taught the natives how to take fish with nets. A tribe of the Algonkins, the Ottawas, venerated a great spirit, Nanabozho, for his having invented nets. The source of the Nanabozho legend could have been the Orkney fisherman, for the evidence is strong that nets were not an invention of an American Indian, but that American Indians and Eskimos became expert net weavers, using many of the techniques of fishermen of the Old World.

Chapter Twelve: "NEW WORLD"

1. In Norse records, 1347 is the date of the last sailing of a ship from Greenland to the southwest to "Markland" (Forestland), which was Nova Scotia.

2. When Antonio Zeno, using a compass, said he sailed "westwards," he may have been sailing in any direction between northwest and southwest.

3. "Ten languages." In the very next sentence of the Zeno Narrative, one of the inhabitants of Estotiland said the island was called "Icaria." This meant there were Irishmen there. Tradition says the Basques and the Portuguese fished on the banks of Newfoundland before Columbus. If we add Irish, Basque, and Portuguese to the languages named in Note 1 of Chapter Eleven, we have twelve or more languages that may have been spoken in Newfoundland when the Orkney Expedition visited it. They are in alphabetical order as follows: Basque, Beotuck (native Indian), Breton, Catalan, English, French (Old French), Gascon, Irish (Gaelic, "West Coast"), Italian, Norse (Icelandic), Portuguese, and Provençaux.

4. Lucas, *Annals of the Voyages of the Brothers Zeno*, p. 69, says: "Neome probably represents Fair Isle." However, logic, in keeping with the Zeno Narrative, would have it as one of the northern of the Shetlands, about three days' sail from Fair Isle (Fer Island).

Chapter Thirteen: SMOKING HOLE AND SPRING OF PITCH

1. G. S. Hume, "Oil and Gas in Eastern Canada," p. 137.

2. *New Glasgow Evening News*, August 1, 1950.

3. George Patterson, *A History of the County of Pictou, Nova Scotia*, pp. 407–409.

4. Henry S. Poole, "Report on the Pictou Coal Field, Nova Scotia," p. 35.

5. *Ibid*, p. 23.

6. John William Dawson, *Acadian Geology*, p. 339.

7. Poole, "Report on the Pictou Coal Field, Nova Scotia," p. 38.

8. Abraham Gesner, *Remarks on the Geology and Mineralogy of Nova Scotia*, p. 136.

9. Clara Dennis, *More about Nova Scotia*, p. 177.

10. There are various theories as to the meaning of the Micmac Indian name "Pictou." A likely derivation was suggested by the Reverend Canon Andrews: PIK (PEK, BIK, or BEG) as meaning "bay," with IKTOOK added to signify "landlocked," so that PIK-IKTOOK by natural elision came to be PIK (ik) TOO or Pictou, meaning "Shut-in Bay." The

missionary to the Micmacs, Silas Tertius Rand, says in *Micmac Place Names* that the word "Pict" means an explosion of gas, as from the bowels, and he supposes the name Pictou to have originated from the sound of gas at the East River being expelled in spurts from the bowels of the earth.

11.   Poole, "Report on the Pictou Coal Field, Nova Scotia," p. 34.

12.   The Micmacs inhabited five districts in Nova Scotia: (1) Cape Breton, (2) Pictou, (3) the south shore between Canso and Halifax, (4) Shubenacadie, and (5) Annapolis to Yarmouth. Their total population has been estimated at about four thousand.

13.   The viking explorer Thorfinn Karlsefni in the early eleventh century found natives on the south shore of "Markland" (Nova Scotia) living in holes in the ground. An official report on caves in Nova Scotia tells us of a gypsum cave near South Maitland, that was "once over twenty feet high. The archaeological value has been much reduced by the enormous quantity of rock continually falling. In its original condition it was doubtless an ideal place for shelter, and was probably so used by the aborigines" (W. H. Prest, *Report of Cave Examinations*, pp. 87–94).

14.   Patterson, *A History of the County of Pictou, Nova Scotia*, pp. 417, 418.

15.   Letter to author from the Reverend Canon A. E. Andrews of Windsor, Nova Scotia.

16.   The only harbor on the south side of Cape Canso that could qualify as even a good one is the small Cole Harbor inside Tor Bay. If the men in rowboats had first pulled ashore in Tor Bay, they would at once have climbed to high ground, the more urgently because Tor Bay is hemmed in closely by hills. The highest of these hills, out of sight from Tor Bay but invitingly near to anyone who climbed from Tor Bay, is Salmon Hill. From Salmon Hill the men could not have failed to look down into Guysborough Harbor near to them, and observe its superior advantages, and also the fact that they were on a cape. Immediately upon receiving their enthusiastic report, Earl Henry would have taken his ships around the cape and to Guysborough Harbor.

17.   N. Denys, *Description and Natural History of the Coasts of North America*, p. 167.

18.   *Ibid*, p. 168.

19.   *Ibid*, p. 166.

Chapter Fourteen :   THE BEGINNING OF A LEGEND

1.   Abby Langdon Alger, *In Indian Tents*, p. 13.

2.   C. G. Leland and J. D. Prince, *Kulóscap the Master*, Preface, p. 16.

3.   Bailey, "The Conflict of European and Eastern Algonkian Cultures," p. 176.

4.   Jeremiah Clark, *Rand and the Micmacs*, p. 45.

5. Silas Tertius Rand, *Legends of the Micmacs*, p. 232.

6. *Ibid*, p. 14.

7. Will R. Bird, "The Micmacs of Canada," p. 6. Leland and Prince, *Kulóscap the Master*, p. 123.

8. Rand, *Legends of the Micmacs*, p. 14.

9. *Ibid*.

10. *Ibid*. Leland and Prince, *Kulóscap the Master*, p. 123.

11. Rand, *Legends of the Micmacs*, p. 14.

12. *Ibid*. Nisbet gives the names of Henry's three daughters as Elizabeth, married to Sir John Drummond, brother of Queen Annabella; Helen, married to John Stewart, Earl of Atholl; and Beatrix, married to John Douglas, Lord Aberdeen. In *The Sinclair Expedition to Nova Scotia in 1398*, I quoted a genealogist who said Henry Sinclair had nine daughters, but later study revealed that Henry and his eldest son Henry, the second Sinclair Earl of Orkney, had by that genealogist been dealt with as one person. I reluctantly relinquished six daughters who were our Henry's grand-daughters, and I did this before the idea first came to me that Henry Sinclair equates with the Micmac's legendary prince.

13. Leland, *The Mythology, Legends, and Folk-Lore of the Algonkins*, pp. 78, 80.

14. Rand, *Legends of the Micmacs*, pp. 228, 229.

15. *Ibid*, p. 24.

16. *Ibid*, p. 75.

17. *Ibid*, p. 14.

18. *Ibid*, p. 73.

19. Alger, *In Indian Tents*, p. 112.

20. Rand, *A Short Statement of Facts*, p. 28.

21. Bird, "The Micmacs of Canada," p. 6.

22. Rand, *A Short Statement of Facts*, p. 28.

23. Since there seemed to be some question as to whether W. D. Wallis and R. S. Wallis had equated "Glooscap" with "Jesus Christ, or the Thunder Christ," on page 392 of their book on the Micmac Indians, I wrote to these authors and received the categorical reply: "We had no intention in the book on the Micmacs to equate Glooscap with Jesus Christ."

24. Geoffrey Ashe, *Land to the West*, p. 234.

25. *Ibid*, pp. 236, 237.

26. Another reference to a smoking hill in Micmac legend is given by Alger, *In Indian Tents*, p. 51: "Seeing a smoke come from the top of a mountain, the children asked the elders what it was, or who could live there." Indians, of course, never lived at the top of a mountain in Nova Scotia, and so the question asked by the "children" reflects the white men's questioning.

27.   Leland and Prince, *Kulóscap the Master*, p. 34.

28.   *Ibid.*

29.   Daniel Garrison Brinton, *The Chief God of the Algonkins*, p. 139.

30.   Leland and Prince, *Kulóscap the Master*, p. 269.

31.   *Ibid*, p. 270.

32.   Rand, *A Dictionary of the Micmac Language.*

33.   Leland and Prince, *Kulóscap the Master*, p. 63.

34.   Harry Piers, "Brief Account of the Micmac Indians," pp. 109, 110.

35.   *Bureau of American Ethnology: 20th Annual Report, 1902–3*, pp. 49, 50.

36.   Rand, *Legends of the Micmacs*, p. 291.

37.   *Ibid*, p. 292.

38.   *Ibid*, p. 291.

39.   Bird, "The Micmacs of Canada," p. 6.

40.   Rand, *Legends of the Micmacs*, p. 236.

41.   Leland and Prince, *Kulóscap the Master*, p. 125.

42.   Rand, *Legends of the Micmacs*, p. 291.

43.   *Ibid*, p. 292.

44.   *Ibid.*

45.   Leland and Prince, *Kulóscap the Master*, pp. 269, 270.

46.   Rand, *Legends of the Micmacs*, p. 292.

47.   *Ibid*, p. 14.

48.   *Ibid*, pp. 228, 229, 292. On the eastern side of the Cape D'Or promontory there are a greater number of habitation sites, but these are of the nineteenth century, associated with the coppermining operations to the north of Horseshoe Cove. I could eliminate these with certainty since I knew their origin and location from a one-time resident of one of the houses, Mrs. Walter E. Wheaton of Parrsboro. When the mining operations ceased, all the houses were moved down to Horseshoe Cove and transported by barge across Minas Basin to the Valley near Grand Pré.

49.   Rand, *Legends of the Micmacs*, pp. 24, 25. Leland and Prince, *Kulóscap the Master*, p. 215.

50.   Bird, "The Micmacs of Canada," p. 6.

51.   Rand, *Legends of the Micmacs*, p. 228.

52.   *Ibid*, p. 228.

53.   Clark, *Rand and the Micmacs*, p. 45.

54.   F. G. Speck, *Some Micmac Tales*, p. 149.

55. Paraphrased into direct discourse from Bailey, "The Conflict of European and Eastern Algonkian Cultures," p. 188.

56. Paraphrased from Bailey, "The Conflict of European and Eastern Algonkian Cultures," pp. 187, 188.

57. Leland and Prince, *Kulóscap the Master*, p. 214.

Chapter Fifteen: A BROKEN SWORD

1. Leland and Prince, *Kulóscap the Master*, p. 17.

2. E. R. Hodgman, *History of the Town of Westford*, p. 237.

3. William B. Goodwin, *The Ruins of Great Ireland in New England*, p. 54.

4. Iain Moncrieffe, *The Highland Clans*, pp. 160, 161.

5. *Ibid*, pp. 167, 168.

6. *Ibid*, p. 161.

7. Rand, *Legends of the Micmacs*, pp. 232, 234, 235, 255–257.

8. Thomas Sinclair, *Caithness Events*, pp. 138, 139.

Chapter Sixteen: BURIED IN ARMOR

1. John Trussell, *A continuation of the collection of the history of England by Samuel Daniel*, p. 69, gives under the year 1401 an attack by the English on the Orkneys, which presumably occurred in 1400.

2. Hay, *Genealogie*, p. 18.

3. John Ruskin, *The Stones of Venice*, vol. 1, Chapter 1, p. 18.

4. George Barry, *The History of the Orkney Islands*, Appendix, pp. 381–89.

5. The Lord Lyon, King-at-Arms, H.M. Register House, Edinburgh, on the eighteenth of March wrote me in regard to the monument in St. Magnus Cathedral: "I would not relate it to the Countess of Angus." It is interesting that Henry's niece had resigned the Earldom of Angus to her son George de Douglas in 1389. A monument that bears record, not to her childhood marriage to the Earl of Angus, whose death had left her a childless widow at fifteen, but to her undying love for Sir William, Earl of Douglas, would have seemed to Henry and to her to be an appropriate memorial for her son George de Douglas. However, George survived Henry.

6. Burke, *Vicissitudes of Families*. The Reverend J. B. Craven, *History of the Church in Orkney*, p. 98, says: "We have many families of ancient descent in Scotland, but it may be questioned if any of these families has produced such a roll of eminent men as that of St. Clair. . . . Although the actual possession of the Earldom of Orkney by the noble family of St. Clair lasted for less than one hundred years, the time of their rule appears to have been

the most successful and prosperous in the history of the northern diocese. The nobility, refinement, justice, and kindly manners of that family appear in all its traditional history."

7. Hay, *Genealogie*, p. 24.

8. *Ibid*, p. 23.

9. *Ibid*, pp. 20–24.

10. Scott, *The Lay of the Last Minstrel*, Canto VI, xxiii, lines 33–44.

11. Hay, *Genealogie*, pp. 79–82. Clouston, *History of Orkney*, p. 259.

12. "It was not from the Sinclairs, so far as all the extant evidence goes, that Orkney suffered during the whole period of their rule, but from other governors who for one reason or another filled their place at times, or from outside foes" (Clouston, *A History of Orkney*, p. 240).

13. Hossack, *Kirkwall in the Orkneys*, p. 25.

14. "Demolition of the Ruins of Kirkwall Castle," *Orkney Herald*, March 7, 1865.

15. Jackson, *Historical Tales of Roslin Castle*, discusses the legend of concealed manuscripts and quotes in that connection from Sir Walter Scott:

> *From the inner edge of the outer door,*
> *At thirty feet of old Scotch measure,*
> *The passage there, that's made secure,*
> *Leads to the holy Roslin treasure.*

Chapter Seventeen: A PARCEL OF OLD LETTERS

1. The original title of the Zeno Narrative is: *Delle scopromente del l'isole Frislanda, Eslanda, Engronelanda, Estotilanda & Icaria, fatto sotto il polo artico, da due fratelli Zeni, Messire Nicolo il Chevaliere e Messire Antonio. Con un disegno particolare di tutte le dette parte di Tramontana da lor scoperte.* The Italian text and an English translation by Richard Henry Major are in the Hakluyt Society Works.

2. The "Book": Antonio's biography of Prince Henry.

3. Lucas, *Annals of the Voyages of the Brothers Zeno*, p. 62.

4. See the illustration of numerous points of comparison between Estotiland on the Zeno Map and Newfoundland on a modern map, in Chapter 10.

5. Zurla, *Dissertazione*, p. 46, asserts that Antonio Zeno could not have begun his voyage to join Nicolò in the North Sea until about 1391.

6. "The honesty of the Zeno narrative has been sufficiently well established, but whether or not the fisherman had the experiences he narrated on Drogio, and whether that may be identified with North America, are

questions that have been much debated." *Encyclopedia Americana*, 1951 edition.

7. Hobbs, "The Fourteenth-Century Discovery of America by Antonio Zeno," pp. 24–31; Pohl, *The Lost Discovery*, pp. 210 *passim*; *The Sinclair Expedition to Nova Scotia in 1398*, pp. 27–30; *Atlantic Crossings Before Columbus*, pp. 248 *passim*.

Acknowledgments

MANY PERSONS assisted me in the research that has brought to light numerous facts that give this biography the status of a new page in history. I am deeply indebted to attendants in the New York Public Library, the Library of Congress, the Library of the British Museum, the New Brunswick Museum, and libraries in various countries. I am particularly grateful to the following: Gerard Alexander, Map Division of the New York Public Library; Dr. C. Bruce Fergusson, Provincial Archivist, Archives of Nova Scotia; Mrs. Phyllis Blakeley and D. C. Harvey, also of the Archives of Nova Scotia; George McLaren, Director, Provincial Museum, Halifax; Dr. Walter Bell, Director, Geological Survey of Canada; Allan M. Fraser, Provincial Archivist and Curator of the Newfoundland Museum; Arthur Fox, Newfoundland Museum; Professor Eugene Gattinger and Dr. V. S. Papezik, Memorial University, St. John's, Newfoundland; Charles T. McInnes, Curator of Historical Records, H.M. Register House, Edinburgh; R. B. K. Stevenson, Museum of Antiquities, Edinburgh; Miss Jean T. Wilson, Library in Crieff; F. W. Robertson and John Glass in Wick; Evan MacGillivray, the County Library, Kirkwall; Dr. George W. Longmuir at the Library of Shetland, Lerwick; Professor Johannes Bøe in Bergen; Dr. Therkel Mathiassen in Copenhagen; Arne Kildal, Department of Education of Norway, Oslo; Professor Holger Arbman, Museum of Lund University; Wilhelm K. Størin in Trondheim; Miss Franca Maria Tiepolo and Dr. Terisio Pignatti, the Correr Museum, Venice.

I name also those who labored and gave invaluable information during archaeological investigations and out-of-door research: Philip Morris, Lighthouse Keeper at Cape D'Or; and with him, Merton Morris, and Weldon Morris; Edward V. McMichael, archaeologist; Dr. Harold W. Borns, Jr., geologist at the University of Maine; Leonard W. Curtis, Jr., and Forrest W. Meader, also from the University of Maine; Arthus C. Ellis; Holiday Phillips of Coatesville, Indiana; Roland Barkhouse of East Advocate, N.S.; Edgar Dunbar, who took me in a motorboat to Spencer's Island at the slack of the tide, and Ratchford Merriam who loaned the motorboat; Gerard Brymer of Guysborough; Mr. and Mrs. Walter E. Wheaton of Parrsboro, N.S.; Chesley L. Allen of Port Greville, N.S.; Eli Janes of Advocate Harbour, N.S.; Mr. and Mrs. Karl G. Parchert of Dearborn, Michigan; Donnell B. Young of North Hanover, Massachusetts.

I owe much to the stimulus of conversations and correspondence with the following: Professor William Anderson, Lund University; Reverend Canon A. E. Andrew, Windsor, N.S.; Dr. W. A. Bell, New Glasgow, N.S.; Professor Jacques V. Borday, Columbia University; Captain Bob Bartlett, of Newfoundland; his nephew, Rupert Bartlett, St. John's, Newfoundland; Professor H. L. Cameron, Acadia University; Tertius Chandler of Berkeley, California; F. M. Cox, Town Manager, Port-aux-Basques, Newfoundland; Miss Mona Cram, Gosling Library, St. John's; Docent Stan Florin, Uppsala; Dr. William S. Fowler, Bronson Museum, Attleboro, Massachusetts; Frank Glynn, Clinton, Connecticut; Arthur Godfrey and his son David, of Pictou, N.S.; Dr. William H. Hobbs, geologist of the University of Michigan; Pall Jacobsen, Oravik, Suduroy, Faeroe Islands; R. F. J. Knutson of Rockville Center, New York; Gunnar Lestikow, representative of *Verdens Gang*, Oslo; Thomas C. Lethbridge, Seaton, Devon; Dr. W. F. Luder, Waltham, Massachusetts; H. P. B. Lund, A. S. Kvaerner Brug, Oslo; Charles W. K. McCurdy, Baddeck, Cape Breton; Dr. T. M. Y. Manson, the *Shetland News*, Lerwick; D. J. Marr, British Vice-Consul,

Thorshavn, Faeroe Islands; Count Marozzo della Rocca, Director of Archives, Venice; Dr. Hugh Marwick, Kirkwall; Dr. George E. McCracken, Drake University, Des Moines; Asger Møller, Tveraa, Faeroe Islands; R. J. Mombourquette, Photogrammetry and Geology Division, Nova Scotia Research Foundation, Halifax; Captain Steve Moodie, Shetlander born; Albert S. Polk, Jr., Johns Hopkins University; Miss Narcie Pollitt, St. Petersburg, Florida; Thomas Raddall, Liverpool, N.S.; Dr. Gad Rausing, Lund, Sweden; Herman L. Reid, West Advocate, N.S.; Mrs. Fred Scott, St. John's, Newfoundland; Dr. Haakon Shetelig, Professor of Archaeology, University of Bergen; Dr. H. D. Smith, President, Nova Scotia Research Foundation, Halifax; William L. Smyth, Winsted, Connecticut; Dr. Vilhjalmur Stefansson; Cecil Strong, Advocate Harbour, N.S.; J. R. H. Sutherland, Publisher-Editor, *Evening News*, New Glasgow, N.S.; Dr. Leif J. Wilhelmsen, University of Bergen; Count Alessandro Zeno, Venice; Dr. Georgio Dalla Zorga, Venice.

Encouragement came constantly from my wife Josephine, to whom I dedicate this book.

Bibliography

Abraham, Herbert. *Asphalts and Allied Substances, Their Occurrence, Modes of Production, Uses in the Arts and Methods of Testing.* 2 vols. New York: D. Van Nostrand & Co., 1938.

Alger, Abby Langdon. *In Indian Tents: Stories told by Penobscots, Passamaquoddy and Micmac Indians to Abby L. Alger.* Boston: Roberts Brothers, 1897.

Allström, Carl Magnus. *Dictionary of Royal Lineage.* Chicago: S. T. Almberg, 1902.

Anderson, James. *Royal Genealogies.* London: the author, 1736.

Anderson, John. *Historical and Genealogical Memoirs of the House of Hamilton.* Edinburgh: John Anderson, Jr., 1825.

Ashe, Geoffrey. *Land to the West.* London: Collins, 1962.

Bailey, Alfred Goldsworthy. "The Conflict of European and Eastern Algonkian Cultures." Monographic Series 2, St. John, New Brunswick: New Brunswick Museum, 1937.

Barry, George. *The History of the Orkney Islands*. Kirkwall, Scotland: W. Peace, 1867.

Beauvois, Eugène. "Les Colonies Européenes du Markland et de l'Escociland—Domination Canadienne au XIVᵉ siècle, et les vestiges qui en subsistèrent jusqu'aux XVIᵉ et XVIIᵉ siècles," *Extrait du Compte-rendu des travaux du Congrès international des Americanistes*. Luxembourg, 1877.

——— *Les Voyages Transatlantiques des Zeno*. Louvain, Belgium: J. B. Istas, 1890.

——— "Le Véracité des Zeno et l'authenticité de leur carte," *International Geographical Congress, 4th Meeting, 1884*, tome 1. Paris, 1890.

Bird, Will R. "The Micmacs of Canada" in *Pictou Advocate* (Nova Scotia), July 29, 1927.

Brinton, Daniel Garrison. "The Chief God of the Algonkins, in His Character as a Cheat and Liar." *The American Antiquarian*, May 1885.

Brögger, Anton Wilhelm. *Ancient Emigrants: A History of the Norse Settlements of Scotland*. Oxford: Clarendon Press, 1922.

Brögger, A. W., and Shetelig, Haakon. *The Viking Ships*. Oslo: Dreyers Forlag, 1951.

Buchanan, William. *An Inquiry into the Genealogy and Present State of Ancient Scottish Surnames*. Glasgow: J. Wylie & Co., 1820.

Burke, Sir John Bernard. *A Genealogical and Heraldic History of the Landed Gentry of Great Britain* (Roslin Sinclairs), 3 supplements, 4. London: Burke's Peerage Ltd., 1939.

——— *Vicissitudes of Families and Other Essays*, vol. 1. London: Longmans, Green, Reader, and Dyer, 1859.

Calder, James T. *Sketch of the Civil and Traditional History of Caithness from the Tenth Century*. Second edition, with historical notes by Thomas Sinclair. Wick, Scotland: William Rae, 1887.

Calendar of Charters, vol. 1 (1142–1406); vol. 2 (1406–1460).

Calendar of Documents, Scotland, vol. 4 (1357–1509).

Cartier, Jacques. *The Voyages of Jacques Cartier*. Publication of the Canadian Archives, no. 11. Toronto: F. A. Acland, 1934.

Champlain, Samuel de. *The Works of Samuel de Champlain in six volumes, reprinted, translated, and annotated by six Canadian scholars*, vol. 1. Translated and edited by Hugh H. Langton and William Francis Ganong. Toronto: The Champlain Society, 1922–1936.

Clark, Jeremiah. *Rand and the Micmacs* (A biography of Silas Tertius Rand). Charlottetown, Prince Edward Island: Examiners Office, 1899.

Clouston, Joseph Storer. "The Battle of Tankernes." In *Proceedings of the Orkney Antiquarian Society*, vol. VI (Session 1927–1928).

————— *A History of Orkney*. Kirkwall, Scotland: W. R. Mackintosh, 1932.

————— "The Orkney Lands." In *Proceedings of the Orkney Antiquarian Society*, vol. II (Session 1923–1924).

————— *Records of the Earldom of Orkney, 1299–1614*, second series, vol. 7. Printed for the Scottish Historical Society, Edinburgh, 1914.

Cochrane, Robert. *Pentland Walks, with Their Literary and Historical Associations*. Edinburgh: Andrew Elliot, 1908.

Cokayne, George Edward. *The Complete Peerage of England, Scotland, Ireland, Great Britain and the United Kingdom*. London: G. Bell & Sons, 1945.

Cowan, Samuel. *Three Celtic Earldoms: Athol, Strathearn, Menteith*. Edinburgh: Norman Macleod, 1909.

Craven, Reverend J. B. *History of the Church in Orkney from the Introduction of Christianity to 1558*. Kirkwall, Scotland: William Peace & Son, 1901.

Dawson, John William. *Acadian Geology; The Geological Structure, Organic Remains, and Mineral Resources of Nova Scotia, New Brunswick, and Prince Edward Island*. London: Macmillan & Co., 1868.

Demmin, Auguste Frederic. *Weapons of War*. Translated by C. C. Black. London: Bell & Daldy, 1870.

"Demolition of the Ruins of Kirkwall Castle" in *Orkney Herald*, March 7, 1865.

Dennis, Clara. *More About Nova Scotia*. Toronto: Ryerson Press, 1937.

Denys, Nicolas. *Description and Natural History of the Coasts of North America (Acadia)*. Translated and edited by William F. Ganong. Toronto: The Champlain Society, 1908.

Dictionary of National Biography.

"Diplomatarium Norvegicum." Vol. 55. Christiania (now Oslo): R. J. Malling, 1852.

Douglas, Sir Robert. *Peerage of Scotland*. Edinburgh, 1813.

Draney, Joseph Rock. "Asphalt—Origin, History," in *Americana Encyclopedia*, vol. 33, pp. 196–221. New York: Grolier, Inc., 1939.

Edmondston, Arthur. *A View of the Ancient and Present State of the Zetland Islands, Including Their Civil, Political, and Natural History*. Edinburgh: J. Ballantyne & Co., 1809.

Evans, Arthur H., and Buckley, T. E. *A Vertebrate Fauna of the Shetland Islands*. Edinburgh: D. Douglas, 1899.

Forster, Johann Reinhold. *History of the Voyages and Discoveries Made in the North*. Printed for G. G. J. and J. Robinson. London, 1786.

Fothergill, George Algernon. *Curiosities of Edinburgh and Neighborhood*. Edinburgh: John Orr, 1910.

Fowler, William B. "Rhode Island Prehistory at the Green Point Site," in *Bulletin of the Massachusetts Archaeological Society*, vol. 15, no. 4 (July 1954): 65–80.

Ganong, William F. See Denys, Nicolas.

Gaudet, Daniel. *Moeurs et coutumes des anciens Souriquois ou Micmacs*. St. John, New Brunswick, Canada: College of St. Joseph, 1895.

Genealogical Magazine. Vol. 6:477–81; vol. 7:101–07. Boston: E. Putnam, 1903.

Gesner, Abraham. *Remarks on the Geology and Mineralogy of Nova Scotia*. Halifax, Nova Scotia, 1836.

Gifford, Thomas. *Historical Description of the Zetland Islands in the year 1733*. Edinburgh: privately printed (only 100 copies), 1879.

Gjerset, Knut. *History of the Norwegian People*. New York: Macmillan, 1915.

Glynn, Frank. "A Unique Punched Portrait in Massachusetts" in *Eastern States Archaeological Federation Bulletin*, no. 16 (January 1917).

Goldthwait, J. W. "Physiography of Nova Scotia" in *Canadian Department of Mines Geological Survey*, memoir 140, no. 122. Ottawa: Geological Series, 1924.

Goodwin, William B. *The Ruins of Great Ireland in New England*. Boston: Meador, 1946.

Goudie, Gilbert. *The Celtic and Scandinavian Antiquities of Shetland*. Edinburgh and London: William Blackwood & Sons, 1904.

Grant, Frances J. W. S. *The County Families of the Zetland Islands*. Lerwick, Scotland: T. & J. Manson, 1893.

Gras, Norman Scott Brien. *Early English Customs System*. Cambridge, Mass.: Harvard University, 1918.

Great Britain Historical Manuscripts Commission Report on Manuscripts in Various Collections.

Groome, Francis Hindes. *Ordnance Gazetteer of Scotland*. London: Caxton Publishing Co., 1903.

Harleian Miscellany, vol. 1. London: R. Dutton, 1808–1813.

Hay, Father Richard Augustin. *Genealogie of the Sainteclaires of Rosslyn*. Edinburgh: T. G. Stevenson, 1835.

Haydn, Joseph Timothy. *The Book of Dignities, Containing Rolls of the Official Personages in the Peerage of England and Great Britain*. London: W. H. Allen & Co., 1851.

Hermannides, Rytger. *R. H. Britannia Magna: sive Angliae, Scotiae, Hiberniae et adjacentium insularum geographico-historica descriptio*. Amsterdam: Ae. J. Valckenier, 1661.

Hibbert, Samuel. *A Description of the Shetland Islands*. Edinburgh: A. Constable, 1822.

Hobbs, William Herbert. "The Fourteenth-Century Discovery of America by Antonio Zeno," *Scientific Monthly*, vol. 72 (January 1951), pp. 24–31.

———— "Zeno and the Cartography of Greenland," *Imago Mundi*, vol. 6 (1949), pp. 15–19.

Hodgman, E. R. *History of the Town of Westford, 1659–1883*. Lowell, Mass.: Westford Town History Association, 1883.

Hoffman, Bernard G. *Cabot to Cartier*. Toronto: University of Toronto Press, 1961.

Hossack, Buckham Hugh. *Kirkwall in the Orkneys*. Kirkwall, Scotland: W. Peace & Son, 1900.

Hume, G. S. "Oil and Gas in Eastern Canada." *Canada. Department of Mines, Geological Survey, Economic Geology Series*, no. 8, 1932.

Jack, David Russell. "The Indians of Acadia," *Acadiensis* (St. John, New Brunswick), vol. 1, no. 8 (October 1901).

Jackson, James (of Penicuik). *Historical Tales of Roslin Castle from the invasion of Edward I of England to the Death of Mary, Queen of Scots.* Edinburgh: Balfour and Jack, 1837.

Jelić, Dr. Luka. "L'Evangélisation de l'Amérique avant Christophe Colomb." *Compte rendu du Congres scientifique international des Catholiques,* vol. 2, part 2 (1891); vol. 3, part 2 (1894).

Johnson, D. Mel. "Observations on the Eskimo Remains on the East Coast of Greenland between 72° and 75° North Latitude." *Gronland. Kommissionen for videnskabelige undersogelser i Meddelelser om Gronland,* vol. 92. Copenhagen, 1923.

Kerr, Andrew. "Roslyn Castle, Its Buildings Past and Present." *Proceedings of the Society of Antiquaries of Scotland* (Edinburgh), vol. 12 (1878), pp. 412–24.

Koch, Lauge. "The Geology of East Greenland." *Gronland. Kommissionen for videnskabelige undersogelser i Meddelelser om Gronland,* vol. 73. Copenhagen, 1929.

Lane, Frederic Chapin. *Andrea Barbarigo, Merchant of Venice, 1418–1449,* The Johns Hopkins University Studies in Historical and Political Science. Series 62, no. 1. Baltimore: The Johns Hopkins University Press, 1944.

Larsen, Helge. "Dodemannsbugton, an Eskimo Settlement on Clavering Island." *Gronland. Kommissionen for videnskabelige undersogelser i Meddelelser om Gronland,* vol. 102. Copenhagen, 1934.

Larsen, Karen. *A History of Norway.* New York: American-Scandinavian Society, 1948.

Leask, J. T. Smith. *A Peculiar People and Other Orkney Tales.* Kirkwall, Scotland: W. R. Mackintosh, 1931.

Leland, Charles Godfrey. "The Mythology, Legends, and Folk-Lore of the Algonkins." *Royal Society of Literature of the United Kingdom Transactions,* series 2, vol. 14, pp. 69–91. (Read in June 1886.)

Leland, Charles Godfrey, and Prince, John Dyneley. *Kulóskap the Master and Other Algonkin Poems.* Translated metrically by Leland and Prince. New York and London: Funk & Wagnalls, 1902.

Lelewel, Joachim. "Tavola di Navicare di Nicolò et Antonio Zeni," *Moyen-Age* (Paris), vol. 4 (1852), pp. 77–108.

Lescarbot, Marc. *History of New France*, vol. 2. Translated by W. L. Grant. Toronto: The Champlain Society, 1911.

Lodge, Eleanor Constance. *The End of the Middle Age, 1275–1453*, Six Ages of European History, vol. 3. London: Methuen & Co. 1909.

Lorris, Guillaume de, and Meun (Meung), Jean de. *Roman de la rose*. Translated by F. S. Ellis. London: J. M. Dent & Co., 1900.

Lucas, Frederick William. *The Annals of the Voyages of the Brothers Nicolô and Antonio Zeno in the North Atlantic about the End of the Fourteenth Century and the Claim Founded Thereon to a Venetian Discovery of America. A Criticism and an Indictment.* London: H. Stevens Son & Stiles, 1898.

Luzio, Alessandro. *Miscellanea de Studi Storici*. Archivi de Stato Italiani. Florence, 1933.

Mackie, Charles. *Historical Description of the Chapel and Castle of Roslin*, Edinburgh: J. Anderson, 1831.

Major, Richard Henry, ed. *The Voyages of the Venetian Brothers, Nicolô and Antonio Zeno, to the Northern Seas, in the XIVth Century.* Hakluyt Society Works, no. 50. London: Hakluyt Society, 1873.

———— "Zeno's Frislanda Is Not Iceland, but the Faeroes." *Royal Geographical Society Journal*, vol. 49 (1879), pp. 412–420.

Marcus, G. F. "The Navigation of the Norsemen," *Mariner's Mirror* (London), vol. 39, no. 2 (May 1953).

Marwick, Hugh. *Orkney*. London: Robert Hale, 1951.

Maxwell, Charles Alfred. *Sea Kings of Orkney; and Other Historical Tales.* Edinburgh: W. P. Nimmo, 1870.

Milner, W. C., compiler. Scrapbook on Indians in Library of New Brunswick Museum, St. John, New Brunswick, Canada.

Moncrieffe, Iain. *The Highland Clans*. New York: Clarkson N. Potter, 1967.

Morrison, Leonard Allison. *The History of the Sinclair Family in Europe and America for Eleven Hundred Years.* Boston: Damrell & Upham, 1896.

Mosto, Andrea da. *Lusio Alessandro*, vol. 1. Florence: Comitato esecutivo per l'onoranza ad Ad. Alessandro Luzio, 1933.

Murdoch, Beamish. *A History of Nova Scotia or Acadia.* Halifax, Nova Scotia: J. Barnes, 1865.

Nicolas, Sir Nicholas Harris. *History of the Earldoms of Strathearn, Menteith, and Airth*. Edinburgh: Wm. Pickering; Stephens and Norton; Clark, 1842.

Nisbet, Alexander. *An Essay on the Ancient and Modern Use of Armories*. Edinburgh: J. Mack-Euen, 1718.

——— *A System of Heraldry*. Printed for W. Blackwood, Edinburgh, 1816. *Orkney and Shetland Miscellany*. Old-Lore Series. Vol. 1 (1907), vol. 3 (1910), vol. 7 (1914). London and Coventry: Viking Society for Northern Research.

Patterson, George. *A History of the County of Pictou, Nova Scotia*. Montreal: Dawson Brothers, 1877.

Peterkin, Alexander. *Notes on Orkney and Zetland; Illustrative of the History, Antiquities, Scenery, and Customs of Those Islands*. Edinburgh: Macredie, Skelly and Co., 1822.

Piers, Harry. "Brief Account of the Micmac Indians of Nova Scotia and Their Remains." *Nova Scotia Institute of Science Proceedings*, Session 1910–1911, pp. 90–125.

Pohl, Frederick J. *The Lost Discovery*. New York: W. W. Norton, 1952.

——— *The Sinclair Expedition to Nova Scotia in 1398*. Pictou, Nova Scotia: Pictou Advocate Press, 1950.

——— *Atlantic Crossings Before Columbus*. New York: W. W. Norton, 1961.

——— *The Viking Explorers*. New York: Thos. Y. Crowell, 1966.

——— "Prince 'Zichmni' of the Zeno Narrative." *Terrae Incognitae* (The Annals of the Society for the History of Discoveries), vol. 2. Amsterdam: N. Israel, 1970.

Pontanus, Joannes. *Rerum Danicarum Historia*. Amsterdam: Sumptibus H. Hondii, 1631.

Poole, Henry S. "Report on the Pictou Coal Field, Nova Scotia," *Geological Survey of Canada, Annual Report*, vol. 14, numbered series (1901), pp. 1m–38m.

Prest, Walter Henry. "Report of Cave Examinations in Hants County, Nova Scotia." In *Nova Scotia Institute of Science Proceedings*, vol. 13 (1910–1914), pp. 87–94. (Read November 13, 1911.)

Ramusio, Giovanni Battista. *Secondo volume delle Navigationi et Viaggi*. Venice: 1559.

Rand, Silas Tertius. *A Dictionary of the Language of the Micmac Indians.* Halifax, Nova Scotia: Nova Scotia Printing Co., 1888.

——— *Legends of the Micmacs.* New York: Longmans, Green & Co., 1894.

——— *Micmac Place-Names in the Maritime Provinces and Gaspe Peninsula Recorded between 1852 and 1890.* Ottawa: Surveyor General's Office, 1919.

——— *A Short Statement of Facts Relating to the History, Manners, Customs, Language and Literature of the Micmac Tribe of Indians in Nova Scotia and Prince Edward Island.* Halifax, 1850.

Rogers, Charles. *Genealogical Memoirs of the Family of Sir Walter Scott.* London: Royal Historical Society, 1877.

Roman de la rose. See Lorris, Guillaume de.

Royal Commission on the Ancient Monuments of Scotland, 12th Report with an Inventory of the Ancient Monuments of Orkney and Shetland, vols. 1, 2, 3.

Russell-Jeaffreson, Joseph. *The Faeroe Islands.* London: S. Low, Marston & Co., 1901.

Saint-Clair, Roland William. *The Saint-Clairs of the Isles, Being a History of the Sea-Kings of Orkney and Their Scottish Successors of the Sirname of Sinclair.* Auckland, New Zealand: H. Brett, 1898.

The Scots Peerage. Edinburgh: D. Douglas, 1910.

Scott, Sir Walter. *The Pirate.* Edinburgh: A. Constable & Co., 1822.

Scottish Notes and Queries. Second series, vol. 4, pp. 65–67, 81–84, 97–99, 122. Aberdeen: A. Brown.

Seaver, Jesse Montgomery. *Stewart Family Records.* Philadelphia: American Historical-Genealogical Society, 1929.

Shearer, John. *Antiquities of Strathearn.* Crieff, Perthshire, Scotland: D. Philips, 1881.

Sinclair, Alexander. *Sketch of the History of Roslin, and Its Possessors,* Irvine, Scotland: M. Dick, 1856.

Sinclair, Catherine. *Shetland and the Shetlanders.* New York: D. Appleton & Co., 1840.

Sinclair, Thomas. *Caithness Events.* Wick, Scotland: W. Rae, 1899.

——— "Orkney and Caithness" (clippings from newspaper articles in County Library), Kirkwall, Scotland, 1901.

———— *The Sinclairs of England.* London: Trübner & Co., 1887.

Sinclair, William. *An Account of the Chapel of Roslin, built by William St. Clare, Prince of Orkney. To Which Is Added a Particular Description of the Costly Housekeeping Kept by the Said Prince.* 1790?

———— "Thomas, Bishop of Orkney and Zetland, and the Chapter of Kirkwall," *The Bannatyne Miscellany*, vol. 3. Edinburgh: Bannatyne Club, 1827.

Smith, H. L. Norton. *A Collection of Armorials of the County of Orkney.* Printed for the author, Galashiels, Scotland, 1902.

Speck, Frank Gouldsmith. "Some Micmac Tales from Cape Breton Island," *Journal of American Folklore*, vol. 28, no. 107 (1915), pp. 59–69.

Steuart, Sir Henry. *Genealogy of the Stewarts Refuted.* Edinburgh: Bell & Bradfute, 1799.

Tancred, George. *Rulewater and Its People.* Edinburgh: Edinburgh University Press, 1907.

Tavel, Emilie. "Rock Sketch Hints Scottish Invasion of America in 14th Century." *Christian Science Monitor*, October 2, 1957.

Thomson, David Patrick. *Orkney through the Centuries; Lights and Shadows of the Church's Life in the Northern Isles.* Crieff, Perthshire, Scotland, 1956.

Torfaeus, Thormodus. *Orcades, seu rerum Orcadensium historiae*, Hauniae, 1697.

Tout, Thomas Frederick. *Edward the First.* London and New York: Macmillan, 1893.

Trevelyan, George Macaulay. *England in the Age of Wycliffe.* London: Longmans & Co., 1899.

Trussell, John. *A Continuation of the Collection of the History of England by Samuel Daniel.* London: the author, 1636.

Tudor, John R. *The Orkneys and Shetland; Their Past and Present State.* London: E. Stanford, 1883.

Venice, Museo Correr. No. 1536 (S–Z). "Discendenza Patrizie" [by Marco Barbaro].

The Voyages of Nicolo and Antonio Zeno, to the Northern Seas, in the XIVth Century. See Major, Richard Henry.

Wainwright, Frederick Threlfall, ed. *The Northern Isles.* London: Nelson, 1962.

Walker, J. Russel. "'Holy Wells' in Scotland." *Society of Antiquaries of Scotland Proceedings*, series 2, vol. 5 (February 12, 1883), pp. 172–175.

Wallis, Wilson D. and Ruth Sawtell. *The Micmac Indians of Eastern Canada.* Minneapolis: University of Minnesota Press, 1955.

Zeno, Nicolò. *The Discovery of the Islands of Frislandia, Eslanda, Engrone-landa, Estotilanda, and Icaria; Made by Two Brothers of the Zeno Family, Namely, Messire Nicolo, the Chevalier, and Messire Antonio. With a Map of the Said Islands* (translated title). Venice, 1558.

Zurla, D. Placido. *Dissertazione intorno ai viaggi e scoperte settentrionali di Nicolô ed Antonio fratelli Zeni.* Venice, 1808.

Index